Understanding Religion and Popular Culture

Understanding Religion and Popular Culture 2nd edition provides an accessible introduction to this exciting and rapidly evolving field. Divided into two parts, Issues in Religion and Genres in Popular Culture, it encourages readers to think critically about the ways in which popular cultural practices and products, especially those considered as forms of entertainment, are laden with religious ideas, themes, and values.

This edition has been thoroughly revised and includes five new chapters, updated case studies, and contemporary references. Among the areas covered are religion and film, food, violence, music, television, cosplay, and fandom. Each chapter also includes a helpful summary, glossary, bibliography, discussion questions, and suggestions for further reading/viewing.

Providing a set of practical and theoretical tools for learning and research, this book is an essential read for all students of Religion and Popular Culture, or Religion and Media more broadly.

Elizabeth Rae Coody is Assistant Professor of Religious Studies at Morningside University, Sioux City, Iowa, United States, and co-editor of *Monstrous Women in Comics* (2020).

Dan W. Clanton, Jr. is Associate Professor of Religious Studies at Doane University, USA. He is the author, editor, or co-editor of a number of books and articles on religion, the Bible, and popular culture.

Terry Ray Clark is Professor of Religion and Chair of the Religion Department at Georgetown College, Georgetown, KY.

Understanding Religion and Popular Culture

Second Edition

**Edited by Elizabeth Rae Coody,
Dan W. Clanton Jr., and
Terry Ray Clark**

Routledge
Taylor & Francis Group

LONDON AND NEW YORK

Designed cover image: Selimcan / Getty Images

Second edition published 2023
by Routledge
4 Park Square, Milton Park, Abingdon, Oxon, OX14 4RN

and by Routledge
605 Third Avenue, New York, NY 10158

Routledge is an imprint of the Taylor & Francis Group, an informa business

First edition published by Routledge 2012

British Library Cataloguing-in-Publication Data
A catalogue record for this book is available from the British Library

ISBN: 978-0-367-52879-9 (hbk)
ISBN: 978-0-367-52883-6 (pbk)
ISBN: 978-1-003-07972-9 (ebk)

DOI: 10.4324/9781003079729

Typeset in Sabon
by SPi Technologies India Pvt Ltd (Straive)

In deepest appreciation of all those who worked with us and helped us to cope through the height of the COVID-19 pandemic.

This edition is humbly dedicated to those who work for the health of the world.

Contents

Contributors

Eric Bain-Selbo is Dean of the College of Humanities and Social Sciences at Southeast Missouri State University (USA). An interdisciplinary scholar, he has authored numerous articles, book chapters, and books. His most recent book is *The End(s) of Religion: A History of How the Study of Religion Makes Religion Irrelevant.*

Dan Clanton Jr. is Associate Professor of Religious Studies at Doane University, USA. He is the author, editor, or co-editor of a number of books and articles on religion, Bible, and popular culture. He enjoys spending time with his family, collecting vinyl records, and watching far too much television.

Terry Ray Clark, Ph.D., is Professor of Religion and Chair of the Religion Department at Georgetown College, Georgetown, KY, USA.

Elizabeth Rae Coody, Ph.D., is assistant professor of religious studies at Morningside University, Sioux City, Iowa, USA and co-editor of *Monstrous Women in Comics* (2020).

Douglas E. Cowan is Professor of Religious Studies and Social Development Studies at Renison University College in Waterloo, Ontario, Canada. He is the author of numerous books on religion and popular culture, including *The Forbidden Body: Sex, Horror, and the Religious Imagination* (NYUP 2022).

Dell deChant teaches at the University of South Florida, Tampa, Florida, United States of America. He is the author of three books, over 30 articles, and chapters in twelve books. deChant's specialization is religion and contemporary cultures. His current research focuses on religious expressions of Agrarianism in popular culture.

Cynthia A. Hogan, Ph.D., is the Visiting Assistant Professor in Religious Studies at Washington & Jefferson College, USA. Dr. Hogan specializes in religious material culture and visual culture of religion, with a particular research interest in the material culture of new and alternative religious movements.

Siobhán Jolley is the Howard and Roberta Ahmanson Research Fellow in Art and Religion at the National Gallery, London, a Visiting Lecturer in Theology and Religious Studies at King's College, London, and an Honorary Research Fellow at the University of Manchester Centre for Biblical Studies.

John C. McDowell is the Associate Dean and Professor in Philosophy, Systematic Theology and Moral Theology at Yarra Theological Union in the University of Divinity, Australia. Among his publications are many studies in popular culture including *The Ideology of Identity Politics in George Lucas* and *The Gospel According to Star Wars*.

Jeremy Rehwaldt was a professor of religion at Midland University in Fremont, Nebraska, USA, and now works for a global health nonprofit.

J. Caroline Toy is Learning Experience Designer in the Center for Learning & Teaching at Champlain College in Burlington, Vermont, USA, and Adjunct Professor in the College's Humanities Core. Her research and teaching focus on religion, popular media, and fan cultures.

Courtney Wilder, Ph.D., is Professor of Religion at Midland University, USA. Her work often focuses on religion, disability and popular culture.

Jonathan Sands Wise is Provost and Executive Vice President at Georgetown College, USA, where he continues to teach regularly as Associate Professor of Philosophy specializing in Ancient and Medieval Virtue Ethics. Jonathan lives in Georgetown, KY, USA with his wife and three children.

America Wolff is a Ph.D. Candidate at Florida State University in American Religious History. She resides in Tallahassee Florida, USA and works primarily in the areas of Religion and Popular Culture and Fan Studies.

Foreword to the Second Edition
How to Use this Book

Elizabeth Rae Coody

In this book, you will encounter a variety of essays that attempt to clarify certain ways in which religion and popular culture are interacting in the contemporary world and the recent past. Each chapter centers a **Theory and Method** that these authors have used to dig deeper into the interactions they have noticed. Theories here are the way that we organize ideas; methods are the way you do your research. These are not hard and fast rules, but organizing principles—ways that people have of communicating ideas and making sense to themselves. Each chapter also, to various degrees, shows you how and why the authors have done their scholarly work with these ideas, often in their **Introduction**. Doing this work is called being "self-reflexive" and it's not an easy task. It's tough to know how much or what to share, and we all struggled. We want to show you that we are imperfect as people always are, so you should use your reason as you evaluate what we say. But we also want you to trust us and understand that we are passionate about our subjects. We sincerely believe in the value of these contributions for helping our readers, especially students, develop skills as interpreters. Each author who contributed here (without exception!) is a real flesh-and-blood person with hopes, dreams, and ideas *beyond* what is referred to in this book, just like you are a person who is *more* than a reader of this book. We invited new voices and engaged with people who have long experience in the field. You should notice that every chapter keeps something of the character of the work of the person who wrote it; they are all a little different by design.

We editors have kept you readers in our minds as real people as we've crafted this book. We wondered whether you would get our jokes or if you would understand our obscure references (which we explain if we at all thought you wouldn't). We encourage you as our readers to enter this book as fellow travelers and contributors to the "understanding" of religion and popular culture that this book is working toward. We want you to be critical readers, so there are a few things about the book we wanted you to know before you dig in.

Notice that this is the second edition of this book. We wanted to update the original from 2012, both because of how quickly the field evolves and to create a new invitation for readers to explore this field of study. There are five entirely new chapters, and the rest have been updated by their authors. Popular culture produces new artifacts to contend with on an hourly basis, so an update a decade later is logical. However, this update is not simply to give new examples. We cleared out creaky older references but also have strived to make sure that this version clarifies its purpose to make the ideas last. The purpose of the book is not to educate the reader on each popular culture topic as the final word on each topic, but to show the reader how each topic might be engaged in a scholarly way. That is, if or when you notice that the examples we use don't feel fresh anymore, this edition of the book invites you to provide your own. In fact, we know for sure that you'll need to add your own examples and point of view. Your own experience happens at the intersection of all the points of your identity and experience with religion and popular culture. Attention generally to "intersectionality" came in the modern academic conversation from law (Crenshaw 1989). When we pay attention to the fact that our readers may share some dimensions of commonality but not others with our authors, this drew us to be more conscious of both the limitations and possibilities. This book is better when you use it.

To help you figure out how to start reading, we structured the table of contents into clusters: "Issues in Religion" and "Genres in Popular Culture." These broad categories might help you find the chapter that applies to your situation more readily. That is, those coming at popular culture from a religious studies point of view could start with the Issues in Religion section to find an applicable chapter. Those coming from popular culture trying to engage religion could start with the Genres section. Every chapter except the Introduction in Chapter 1 will have a **Case Study** to show you how the author of that chapter might use the issues from religion or genres from popular culture to address a problem or play with an idea. The **Summary** at the end of each chapter is there to help you track the ways the **Theory and Method** section interacts with the **Case Study**.

In this edition, we still hope you will acquire a set of introductory tools for analyzing important places in society where religion and popular culture intersect. To help you go beyond the page, we've given you **Discussion Questions and Activities** to engage individually with your own research or with a class. Conversation about religion and popular culture can be a challenge, but we think these kinds of discussions are key to the field and wonderful training for all kinds of topics beyond this book. Some of the questions or suggestions for activities are projects we wish someone would take up so that *we* can read them! We invite you to mix and match ideas and chapters. In this way, you can make your own projects and engage the popular culture you want to learn from or about the most.

The **Glossary** in each chapter gives you a handy list of the most complicated or important terms that the author wants you to know. You'll notice that some terms are defined differently by different people. That's as it should be! Words are slippery, especially in the academic field of Religion and Popular Culture. But the chapter isn't the end of the story. At the end of each chapter, there is a list of **Suggested Further Reading** that shows you important and useful books, articles, and websites that can take you further forward into that part of the field. We all also have a **Bibliography** that can lead you back to the authors we read and engaged in the chapter you read.

Where to start? I hope you start with the **Introduction** in the first chapter. My fellow editor lays out several ideas and theories in this first chapter that will serve you well through the rest of the book. We hope that using the unique lenses provided by the academic field of Religion and Popular Culture is a valuable way to study the culture that you live in—whatever that is and whoever you are. If you do find this work valuable, then we hope you're inspired to pursue further study, eventually making your own contribution to the development and application of new theories and methods in this rapidly expanding subject area. The world could do with more people who use robust theories and methods when talking about popular culture and religion; we would all be richer for hearing your voice added to the chorus.

Bibliography

Crenshaw, Kimberlé (1989) "Demarginalizing the Intersection of Race and Sex: A Black Feminist Critique of Antidiscrimination Doctrine, Feminist Theory, and Antiracist Politics." *University of Chicago Legal Forum.* v. 1989, Issue 1, Article 8.

1 Introduction

What Is Religion? What Is Pop Culture? How Are They Related?

Terry Ray Clark

I was introduced to the academic study of religion and popular culture somewhat by accident. A recent graduate of the same PhD program where I was enrolled (one of my co-editors for this volume, Dr. Dan W. Clanton, Jr.) invited me to teach a course on this topic alongside him at the University of Colorado at Colorado Springs. I had no idea what I was getting myself into. Up to this point in my life, I primarily considered popular culture to consist of a variety of things related to entertainment: comics and graphic novels, TV, film, music, novels, video games, etc. Teaching on such things sounded more like a way to indulge my recreational interests than a serious academic endeavor. I practically learned to read with the help of Marvel Comics, and who isn't interested in watching films? [*Star Wars* was the first blockbuster film I saw in a movie theater; I was nine years old, and I was mesmerized. You'll get to read a chapter about *Star Wars* later in this book!] I figured, why not combine my natural interests (religion, pop culture, and academic pursuits) and get paid for it? I had so much to learn. I never dreamed that a few years after teaching that first Religion and Pop Culture class, I would be co-editing an introductory book on the topic!

Back then, when the first edition of this book was published (2012), the field seemed to just be building momentum. Introductory courses were emerging across the country, no doubt fueled by student interest in "studying" things they were already interested in as consumers of pop culture products. A lot has transpired since I first began this mixing of business and pleasure in the classroom. The field has exploded and established itself as a respected subset of cultural studies, a critically important way to better understand the ideology of both producers and consumers. Its greatest value probably lies in providing us a way to better understand ourselves. What are our society's greatest hopes and dreams? What are our greatest obsessions, and why? Why is our culture so saturated with religion even *outside* of (or in addition to) traditional religious contexts and institutions, so much so that unless we're really paying attention, much of the religion around us is barely noticed, much less scrutinized? [If you haven't yet noticed this yourself, my hope is that after reading this book, you will begin to take note.]

DOI: 10.4324/9781003079729-1

What hasn't changed, in my opinion, since the early days of this still growing field, is the need for good introductory texts that can make the academic study of popular culture accessible to undergraduate students, a way for them to "get their feet wet" without being overwhelmed by the vast amount of theoretical approaches and practical applications that now exist. So, when Routledge asked for an updated version of this text, Dan recruited some new help (co-editor, Dr. Elizabeth Coody) and together they dragged me along for a second round. I'm glad they did.

For the current volume, we kept some of the original material, not because the practical examples they offer are the most recent material available for study (staying on the cutting edge of popular culture is a never-ending challenge), but because we felt the theory in some chapters is still highly relevant and applicable to other current and future material. We hope you will agree. We added some new chapters, updated others a bit, and dropped a few from the first volume. We hope this revision is worthy of your time and intellectual energy.

What follows in the rest of this chapter is merely a slight revision of the original introduction, a rather short, sweet, and, for some discerning scholars, perhaps too simple a treatment of several important concepts related to this field. Please keep in mind, this book is intended as a starting point for what we hope will become a lifetime of further analysis. In our collective experience teaching Religion and Popular Culture, too much complicated theory up front tends to discourage students from pursuing a new course of academic study, which is the exact opposite of what the editors of this book want to accomplish. So, without further delay, let's begin.

Welcome to the exciting and rapidly evolving field of study known as Religion and Popular Culture! This still relatively new area of study is establishing itself as an important subset of two larger subject areas known as Religious Studies and Cultural Studies and is represented by a growing number of college and university courses across the country, as well as academic publishing. These include, but are not limited to, such things as: Religion and Media Studies, Religion/Theology and Film, Religion and Literature, Ethics in Pop Culture and Entertainment, Religion in Contemporary America, Religion and Politics, Communication Studies, and of course, Religion and Popular Culture.

The chief purpose of this book, as stated above, is to provide an entryway for introducing this field, providing teachers, researchers, and especially students, with a set of practical and theoretical tools for beginning their own academic investigation of this vast terrain of subject matter. The book is designed to assist readers in beginning to think critically about the ways in which popular cultural practices and products, especially those considered to be forms of entertainment, are laden with religious ideology, that is, with religious ideas, themes, and values. Some of this ideology is encountered so regularly in everyday life that it goes unnoticed unless one is specifically trying to locate, identify, and study it. Similarly, it is so widespread and common that a vague familiarity often winds up serving as a poor substitute for real understanding, and therefore the material fails to be critically examined by the very culture that inherits, adapts, produces, or reproduces it. However, a culture's popular ideas, products, and practices have much to teach its own members about themselves, including their religious assumptions, their foundational beliefs, and their motivations for certain behaviors. Recognizing this can be the starting point for encouraging people to begin thinking critically about their own society as well as equipping themselves to interact more meaningfully and effectively with others located either inside or outside of their own unique cultural setting.

In addition to these justifications, the academic study of Religion and Popular Culture has the advantage of being, from the outset, less intimidating to new students because much of the subject matter is perceived as being, at least in part, something with which they are already familiar and interested. This is due in large part to the fact that today many of the earth's inhabitants live in an environment of mass communication, a world in which modern technology (e.g., satellite or digital TV, radio, mobile phones, internet, etc.) makes the ideas, products, and practices of others accessible around the globe in the blink of an eye.

This chapter attempts to lay a very basic, theoretical foundation for readers to begin exploring some specific ideas, products, and practices in Western popular culture that specifically reflect religious influences, and which therefore contain some amount of religious content. The essays that follow in the remaining chapters provide examples of how some scholars have begun to analyze this seemingly inexhaustible and ever-evolving subject matter. They are not the only legitimate ways to understand the material. Rather, they are intended to provide readers with a starter toolbox, that is, with helpful strategies for beginning their own intellectual journey through this exciting and complex cultural terrain.

Theory and Method

A Practical Foundation for Studying Religion and Popular Culture

It is often considered helpful when immersing oneself in a new subject of study to define, as clearly as possible, what the boundaries of that subject should be. Therefore, the editors here have chosen to begin this study by providing readers with a set of working definitions of Religion, Culture, and Popular Culture. Working definitions are not necessarily perfect, complete, or universally accepted, but they can provide a practical starting point for further exploration. They can highlight some of the major, foundational challenges that scholars face in a particular field. From our own teaching experience, we have discovered that if too much emphasis is placed on all the challenges, obstacles, or problems of studying Religion and Popular Culture from the outset, new students often become discouraged, disillusioned, and too frustrated to proceed. Hence, this book will provide just enough information to allow the novice to get a foothold in the material, without getting lost in the complexities and difficulties of foundational theory and method. For those who choose to pursue further work in the field, there will be plenty of time to revisit such matters in the future. The theories and methods provided in this book assume that they are merely a starting point for more in-depth study. Furthermore, each contributor hopes to inspire ongoing conversations with other scholars who likewise recognize the value of pursuing a critical analysis of the religious characteristics of the popular cultural products and practices of our world, in spite of the technical difficulties of defining our subject matter.

Although perfect, universally accepted definitions for Religion, Culture, and Popular Culture have not been produced, scholars agree that religion has been and continues to be one of the most pervasive and important characteristics of human society. Similarly, culture and popular culture are undeniable realities of human existence. They provide real phenomena worthy of academic analysis, and they reflect real ideas, beliefs, and values; they are not merely figments of human imagination. Culture, including popular culture, refers to all the ideas, products, practices, and values of human society. These things emerge from and reflect the hopes, fears, dreams, goals, and struggles of real people. Thus, their study provides an opportunity to better understand human society, as well as more specific parts of society, including all the groups, sub-groups, and individuals that interact with one another, sometimes cooperatively, and sometimes in a context of competition and conflict.

What Is Religion?

The problem of defining religion is one of the most difficult, foundational, and pervasive issues plaguing the field of Religious Studies today. Yet, it is usually never even considered outside the realm of academia. Why is this? The answer lies in the simple fact that most people inherit from the beginning of their lives—from their elders, family, religious tradition or larger society—a working concept of what religion is, and what it means to be religious. Most do not need to be taught how to recognize something as religious, at least not within their own tradition. Religion, generally speaking, refers to those practices of any society that are attentive to what is believed to be a sacred, unique, or extraordinary element or quality of human experience. Even societies that do not always clearly delineate what is considered sacred from what is not sacred (i.e., the mundane or ordinary) seem to understand what these terms refer to. Theoretically speaking, they might consider all reality to be sacred, but for all practical purposes they will usually distinguish between certain elements of life that are more sacred than others. How can this be? What is it that makes some things at least appear to be religious or sacred, and other things ordinary? What is the nature of so-called 'sacred reality?' Does it really exist, or is it merely a product of human imagination?

There is no lack of scholarly attempts to address these questions. Some definitions assert the existence of a unique substance in the universe that human beings have a special, inexplicable way of sensing. It is believed that this substance can be directly experienced and immediately recognized for what it really is, even though a complete understanding of its nature eludes our grasp. Hence, it remains at least partially **transcendent**. This reality is considered the cause of the human experience and practice of religion. It is assumed that because many, if not most, human beings describe some of their experiences as religious in nature, there must be a separate or unique reality that causes it. From this perspective, 'The Sacred' truly exists as a causal substance or entity that normally lies hidden from the naked eye (as well as the other four senses of human perception that make up the approach known as scientific observation: sight, sound, smell, taste, and touch). Nevertheless, 'The Sacred' is believed to exist because its effects, if not its cause(s), are considered to be apparent in the observable world.

While this assumption represents a logical fallacy from the perspective of pure, rational analysis (e.g., there could be other reasonable explanations for humanity's religious beliefs and behaviors), believers are undeterred. Of course, no one can really prove or disprove someone else's (or even one's own) claim to have had a genuine encounter with a sacred reality. Likewise, no one can prove or disprove, at least not with scientific evidence, that a sacred reality is or is not the cause of a religious experience (some of which believers might describe as a religious "encounter"). Thus, many scholars direct their attention toward better understanding the observable human phenomena that tend to accompany alleged religious experiences. This is because human behavior, unlike any theoretically existing sacred reality, does provide a substance or **phenomenon** that can be examined, measured, described, and verified by multiple witnesses. This approach is referred to as the phenomenological approach to religion. If nothing else, the phenomenon of religion clearly does exist. Many, if not most, people throughout recorded human history have either claimed to have religious experiences or exhibit beliefs and behaviors they consider appropriate in response to the sacred or ultimate reality. They believe that at least some aspects of life have, or should have, a sacred quality. This makes their lives more meaningful, fulfilling, and practical (i.e., successful).

So, for pragmatic reasons, many approaches to the study of religion choose to focus exclusively on those beliefs and practices that a particular society understands as their own appropriate response to what is perceived to be a sacred reality. This is the approach to religion adopted by this book. Sacred or Ultimate Reality can refer to whatever a particular person or group considers the most enduring, foundational, and important substance or reality in the universe. 'The Sacred' is something that is considered to be deeper, more powerful, and more valuable than the normal, everyday things with which it is often contrasted, although it is also often considered a reality that creates and/or sustains all other reality. It is a reality that deserves appropriate human attention, and for many, this includes all the various forms of human activity known as worship. It need not be something that is focused upon all the time. For some people, "orientation to ultimate reality takes place by degrees and is restricted to certain times and places, even among 'very religious' people" (Deming 2005: 15). And yet, evidence of one's acknowledgement and orientation to 'The Sacred' may still be found scattered throughout one's culture, including one's everyday routines, sometimes without one even being aware of it. Religion is not something that is simply relegated to 'official' holy days, times, and festivals; it does not merely occur in formal, ritual, or sacred time, in which special religious authorities often perform the task of conducting formal worship activities. Religion, for many, is something that may occur on any day of the week, at almost any time, and in nearly any place. Sacred reality is something that is believed to permeate most, if not all, reality, and therefore all aspects of human culture.

Granting these general parameters for understanding the concept of sacred reality, what then is a good, working definition of religion? One that is helpful for beginning an academic exploration of the subject matter may be derived from the approach taken by John C. Livingston in his book *Anatomy of the Sacred: An Introduction to Religion* (2008): Religion is a coherent system of beliefs and practices that are "directed toward that which is perceived to be of sacred value and transforming power" (10). The reference here to "power" is an essential aspect of a good definition of religion, because it highlights the practical benefits sought by the religious activities of those who engage in them. Religious observance is believed to be a source of help for living a more meaningful and fulfilling life, and often this includes the belief that it provides a viable path for life beyond this world. Put succinctly, "whatever powers we believe govern our destiny will elicit a religious response from us and inspire us to wish 'to tie or bind' ourselves to these powers in relations of ritual obligation" (Esposito, Fasching, and Lewis 2009: 7).

This reference to "bind[ing]" is important, because it highlights what many scholars believe is the root meaning of the word "religion." This English word is most likely derived from the Latin prefix *re*, which means "again," combined with the root *lig*, which means "to join" or "connect," thus producing the meaning "to re-connect" or "to join again" (Molloy 2010: 5). This suggests that, at its root, religion refers to any practice that serves to bring back together or to bring back into harmony the sacred and mundane realms of reality that, for various reasons, are often perceived as being disconnected. Religion provides not only an explanation for why human life is in some ways chaotic, problematic, or difficult, but it also seeks to provide a solution to this problem. In the words of Jonathan Z. Smith, "Religion is the quest, within the bounds of the human, historical condition, for the power to manipulate and negotiate one's 'situation' so as to have 'space' in which to meaningfully dwell" (Smith 1993: 291). Religion provides human beings with "a strategy for dealing with a situation," in this case, the human situation (Smith, 299, following Burke 1957: 256). By performing ritual acts of worship, humans hope to "oblige" the 'powers that be' to reward us with a more orderly and successful life in the present and a more rewarding existence in the future.

Thus, for many, if not most, people, religion provides a means of helping us "relate to the unknown universe around us by answering the basic questions of who we are, where we come from, and where we are going" (Molloy, 10). However idealistic it sometimes seems to be, religion provides its practitioners with what are believed to be very rational and practical strategies for coping with the challenges of everyday life. Some of these strategies include **ritual** behaviors that help orient the mind and body toward proper (i.e., religious) ways of thinking and acting. Often, this follows from the belief that a sacred reality represents and/or imposes a value system on the universe that obligates humans to live in accordance with it, and doing so brings more meaning, purpose, and success in life for oneself and for others.

What Are Culture and Popular Culture?

Like the phenomenon of religion, which in all its myriad forms falls within the larger domain of human culture, so also popular culture is merely a subset of this larger category of human activity. It is not something that is ever, entirely distinct from the larger context in which it occurs and in which it is defined. But what do these terms really refer to? Like the term religion, scholars have had a difficult time agreeing on what "culture" and "popular culture" really represent. In fact, some scholars treat each of these terms as "an *empty* conceptual category, one that can be filled in a wide variety of often conflicting ways, depending on the context of use" (Storey 2009b: 1). However, if the terms are to be worthy of any use at all, they must be clarified in some fashion.

Historically speaking, the term culture has at times been used to designate what some would consider a distinctly higher form of "intellectual, spiritual, and aesthetic development" than that found among the more common masses of society (Williams 1983: 90). In other words, culture here refers to so-called 'high culture,' or what more privileged or wealthy members of society consider to be most valuable. This use of the term, however, reflects a biased judgment on the part of those individuals who have the power to impose their own preferences or value system upon others, and may serve to maintain a distinction in society between people of different economic and political standing. Two other definitions of culture have served as attempts to correct this bias. One considers the term "culture" merely to designate the "particular way of life...of a [particular] people, a period or a group" (Storey 2009b: 1), without necessarily evaluating one culture as better than another. In this approach, culture includes practically every idea, product, practice, and value of a society, regardless of the socioeconomic class in which it originates. Finally, a third approach attempts to find a middle ground by using the term culture in a more limited fashion to refer only to those products and practices "whose principle function is to signify, to produce or to be the occasion for the production of meaning" (Storey 2009b: 2). In other words, this third use is more specifically geared toward recognizing those products and practices that are purposely designed to communicate ideas in a symbolic way.

Right away, it should be obvious that any product or practice in a society has the power of signifying and/or producing meaning, even if this is not the primary, intended purpose for its existence. Thus, the least biased definition, and the one preferred here, is also the most general and inclusive one. The term "culture" should be used to refer to *all* the potentially signifying products and practices of a society, regardless of the economic, political, religious, or social class in which they originate. Immediately, the reader should recognize that our preference here for this particular definition necessarily reflects its own bias in the direction of such values as objectivity and inclusiveness, as opposed to other possible criteria. From an academic perspective, these biases are ones that the authors of this book are willing to take ownership of. However, this does highlight the fact that all definitions contain, to some extent, their own subjectivity, just as all cultural products and practices contain their own subjectivity. They always simultaneously both represent and "present a particular image of the world," including what that image considers to be of greater value (Storey 2009b: 4). Every product and practice of every culture reflects its own assumptions about "the way the world is or should be," and the definitions put forward in this book are no exception (Storey 2009b: 4). One of the foundational goals of the critical study of Religion and Popular Culture should always be to clarify, as much as possible, the ideological values reflected in every popular cultural practice or product, because often these are never discussed directly or openly by their originators, practitioners, and/or consumers. Usually, these things are communicated implicitly rather than explicitly.

This leads us to another important term (and aspect) of culture that needs to be defined, namely, "ideology." Ideology, most literally, refers to "a systematic body of ideas" that, to various degrees, is "articulated by a particular group of people" (Storey 2009b: 2). All individuals, and all groups of people, have an ideology, however clearly it is articulated, just as every product and practice of individuals and groups will reflect the ideology of their makers and users. Therefore, the study of culture, including popular culture (which will be defined in more detail below), necessarily involves the recognition and analysis of competing ideas, beliefs, and values inherent within every cultural product and practice one encounters. Culture should be recognized as a realm of human political activity in which various ideas "are created" and in which various ideas compete with one another (Hall 2009: 122–123). In other words, culture is often a realm of conflict, where different ideas are always being defined, redefined, negotiated, reinforced, and/or rejected. Relations of power, therefore, always lie beneath the surface of cultural activity.

Given these understandings, how should we delineate the realm of popular culture from that of culture in general? John Storey helps to highlight the fact that the term "popular culture" should at least refer to those aspects of culture that are widespread and which may be appreciated by a significant number of people (2009: 5–6). But even this description can be misleading if it fails to acknowledge that products and practices which are widespread and widely appreciated can achieve this status in a variety of ways. They do not necessarily appear simply by accident, but instead may arise as a result of the conscious efforts by some to influence the values of others. Hence, the issues of opportunity, influence, and power discussed above in relation to the term ideology also apply to the realm of popular culture. This is especially the case in the modern world where advances in technology make the dissemination and proliferation of ideas to a large audience much easier to accomplish. We live in a world of so-called 'mass communication,' where competing ideas and values clash on a daily basis, where various forms of media often serve as tools of rhetoric (argument) and potential manipulation. This has become far more pronounced since the industrial revolution in the 18th and 19th centuries (cf. Williams 1963; Burke 1994; and Storey 2003). But prior to this, even more basic developments of human society, such as the rise of empires and nations, the growth of international commerce, and the invention of the printing press have all served as important precursors to the modern age of mass communication. Today, most of us recognize that we now live in a global or worldwide society, where a great number of humans around the planet are connected by a variety of satellite-assisted technologies such as radio, television, internet, cell phones, and video game platforms. Thus, many of the planet's residents have multiple ways of communicating with one another, and many of the messages they send, including those with religious content, have the potential to develop a large audience. As a result, this book will use the term "popular culture" to refer to widespread and well-liked products, practices, themes, and values that have achieved their popular status because of their dissemination through the vehicles of modern technology, including **mass marketing**.

How Do Religion and Popular Culture Interact?

Conrad Ostwalt provides an extremely useful model for understanding the ways in which religion and popular culture have related in the past and continue to relate to one another today. They are not entirely separate things, and never have been. Each finds its meaning in relation to the other. Religion is an element of nearly every human culture, one "strand among many cultural strands that are interrelated in society" (Ostwalt 2003: 23; cf. Geertz 1973: 3). As Oswalt puts it, "Religion … [is] a cultural form that is directed toward the sacred, and that exists in dialectical relationship with other culture forms that sometimes explore religious content" (2003: 23). "Religion is necessarily entangled with secular culture" (Ostwalt 2003: 23); it is not something that is itself utterly distinct from other cultural forms, nor does it occur in any completely distinct way.

While it is undeniable that something we call religion 'happens' quite often throughout the world, whenever something religious occurs, it does so within the confines of other cultural events, that is, within a complex cultural context. This becomes clear when one recognizes that distinct cultures and subcultures regularly define the sacred in their own unique ways. There is no universally agreed upon way that all humans delineate the sacred from the mundane. This varies from people to people, and place to place. In the words of J. Z. Smith, "There is nothing that is inherently sacred or profane. These are not substantive categories, but rather situational or relational categories" (1988: 55). These terms serve as functional "labels" to designate and represent the way humans order their spatial environments and their activities within space (Smith 1988: 54–56; cf. also Smith 1992: 11). Religion is one way that humans uniquely organize their environments. And the significance of this is that, whenever something religious can be said to have happened, it must be understood as doing so in relationship to other things that are not considered sacred.

This insight represents a revolution in thinking about the role of religion in culture, especially in the Western world. Prior theories typically drew a fine line of separation between that which a society considered sacred and that which it considered non-sacred or secular (Ostwalt 2003: 8–14). Ostwalt, in his own treatment of so-called **secularization theory**, refers to this as a false or artificial dichotomy. His response is to argue for a more nuanced approach that recognizes how sacred and non-sacred elements of society are always interacting because the boundaries between the two are not firmly fixed (2003: 29). In fact, in the current situation, especially in contemporary America, there are two directions or movements of secularization that must always be considered. In the first, traditional sources of religious authority in society (i.e., those that have held sway for some significant amount of time) "are becoming increasingly more attune[d]" to those things that are typically considered non-religious, especially those things that are highly popular (Ostwalt 2003: 29). In some cases, these traditional religious authorities (i.e., religious institutions, leaders, texts, etc.) even "seek to emulate [secular practices and products] in the effort to remain relevant" to those audiences that value them (Ostwalt 2003: 29). For example, in the case of sacred texts, this is clearly seen in the way modern readers tend to interpret scriptures in light of their own, modern-day concerns, often with little reference to the ancient contexts in which they were originally composed. In the second direction or movement, Ostwalt recognizes that "popular cultural forms, including literature, film, and music, are becoming increasingly more visible vehicles of religious images, symbols, and categories" (2003: 29). In other words, modern-day products, practices, ideas, values, and voices are always influential on the way people understand religious truth. We should conclude from this insight that there is an ever-present flux, negotiation, or re-negotiation that occurs in any society between those elements or sources that are considered predominantly religious authorities and those considered to be predominantly secular or non-religious authorities. According to Oswalt, over time, societies do not necessarily become more secular or more religious, but differently-secular or differently-religious (2003: 31). Those things in society that are considered to be either religious or secular are always being defined or redefined in relation to one another.[1]

Summary

- The field of study known as Religion and Popular Culture is complex, interdisciplinary, and still relatively new to the academy, requiring foundational work in defining and delimiting its boundaries and definitions.
- Despite the difficulties and imperfections, working definitions for Religion, Culture, and Popular Culture are available and adequate for further study to proceed.
- 'Sacred' and 'Mundane' are empty conceptual categories used uniquely in different cultures to order the worldviews of their participants.
- Ostwalt's more nuanced theory of secularization better explains the complex, fluctuating relationship between religious and secular authorities in our world.

Discussion Questions/Activities

- Keep a log for one full day, recording every instance of a religious message found in the various pop cultural products and practices encountered, including everyday language or phrases (e.g., references to biblical material), song lyrics, TV commercials and shows, movies, advertisements, sports events, newspapers, literature, internet material, etc. Discuss the pervasiveness of religion in pop culture today.
- What is the nature and intended purpose of various religious content found in today's pop culture, and how do these reflect the negotiable boundaries between competing religious voices/authorities in your particular societal context?
- Discuss whether you agree with the idea that the concepts of sacred and profane represent empty conceptual categories for ordering human existence, versus realities in and of themselves. How would one go about proving or disproving that a unique, sacred reality truly exists and/or can be encountered in some fashion by human experience?
- What are the potential risks or dangers associated with people becoming differently religious over time? Who or what is most at risk, and how?

Glossary

Mass Marketing   The attempt to sell some commodity or product to a very large audience, often by utilizing some form of modern technology.

Phenomenon   An experience, event, or reality that is observable by the human senses, and which can be verified by factual data.

Ritual   A sequence of actions performed in a strict, pre-established pattern whose purpose is to reinforce certain beliefs, practices, and values as well as to produce some real benefit for the participant(s).

Secularization Theory   Traditionally speaking, the idea that human religious behavior is a primitive holdover from ancient times that will eventually fade away as society evolves.

Transcendent   Something that remains at least partially beyond full human apprehension and/or comprehension.

Note

1 Please note that, due to the nature of this introductory chapter, there is no Case Study section, such as will be found in the remaining chapters. Every other Case Study and chapter is in some way engaging with these ideas.

Further Reading

Paden, William E. (1994) *Religious Worlds: The Comparative Study of Religion.* Boston: Beacon Press.
   This is a very readable introduction to the academic study of religion, geared toward undergraduate students, which attempts to simplify the comparative method by focusing on a limited number of universal religious categories such as Myth, Ritual and Time, Gods, and Systems of Purity.

Kessler, Gary E. (2008) *Studying Religion: An Introduction through Cases.* 3rd edn. New York: McGraw-Hill.
   This text has the advantage of introducing new students to the phenomena of religion (power, myth, ritual, etc.) while also providing real-life examples of how they occur in various traditions through a case-study approach.

Storey, John (ed.). (2009a) *Cultural Theory and Popular Culture: A Reader.* 4th edn. Harlow: Pearson Education.
   Designed as a potential supplement to Storey's *Cultural Theory and Popular Culture: An Introduction* (2009), this is a sizable collection of readings on various theoretical approaches to understanding the workings of culture and pop culture. It includes units on Marxism, Feminism, Structuralism, Racism, Postmodernism, and Politics.

Journal of Religion and Popular Culture (n.d.) University of Toronto Press. Edited by David Feltmate and Jennifer E. Porter. Online. Available https://www.utpjournals.press/loi/jrpc.
   This subscription-based, online, peer-reviewed journal provides relevant, timely articles that explore the "interrelations and interactions between religion … and popular culture."

Lynch, Gordon (2005) *Understanding Theology and Popular Culture*. Malden, MA: Blackwell Publishing.

An introduction to studying popular culture from several different theological perspectives, including text-based, ethnographic, and aesthetic approaches. Lynch also provides a definition of popular culture and discusses the technological and consumer-oriented nature of "everyday life in contemporary Western society."

Mazur, Eric Michael and McCarthy, Kate (eds.) (2000) *God in the Details: American Religion in Popular Culture*, New York: Routledge.

A collection of essays on the intersection between religion and popular culture in America, covering a variety of products, practices, and themes including civil religion in popular music, popular morality and the supernatural in television, apocalyptic in film, secular rituals in religious holidays, consumerism and religion, and internet religion.

Forbes, Bruce David and Mahan, Jeffrey H. (eds.) (2017) *Religion and Popular Culture in America*. 3rd edn. Berkeley, CA: University of California Press.

An updated collection of essays on religion in modern day film, internet, literature, music, sports, television, and other cultural products, practices, and themes.

Culbertson, Philip and Wainwright, Elaine M. (eds.) (2010) *The Bible in/and Popular Culture: A Creative Encounter*. Semeia Studies: 65. Atlanta, GA: Society of Biblical Literature.

A collection of essays specifically focusing on the adaptation and interpretation of biblical images, texts, and themes in popular cultural products like literature and music.

Bibliography

Burke, Kenneth (1957) *Philosophy of Literary Form: Studies in Symbolic Action*. Rev. and abr. edn. New York: Vintage.

Burke, Peter (1994) *Popular Culture in Early Modern Europe*. Aldershot: Scholars Press.

Deming, Will (2005) *Rethinking Religion: A Concise Introduction*. New York: Oxford University Press.

Esposito, John; Fasching, Darrell J., and Lewis, Todd (2009) *World Religions Today*. 3rd edn. New York: Oxford University Press.

Geertz, Clifford (1973) "Thick Description: Toward an Interpretive Theory of Culture." Pages 3–30 in *The Interpretation of Cultures: Selected Essays*. New York: Basic Books.

Hall, Stuart (2009) "The Rediscovery of Ideology: The Return of the Repressed in Media Studies." Pages 111–141 in John Storey (Ed.), *Cultural Theory and Popular Culture: A Reader*. 4th edn. Harlow: Pearson Education.

Livingston, John C. (2008) *Anatomy of the Sacred: An Introduction to Religion*. 5th edn. Hoboken, NJ: Prentice Hall.

Molloy, Michael (2010) *Experiencing the World's Religions: Tradition, Challenge, and Change*. 5th edn. New York: McGraw-Hill.

Ostwalt, Conrad (2003) *Secular Steeples: Popular Culture and the Religious Imagination*. Harrisburg, PA: Trinity Press International.

Smith, J.Z. (1993) *Map Is Not Territory: Studies in the History of Religions*. Chicago: University of Chicago Press.

———— (1992) *To Take Place: Toward Theory in Ritual*. Chicago: University of Chicago Press.

———— (1988) *Imagining Religion: From Babylon to Jonestown*. Chicago: University of Chicago Press.

Storey, John (2009b) *Cultural Theory and Popular Culture: An Introduction*. 5th edn. New York: Pearson Education.

———— (2003) *Inventing Popular Culture: From Folklore to Globalisation*. Oxford: Blackwell.

Williams, Raymond (1983) *Keywords*. London: Fontana.

———— (1963) *Culture and Society*. Harmondsworth: Penguin.

Part I

Issues in Religion

2 Pop Culture's Critique of Sacred Traditions

South Park and Satire

Terry Ray Clark

Introduction

When I first began teaching Religion and Popular Culture as a college course around 15 years ago, I was surprised to find that a significant number of students failed to appreciate religious satire. It seemed that from their perspective, a fair amount of television programs, films, and literature, while occasionally humorous, contain highly exaggerated and mean-spirited depictions of religious people and their practices. The general tone was perceived to be mocking, and as a result, students often found these cultural products offensive. They therefore failed to appreciate their value both as entertainment and as educational tools for critically understanding their own culture.

Over time, it seemed that this sort of reaction was more common among students who self-identified as belonging to more conservative religious traditions. In addition, it appeared that such students were, by and large, more offended when their own traditions were satirized than when they encountered satires of someone else's traditions. While shifting cultural trends, including social media proliferation, and perhaps the fact that I now teach in a different institutional setting may explain why it seems that fewer students today take offense at religious satire, the phenomenon persists, and the following questions remain relevant. Does the failure of some students to appreciate religious satire derive from a lack of understanding about what satire really is and how it works? Are some students simply insecure about their own religious beliefs and practices? Are certain religious topics considered off limits for critique or humor? And is there an important role for religious satire in a healthy democracy that my students would benefit from exposure to?

Although I never performed a scientific study to identify the exact causes, I concluded then, and remain convinced today, that most of my students would benefit from being better educated about the nature of satire as a genre, as a method of communication, and as a contributor to the maintenance of a free and open society that ascribes value to the notions of freedom of religion and freedom from religion. This essay is an attempt to make

DOI: 10.4324/9781003079729-3

available to students and educators a useful, **genre**-based approach to understanding religious satire when it occurs in the context of popular cultural media.

I would like to begin by briefly reviewing a few of the real-life examples that convinced me of the value of this endeavor. One day while teaching a college course on Religion and Pop Culture, I made reference to the highly provocative episode of *South Park* titled "Christian Rock Hard" (S7E9, 2003). The episode critically examines the degree to which a contemporary Christian may actually have a "personal relationship with Jesus." This focus was apparently in response to the pervasiveness of the language of personal relationship in evangelical Christian circles. To demonstrate their conviction that some Christians take this idea too literally, the creators of the show decided to explore the notion of an intimate relationship with Jesus to a ludicrous and blasphemous degree.

In the episode, the character named Cartman, who regularly functions as a stereotype of bigotry and selfishness, creates a Christian rock band in an attempt to win a bet with his friends to see who can be the first to make a platinum album. Cartman chooses the genre of Christian music for his band because he believes Christians are gullible and easily persuaded into buying a product simply because it has a Christian label or Christian lyrics, regardless of how superficially religious the band members or message truly are. After quickly securing a record deal, Cartman's band makes a television commercial in which he sings a few lines from a number of cheesy love songs that treat Jesus as the object of the singer's romantic feelings. In one particular song that parodies the prayer life of the believer, Cartman's lyrics suggest that he would like to have oral sex with Jesus: "I wanna' get down on my knees and start pleasin' Jesus; I wanna' feel his salvation all over my face..."

To this day, I find this to be one of the most provocative and potentially offensive treatments of Christianity I have ever encountered in a popular culture product, and I still cringe whenever I show the episode in my classroom. However, I continue to use it because I consider it extremely effective for demonstrating several important characteristics of religious satire (which will be elaborated below). I have learned over time that when viewers fail to understand the nature of satire—what it really is and how it really works—it can be mistaken for being utterly antagonistic to the audience that might benefit most from understanding its intent. For example, one day after merely referring to in class (rather than showing) the *South Park* scene described above, one of my students was so offended that he accused me in a private e-mail of making fun of Christianity "as a matter of principle," and went on to recommend that I make fun of Muhammad, the prophet of Islam, instead of Jesus. I never quite figured out if the student considered it more appropriate to disrespect Muhammad than Jesus, or if perhaps he was wishing upon me some kind of violent retaliation, as this incident occurred around the same time that a Danish newspaper was facing backlash for printing satirical political cartoons about Muhammad that many of the world's Muslims considered highly offensive. Given the highly publicized nature of that event, I feared that my student did not wish me well. [Cf. *Jyllands-Posten* Cartoon Controversy that began in 2005.[1]] Regardless, it appeared that, from the student's perspective, my reference in the classroom to the satirical *South Park* material was equivalent to agreeing with and/or advocating the disrespectful ideology it was perceived to express. I concluded that I had failed to communicate clearly and convincingly why I considered this material worthy of my students' time, attention, and tuition dollars. I hope this chapter does not repeat that mistake.

A second enlightening incident occurred one semester when a particular student asked in advance to be excused altogether from viewing any episodes of *South Park*. The class had been forewarned in the syllabus about the potentially offensive nature of certain course material, but as a concession to the student, I suggested that she view some episodes of *The Simpsons* instead. I assumed that this other satirical material would serve as a less provocative and offensive substitute, while still demonstrating some of the key principles of satire that I wanted my students to learn. The student's reaction, however, was to say in so many words, "I'd rather not. I really don't want to fill my head with that kind of stuff." I was stunned, and temporarily found myself in a rare situation as a professor—I was at a complete loss for words. How could I teach the nature of religious satire in a Popular Culture class without actually introducing the student to real life, modern-day examples? What was it about religious satire that made it so offensive that students didn't care if they understood it or not? How could I impart a deeper understanding and appreciation for satire as an important form of communication? This chapter is, in part, an attempt to answer these questions.

First, I believe the reason for exposing students to religious satire, and the goal for any other teaching endeavor, should never be simply "to fill a student's head with something," as if education were merely an exercise in indoctrination, rather than the application of critical analysis to various subject matter. Likewise, I believe that educators should never seek to "make fun of" any religious tradition "as a matter of principle" (whatever that principle might be). While I will admit that all education has its ideological slant, ultimately, good education seeks to develop important skills in the student, including the ability to analyze data in intelligent ways. Education also necessarily requires students to be exposed to new ideas and new ways of viewing old ideas, but it need not require them to agree with everything they hear, read, see, and reflect upon. In the case of teaching Religion and Popular Culture, the goal should be to enlighten students about the nature of popular culture and its religious aspects, particularly the ways in which Western culture typically provides room for religious ideas, themes, and values to be communicated, explored, and evaluated in various forms of so-called "secular" media. Second, and conversely, students should be taught to recognize ways in which religious communities sometimes make use of popular secular ideas, products, and practices to further their own so-called "sacred" goals.[2] Students should never be required to agree or disagree with a particular ideological perspective, and all participants in the academy should be expected to provide supporting evidence for their positions. So, given these clarifying and apologetic comments about the study of religious satire, what is it about the nature of this material that makes it so difficult for some to appreciate or even study without revulsion?

Theory and Method

What Is Satire, and How Does It Work?

Satire, and more specifically, religious satire, is not a new phenomenon. One of the earliest written examples can be found in the Hebrew/Jewish canon of scriptures (equivalent in content to the Protestant Christian Old Testament). In the second major unit of the prophetic Book of Isaiah (Chs. 40–55), probably written sometime in the early post-exilic period (late 6th– early 5th century BCE), one encounters an ancient Israelite **caricature** of the religious practices of non-Israelite nations. One particular text pokes fun at those who worship their god(s) by constructing images out of wood and/or stone and bowing down before them (Isa 44:9–20). The depiction is far from flattering. In fact, it is downright inaccurate and unfair, grossly misrepresenting the religious beliefs and practices of many ancient Near Eastern peoples. It suggests that foreign worshipers are delusional (and downright stupid) for bowing down before what the text considers an obviously inanimate object that their own hands have fashioned, and which therefore has no real life or saving power within it. The real intentions of such worshipers are treated in a highly exaggerated and distorted fashion.

The purpose of this ancient caricature is **polemical**, that is, it is designed to discourage such a practice among the originally-intended ancient Israelite readers of the text. It represents a particular type of religious rhetoric (i.e., argumentation). It does not matter to the original author that this tradition exaggerates or misrepresents the foreigner's real intentions and understandings about the way the god(s) might inhabit a divine image in order to be present in some meaningful way to the worshiper. From the author's perspective, this is simply a ridiculous superstition (because it is considered to be false), and therefore it should be harshly criticized. The implicit point is this: if some belief or practice is considered to be false, it can and should be made fun of, even if it belongs to the sacred beliefs and practices of some other culture. In fact, some believers consider it a sacred task to do this sort of thing, because such religious satire holds the potential to improve the world by abolishing what is believed to be a false and foolish tradition.

A number of ancient Greek writers also incorporated satire into their compositions in order to criticize their rivals and what they considered the ludicrous beliefs and practices of their own cultures. Aristophanes, a famous Athenian playwright of the late 5th century BCE, provides a famous example in his comedic play *The Frogs*. In this work, Aristophanes implicitly ridicules the religious beliefs and practices surrounding the worship of the sensual god Dionysus. The god is depicted in stereotypically effeminate ways and is made to look the fool by his own slave. Eventually, Dionysus holds a satiric contest in Hades with two famous, but dead playwrights, Aeschylus and Euripides, whereby the dead poets also use satire to criticize one another's work. The winner of the contest is promised rescue from the underworld and an opportunity to revive Athenian society with his own literally resurrected career.

Humor, including what some would consider mean-spirited humor, has been used by countless individuals for centuries as a tool for critiquing what some consider potentially dangerous, excessive, or just plain silly beliefs and practices. It has served, and continues to serve, an important educational function. The modern era is no exception. Not only is satire regularly utilized by political cartoonists to critique what they consider the failings of governmental leaders, but many standup comics also discuss the subject matter of religion and politics for the chief purpose of entertainment, artfully and effectively tying together education and humor. Here, the subject matter of religion, often considered a topic off-limits to frivolity, is effectively used for entertainment for the very reason that people need an occasional break from too much seriousness about anything, including, and perhaps especially, religion. But how, exactly, does satire work?

One of the most helpful resources for understanding the nature and function of satire is Dustin Griffin's *Satire: A Critical Reintroduction* (1994). Although originally intended to clarify the nature of ancient satirical works, Griffin's theory applies quite readily to modern day manifestations of the genre, such as that found in literature, television, and film. I have adapted here the basic principles of Griffin's approach for the sake of helping others better appreciate what satire is and how it works.

According to Griffin, while satire is often, by design, both humorous and entertaining, it is primarily intended as an act of inquiry or exploration into the truth, falsity, or reasonableness of a particular idea or practice. It does not necessarily provide answers for all the questions that it raises and explores, nor does it necessarily prescribe alternative beliefs and practices to replace those that it criticizes. Satire is not simply a straightforward act of rhetoric or argumentation, with a predetermined conclusion that it seeks to persuade its audience to agree with. Instead, its ultimate goal is to create a more reflective, more critical thinking, and therefore wiser audience. Here, Griffin asserts a clear contrast between the purpose of satire, which is primarily exploratory, and that of classical rhetoric, which is argumentative and conclusive. Ultimately, however, at least in practice if not theory, this assertion by Griffin is somewhat overstated.

In reality, satire often does put forward an argument—an alternative version of the truth—albeit sometimes in rather subtle ways. Even if an argument is not explicit, an implicit truth claim is present in many satirical works. It should be noted that the vast majority of arguments, always and everywhere, are conducted by means of implicit, rather than explicit, truth claims. In normal, everyday language, as opposed to the kind of language one finds in a logic textbook, one rarely tries to persuade with very explicit language. In other words, satire often *does* intend to move an audience to agree with its own alternative version of reality, even if it requires analysis to expose the implicit meaning, as we will see in modern-day examples in this chapter.

Aside from his somewhat overreaching claim about the difference between rhetoric and satire, Griffin provides an extremely useful method for analyzing satirical texts, which he sees as made up of the following key components: Inquiry, Provocation, Display, and Play, with the occasional added element of "Unstable Irony" (1994; cf. also Booth 1974: 248). Inquiry and provocation work hand in hand, and the latter primarily serves the former. For Griffin, the most important characteristic of satire is that it is designed to explore the truth or validity of a particular idea or practice. It asks the question, "Does this really make sense?" or "Is this really true?" Satire is chiefly intended to examine something more critically than it has thus far been examined by a particular audience: "The satirist writes in order to discover, to explore, to survey, to attempt to clarify" (Griffin 1994: 39). Often, according to Griffin, the satirist has no pre-determined plan for what the outcome of the inquiry will be; there is no "predetermined argument," although as I have suggested above, many satires suggest otherwise (Griffin 1994: 39). But by and large, the purpose of a satire is to provide an opportunity for cultural critique, for an audience to begin thinking for itself and perhaps reach a new level of insight, especially in the area of self-understanding. I would also argue that sometimes the satirist would like to encourage an audience to respond by changing its behavior as well as its thinking, and this represents a form of **deliberative rhetoric**.

The second, and perhaps most controversial component of satire, is **provocation**. Provocation seeks to inspire critical thought by raising questions about things previously deemed unquestionable. Figuratively speaking, provocation seeks to "pull the carpet out from under" the audience, leaving it naked and exposed to its own folly. Provocation is, by design, rather abrasive. As Griffin puts it, "If the rhetoric of inquiry is 'positive,' an exploratory attempt to arrive at truth, the rhetoric of provocation is 'negative,' a critique of false understanding" (Griffin 1994: 52). The questions that satire raises are "designed to expose or demolish a foolish certainty" (Griffin 1994: 52). In other words, something that the intended audience simply takes for granted as true is targeted for serious scrutiny, if not outright annihilation! But it should be remembered that satire's purpose is not simply for the satirist and his/her allies to enjoy the (sometimes twisted?) pleasure of unleashing destruction upon something that their enemies smugly assume to be unassailable: "Its function is less to judge people for their follies and vices than to challenge their attitudes and opinions, to taunt and provoke them into doubt, and perhaps into disbelief" (Griffin 1994: 52, citing Elkin 1973: 201).

Provocation may take the form of an intentional obscurity, difficulty, puzzle, or absurdity, not merely to confuse the audience, but to gain attention and encourage concentration (Griffin 1994: 52–53). This could take the form of a paradoxical truth, in the popular sense of combining things that are normally considered opposites. For instance, *South Park* will often depict characters like Jesus or Satan behaving as mere mortals, with very human desires and weaknesses, rather than as superhuman beings. However, there is another, classical and more literal sense in which paradox, "another voice," is used as a means of provocation to present an alternate opinion to the so-called majority view, the latter of which often goes unquestioned (Griffin 1994: 53). The purpose of such paradox is to "rouze and awaken the Reason of Men asleep, into a *Thinking and Philosophical Temper*" (Griffin 1994: 53, citing Dutton 1707: 1, as quoted in Morris 1984: 169).

Provocation sometimes takes the form of holding up for the audience a mirror by which they may more accurately view themselves. This includes revealing to viewers their highly idealized self-images, desires, and goals, demonstrating that they are impossible to obtain, or alternatively, that they might actually disappoint them were they to be achieved (Griffin 1994: 62). The satirist "embod[ies] our highest image of ourselves and show[s] us that we are not it" (Griffin 1994: 62). And what some find even more disconcerting about satire is that it sometimes either offers no real solution or suggests that no solution even exists.

> The ultimate provocation—what Swift calls vexing the world—is to make readers look in the mirror and see that they are not and can never be what they claim to be. Satire cannot mend them; it can only hope to make them *see*.
>
> (Griffin 1994: 62)

Griffin suggests, therefore, that for some satirists, the only positive contribution of their work is to tell the truth, simply for the sake of revelation itself (Griffin 1994: 63). But I suspect there is also hidden beneath the rough exterior of many satires an ulterior motive of sharing the cold, hard facts of reality with others, if for no other reason than the simple fact that sometimes "misery loves company." However, the danger of such an assumption is that it may unfairly paint the satirist as too much of a pessimist or skeptic than is really necessary.

One of the challenges of using provocation effectively is knowing where to draw the line between seizing the attention of one's audience, perhaps with shocking material, and offending them to the point of driving them away. One needs to *maintain* an audience in order to communicate with them. But as Griffin points out, "An unregulated spirit of ridicule arouses concern, not just for decorum ... but for the safety of whatever one holds dear," and this can undermine one's underlying purpose (Griffin 1994: 55). Too strong a defensive reaction from the intended audience can make them deaf to what the satirist ultimately hopes to communicate.

The next two features of satire are display and play, and they are closely related. Both reflect the artistic skill of the satirist, and, like provocation, are ultimately designed to serve the goal of inquiry. Display refers to any satiric feature intended to demonstrate the satirist's gifts and talents for entertaining, for acquiring the audience's admiration and respect, even if it occurs in the context of being highly critical of something the audience holds dear. It builds respect and trust, both of which are useful for keeping an audience's attention, and for softening the abrasiveness of, or building tolerance for, the author's provocation. According to Griffin, "Anybody can call names, but it requires skill to make a malefactor die sweetly" (Griffin 1994: 73).

For example, in *South Park*, while Cartman regularly infuriates the other characters around him (and the audience as well) with his extreme bigotry and racism, the audience celebrates much more enthusiastically when his evil plans (which are often a key plot element) fail miserably. He is the character that every viewer loves to hate, and as such, he is a highly effective negative example that clarifies what are more appropriate attitudes and behaviors for the rest of the world. He helps to highlight any latent, revolting attitudes in the audience, and brings these things out into the open, expressing that which is, under normal circumstances, taboo (i.e., off-limits or unholy). In doing so, he earns a certain amount of embarrassing respect from the audience for his unbridled honesty. Ultimately, Cartman plays the role of the sacred clown, teaching that the opposite of Cartman is really what the creators are advocating. This, in fact, is one of the strategies of satire that immature or unenlightened viewers most often fail to understand.

Play refers to any element of fun and humor, any delightful or "self-delighting activity that has no concern for morality or for any real-world consequences save the applause of the spectators" (Griffin 1994: 84). Play is a "joyous exercise or movement," which not only entertains, but also provides an "arena...marked off from business or serious purpose" (Griffin 1994: 84). As a result, satiric play makes room for the treatment of otherwise serious subject matter in ways not normally allowed. This technique is clearly seen in the amount of religious satire found in standup comedy, as well as in the effective use of caricatures, for some of the most provocative satiric messages. It is no accident that some of the most potentially offensive religious satires occur in cartoon sitcoms. A fictitious character like Cartman, in a cartoon where all the characters are depicted in a rather flat, two-dimensional, or stereotypical way, can get away with much more provocation than a more realistic, human character. What some may initially criticize as uninspired or unrealistic artwork in *South Park* is actually an important and ingenious display of skill for more effective provocation, allowing the creators to push the boundaries of socially acceptable norms much further than human actors or otherwise more realistic depictions of human actions. For example, Cartman's frequent racial and anti-Semitic slurs directed toward the characters of Token and Kyle, respectively, would be less likely tolerated by viewers if depicted in a more realistic fashion.[3]

The last element of satire to be discussed here is unstable **irony**. According to Griffin, satire sometimes "acquires a momentum of its own" and spins out of control (Griffin 1994: 64). The satirist can display an almost devilish attack on anything deemed worthy of destruction, even if this undermines the overarching purpose of inquiry. Here one encounters an "ambivalence" that makes it difficult to "reconstruct that author's precise meaning with any confidence" (Griffin 1994: 67). This kind of satire primarily "takes the form of an evasion, a refusal to commit, a negative rather than an assertion" (Griffin 1994: 69, following Kierkegaard 1968: 263–281). Griffin suggests that sometimes "the process of inquiry is truly open-ended; its exploration has no territory or map, no particular complacency to disturb," and the satirist "fall[s] into a mindless cynicism where everything is subject to" attack (Griffin 1994: 69–70). The danger in this is that "the satire that attacks everybody [and everything] touches nobody. And the satirist who laughs too widely may be... dismissed as a buffoon," or, I would add, as simply evil (Griffin 1994: 70).

Case Study

Numerous early-season episodes of *South Park* deal with religious topics, addressing both practical ethics for living a meaningful life and issues related to the afterlife, including farcical depictions of heaven, hell, and their residents. Two of my favorite episodes with religious content are "Christian Rock Hard" (Season 7), mentioned above, and "Best Friends Forever" (Season 9).

South Park episodes often contain two story lines that are related and woven together in various ways, and "Christian Rock Hard" is no exception. How the two plots are related in a given episode is not always obvious, but this design encourages viewers to reflect upon the structure of each episode and usually provides a **cipher** for understanding the creators' intended message. As state above, in "Christian Rock Hard" the first story line involves Cartman's attempt to use superficial Christian music to create a platinum rock album before his friends, Stan, Kyle, and Kenny, can. This plot explores such things as the real nature and purpose of Christian music, the potential gullibility of Christian consumers, and what it really means to have a "personal" relationship with Jesus. The second story line explores the ethics of Stan, Kyle, and Kenny illegally downloading secular music from the internet in order to inform their developing style of music. It inquires about whether secular artists should produce music purely for the money or because they love art for art's sake. It asks whether it is unethical for average consumers to steal music if the artists are already "filthy" rich or if they can still make a good living on the proceeds from concerts and the sale of memorabilia.

The relationship between these two plots is quite easily grasped with a little bit of reflection. Both inquire about the ethics of exploitation in a pop culture world of mass marketing and mass consumption. Both inquire about the integrity of consumers and producers. Together, they raise questions about who is the victim and who is the criminal when greed combines with high tech media to compete for the average consumer's hard-earned dollars. Should musicians consider themselves artists, first and foremost, or are they merely greedy salespeople? Are consumers merely powerless, gullible pawns at the mercy of greater economic forces? Is Christian music any different from secular music? Are Christian consumers significantly different from secular ones?

In light of the fact that "Christian Rock Hard" is primarily focused on dealing with such complex ethical issues, the highly provocative exploration of the topic of a personal relationship with Jesus, while certainly an attention-grabbing and playful display, is treated quite superficially in comparison. It appears to be designed more for fun and for maintaining viewer interest, rather than as the central topic of inquiry. In the end, the episode asks far more questions than it answers. Yet it is understandable that some viewers interpret this episode as going well beyond merely raising the question of how intimately a believer may know an invisible god and feel instead that their religion is being aggressively mocked.

As stated above, most rhetoric is communicated implicitly, and this episode's critiques of secular music are no exception. For instance, in one scene, a police officer takes Stan, Kyle, and Kenny on a tour of famous music artists' homes in order to demonstrate the so-called devastating effects of consumers downloading music for free from the internet. Here, the boys learn that Lars Ulrich, drummer for the rock band *Metallica*, is in a deep state of depression because he will have to wait a few months before he can afford to install a "gold plated shark tank bar" next to his outdoor pool, all because of people downloading his music for free, rather than purchasing it legally. The boys are stunned, and quite sympathetic. Likewise, Brittany Spears is depressed because she has to downsize her private jet from a Gulfstream 4 to a Gulfstream 3, the latter of which doesn't even have a remote control for its surround sound DVD system. And finally, the tour ends with a visit to the home of rap artist Master P, who will likely be unable to buy his son an island in French Polynesia for his birthday this year. The boys are distraught over the thought that this child's wish of owning his own tropical paradise will not be fulfilled.

A second example of a more implicit argument occurs when Cartman loses his temper at a public award ceremony upon learning that his album did not go platinum, but instead earned a uniquely Christian Myrrh award. Cartman begins cursing and smashes his award, complaining that he will never be able to produce a platinum album with Christian music, because such music is only awarded Gold, Frankincense, and Myrrh albums. The presenter of the award protests, "But you spread the word of the Lord; you brought faith in Jesus," to which Cartman responds, "Ahh, fuck Jesus!" Butters, one of the other band members, then states, "Eric, I'm pretty sure you shouldn't say the f-word about Jesus." Cartman, however, doesn't care about the well-being of the band, or blasphemy, and his tirade drives away the entire audience. This is when the third band member, named Token, also responds, criticizing Cartman's self-centered behavior, which has now destroyed the band: "Good job dickhead; you lost the entire audience." His words here reflect the perspective of the creators about the risk artists take by being too self-absorbed and greedy to care about the audience that has made them successful. Having heaped racist verbal abuse on Token throughout the episode, Cartman then refers to Token one last time as a "Black asshole." Token finally loses control and, to use the kind of crude language typical of the show, kicks Cartman's ass. Stan then tells Kyle and Kenny, "Hmmn, I guess he got what he deserved," and even Butters, one of the show's most timid and naive characters, swears at Cartman and walks away.

Here, one encounters not an explicit argument against Cartman's (and the music industry's) greed and hypocrisy. Instead, the creators make the argument implicitly through the reactions of other characters. This closing moment suggests that the creators of the show are not simply anti-religious, anti-Christian, or anti-music industry. They do not advocate Cartman's sacrilegious behavior any more than they support greed among secular musicians. In fact, for the most part, the Christian characters in the episode are treated rather sympathetically. They may be presented as somewhat gullible and misled, but their behavior is well-intentioned. Likewise, everyday consumers of secular music, including those who download songs illegally, are also handled sympathetically. Provocation in the episode is designed more to help the audience think critically about not just the way some relate to Jesus, but also how they behave as producers and consumers of both religious and secular goods. Do believers conduct the business of Christian music any differently than that of secular music? Secular musicians are chided here for the hypocrisy of considering themselves artists when many are only in the music industry for the money. Their potential smugness and greed are highlighted by their petty, superficial concerns for outdoor bars, private jets, and private islands.

Griffin's categories of inquiry, provocation, display, play, and unstable irony can greatly assist the viewer's understanding of the real intentions behind such an example of religious satire. While some of my religious students initially react to *South Park* by focusing too much attention on the provocative religious material, critical analysis in light of the true nature of satire can redirect their attention to the more important object of inquiry. This helps them see that the provocation is normally placed in service of the inquiry, as are the display and play. Those who focus too much on the graphic language, potty humor, and disrespectful treatment of certain characters, beliefs, and practices in *South Park* fail to grasp that these are usually just a means to an end, not the end itself. They are often playful elements or an attempt merely to display the author's creativity. There are moments, of course, when play for play's sake takes center stage, and sometimes irony or an outright attack on something deemed ridiculous temporarily spins out of control. But the moralistic teaching emphasis of most *South Park* episodes suggests that cultural critique in the form of satire is the chief purpose. Many episodes include a so-called teaching moment near the conclusion, when a character (usually Stan or Kyle) raises questions for reflection, many of which are merely rhetorical, in order to suggest a better course of action for the viewer than what has been displayed thus far. This is typical of *South Park*, where the starring children often display more common sense than their parents or adult neighbors.

Sometimes, these moments do not implicitly clarify what the authors consider the correct response, but merely highlight what are considered incorrect ones. For example, near the end of the "Best Friends Forever" episode, in which Kenny has become brain dead and his situation has been seized upon by both right-to-life and right-to-death advocates to promote their respective causes, Kyle steps forward, as if speaking directly to the viewer, and makes a series of mature and rational statements: "Maybe we let this thing get out of hand. This issue is so complicated, but maybe we should just let Kenny go in peace." Kyle also suggests that people can do the right thing for the wrong reason, and the wrong thing for the right reason. He ends by saying, "C'mon everybody, I think Kenny wants to be left alone."

These statements are intended to sum up the lessons that the viewer should have learned throughout the viewing experience. They are not necessarily profound, or incredibly insightful. They simply reflect common sense. This episode never provides a conclusive answer to the right-to-life debate, but it does suggest some respectful ground rules for all parties involved, primarily focusing on trying to determine what the patient would have wanted. The purpose of this episode is to explore issues surrounding the right to life debate, specifically concerning disabled and potentially brain-dead individuals in the wake of the famous Terri Schiavo case (1998– 2005), in which the patient's husband sought to remove her feeding tube, against the wishes of other family members. The incident became a media sensation, and the Schiavo family found themselves at the center of a political battle in which few parties really cared about their gut-wrenching dilemma. Instead, various groups manipulated the situation to further their own agendas. Unfortunately, simple human decency and dignity were lost in the midst.

But the episode does not end on this note. Instead, irony prevails, because Kenny was initially killed by divine design before his body was revived in a vegetative state by human hands (i.e., doctors playing God, just because they can). God had chosen Kenny to lead the forces of heaven in an epic battle against the forces of hell, by intending him to control a golden PSP (PlayStation Portable; a handheld video game), which Kenny had mastered before his death. Eventually, and unbeknownst to all those on earth who fought over his right to life, it is only when Kenny is finally allowed to die that his soul is finally able to lead the forces of heaven to victory. This irony suggests that no one on earth can truly claim to know the will of heaven on certain issues, and it is presumptuous to assume such knowledge in order to manipulate others.

Conclusion

In conclusion, it should be clear that Griffin's categories may be readily applied to a variety of satiric texts, including both animated and live action television and film. This should be done carefully, with critical reflection. Over against one of Griffin's conclusions, some satires do more than simply point out something that is deemed incorrect or present the viewer probing questions for reflection. Rather often they suggest by implication what is considered a more appropriate position or a solution to certain problems. Nevertheless, Griffin's approach is helpful for better understanding a satiric author's intentions, regardless of which satiric element dominates. It would behoove all students of satire to clarify the chief topics of a satire's inquiry, asking what issues are being explored, what assumed positions are being questioned, and what more appropriate advice or course of action may be advocated. This should lead to a greater appreciation for the genre and a better understanding of the role of such elements as provocation, display, and play. Ultimately, if one better understands the nature of satire, there is a greater potential for one to learn from it, and therefore become a more critical thinking, self-aware, and wise consumer of popular culture. This would fulfill the overall goal of most satires quite nicely.

Summary

- Satire is a complex genre often misunderstood by those who are unfamiliar with its true nature and purposes.
- Griffin's approach provides an important resource for better appreciating satire's component parts and intentions, especially in pop cultural versions.
- The chief purpose of satire is inquiry, but provocation, display, and play are key tools for grabbing an audience's attention and keeping it.
- Sometimes the abrasiveness of provocation, as well as unstable irony, can undermine the goal of inquiry, and drive an audience away.
- Often satires go beyond mere inquiry and therefore function more rhetorically.

Discussion Questions/Activities

- How many examples of modern-day religious satire can you think of, and how many different pop culture genres do they represent (e.g., TV series, film, music, literature, video games, social media, etc.)?
- Thinking about these examples, are you convinced that their chief purpose is simply creating a more critically informed audience? Who do you think is their intended audience?
- For how many of your examples can you identify a rhetorical (argumentative) message? How would you describe this message?
- How many of your examples do you think are effective for accomplishing their chief purpose? Why or why not?

Glossary

Caricature   A literary or visual depiction of a person that exaggerates or otherwise distorts certain characteristics of his or her image and/or behavior.

Cipher   Either a means of encrypting or hiding one's intended message or the interpretive key to revealing or understanding a hidden message.

Deliberative Rhetoric   Argumentation whose purpose is to convince the audience to change their behavior or take up a new course of action.

Genre   A particular category of expression characterized by a cluster of conventional, recognizable stylistic elements employed for a specific purpose or goal.

Irony   A situation in which the expected outcome or intended effect is subverted, and the opposite occurs.

Polemic   An argument intended to dispute a position or person that is considered false or heretical.

Provocation   A deliberately annoying or irritating act intended to elicit a particular kind of emotion, thought, or deed from a target audience.

Notes

1 For access to a whole series of articles about this controversy, visit the following: https://www.nytimes.com/topic/subject/danish-cartoon-controversy
2 Conrad Ostwalt, Secular Steeples, 2nd edition, New York: Bloomsbury Academic, 2012, discusses the complex relationship between secular and sacred in popular culture in great detail.
3 Token, as his name suggests, plays the role of the primary Black child in the series, while Kyle serves as the primary Jewish child, both of whom, ironically, regularly challenge social stereotypes for their respective racial/ethnic categories.

Further Reading

Aristotle (1926). *The Art of Rhetoric*, trans. J. H. Freese, Loeb Classical Library 193, Cambridge, MA: Harvard University Press.
One of the most ancient and famous works ever written on rhetorical theory.
Arp, Robert (ed.) (2006). *South Park and Philosophy: You Know, I Learned Something Today*, Blackwell Philosophy and Pop Culture Series, Malden, MA: Blackwell Publishing.
A collection of essays on various aspects of the world of South Park, some more insightful than others, which address interesting philosophical, political, and religious topics. These are helpful for better appreciating the intellectual depth and educational value of the show.
Perelman, C. H. and Olbrechts-Tyteca, L. (1971). *The New Rhetoric: A Treatise on Argumentation*, trans. John Wilkinson and Purcell Weaver, Notre Dame, IN: University of Notre Dame Press.
The most extensive single volume on argumentative strategies and techniques. This is a very technical, but exhaustive resource on the topic of rhetoric.

Walls, Neal H. (ed.) (2005). *Cult Image and Divine Representation in the Ancient Near East*, Boston: American Schools of Oriental Research.

An insightful but technical collection of essays about the form and function of divine images in the ancient Near Eastern world.

Wisnewski, J. Jeremy (ed.) (2007). *Family Guy and Philosophy: A Cure for the Petarded*, Blackwell Philosophy and Pop Culture Series, Malden, MA: Wiley-Blackwell Publishing.

A collection of essays on various aspects of the world of Family Guy, some more insightful than others, which address interesting philosophical, political, and religious topics. These are helpful for better appreciating the intellectual depth and educational value of the show.

Bibliography

Aristophanes (1993). *Frogs*, ed. Kenneth Dover, Oxford: Clarendon Press.

Booth, Wayne (1974). *The Rhetoric of Irony*, Chicago: University of Chicago Press.

"Danish Cartoon Controversy." *New York Times.* Accessed 31 December 2021. https://www.nytimes.com/topic/subject/danish-cartoon-controversy

Dutton, John (1707). *Athenian Sport: or, Two Thousand Paradoxes Merrily Argued, to Amuse and Divert the Age*, London: Paternoster.

Elkin, P. K. (1973). *The Augustan Defence of Satire*, Oxford: Oxford University Press.

Griffin, Dustin (1994). *Satire: A Critical Reintroduction*, Lexington, KY: University of Kentucky Press.

Kierkegaard, Søren (1968). *The Concept of Irony*, trans. Lee Capel, Bloomington, IN: University of Indiana Press.

Lucian (1913–1936). *Volumes I–V*, trans. A.M. Harmon, Loeb Classical Library, Vols. 14, 54, 130, 162, 302, Cambridge: Harvard University Press.

Morris, David (1984). *Alexander Pope: The Genius of Sense*, Cambridge: Harvard University Press.

3 A New Myth

The Critical Study of *Star Wars* as Myth

John C. McDowell

Introduction

The concerns that have predominantly determined my research have to do with popular culture's contributions to the shaping of how people understand themselves, the world, and the politics of the good life, and more specifically how certain forms of violence are encouraged to be desirable or inevitable. As Terry Eagleton argues, "What may persuade us that certain human bodies lack all claim on our compassion is culture. Regarding some of our fellow humans as inhuman requires a fair degree of cultural sophistication" (Eagleton 2003: 156). To put this in more technical terminology, my work reflects on movies as ways of disciplining the imagination through "symbolic violence" (Žižek 2008: 1). The Latin word *cultura* (culture), after all, has an agricultural foundation, and means something like the soil in which crops grow.

George Lucas, the celebrated creator of *Star Wars* (hereafter this will be referred to be the abbreviation *SW*), recognises the significance of film for shaping the growth of audience's understandings of the moral life, the common good, and personal responsibility. He has spoken of filmmaking as involving, among other things, talking through "a very large megaphone" (Lucas, in Kline 1999: 90). In a number of interviews, he has even made grand claims about his purposes behind designing the *SW* saga. Quite early on Lucas began to describe this educative dimension of his work of cinematic storytelling through a term that has generated significant repetition among scholars of the franchise. In an article published the month before *SW*'s theatrical release, Lucas admitted to his interviewer that "I wanted to do a modern fairy tale, a myth" (Lucas, in Kline 1999: 53). Because of the connection between the *SW* sensation, the prominence of the myth-scholar Joseph Campbell's PBS interviews, and the popularity of the 1997 Smithsonian Institution's National Air and Space Museum exhibition, "In the public's imagination, the terms 'myth' and '*SW*' are very closely linked" (Silvio and Vinci 2007: 2).

What this means, and the character of what is meant by 'myth' in relation to a cinematic text (or, rather, set of texts) such as *SW* is not as simple as it might otherwise appear. After all, one must ask the telling question: what are Lucas' mythic *SW* movies an education in?

DOI: 10.4324/9781003079729-4

Theory and Method

'A Long Time Ago…': Star Wars, Genre-Pastiche and the Fairy Tale

An early draft summary (May 1973) of what was then tentatively titled *The Star Wars* was set in the thirty-third century. Lucas had in mind a *Buck Rogers/Flash Gordon* type action-adventure, but failing in the quest to procure the rights to remake *Flash Gordon*, however, he began to develop an 'original' hero-in-space adventure story (see Lucas, in Jones 2016: 172). The story gradually was removed from a future-of-this-world setting, and early in 1976 the script for *The Adventure of Luke Starkiller as Taken from the Journal of the Whills: Star Wars* opened with a longer version of the now famous scene-setting line: "A long, long time ago in a galaxy far, far away…" Possibly as a result of familiarity with Bruno Bettelheim's *The Uses of Enchantment* this is a conceptual link to fairy tales ('Once upon a time') and legends, in other words to the stories of our past.

Like Tolkien's *Hobbit* and *The Lord of the Rings*, Lucas had conceived of *SW* as being part of a grand narrative being recounted many years later. To that end he developed the idea of the *Journal of the Whills*, similar in function to Tolkien's ancestral mythology of Middle-Earth, *The Silmarillion*. This, Lucas claims, "was meant to emphasize that whatever story followed came from a book", an inspirational piece of heroic folklore in a 'holy book' (Lucas, in Rinzler 2008: 14). The second draft of Lucas' script even opens with a prophecy of a saviour.

The screen-crawl refers to a 'princess', but this is an echo not merely of the fairy story link but of another influence. Initially, when searching for a story to tie a few visual ideas together (principally, the cantina scene and the space battle), the story became shaped around Akira Kurosawa's sixteenth-century adventure, *The Hidden Fortress* (1958). The influence of this remains in several places in the final version: in the perspective on the story of the two squabbling peasants, Tahei and Matashichi (in *SW*, C3PO and R2D2); in General Rokurota Makabe's (in *SW*, General Obi-Wan Kenobi) rescue of the young Princess Yuki (in *SW*, Princess Leia Organa) to return her to her own people (in *SW*, Leia's family on Alderaan, and then the Rebel Alliance on Yavin IV). Lucas also named his religious order the 'Jedi' after the Japanese term 'jidai geki', meaning period film; and the Jedi were dressed in Buddhist-like monastic robes with kimonos underneath. At one stage Lucas had even toyed with the idea of making *SW* a wholly Japanese affair.

The director from Modesto was keen, too, on the swashbuckler movies of old, such as those starring Errol Flynn, and from this comes the notion of the Jedi as *knights* and of their weapons as *sabres* (albeit a technologically sophisticated version, *lightsabers*). The eminently popular Westerns of Lucas' youth had enough of an impact upon him for *SW* to raid that particular genre, with its frontier hero-mythology, for some of its inspiration. The saloon scene in John Ford's *The Searchers* (1956) "partially inspired the treatment's [Mos Eisley] cantina sequence" (Rinzler 2008: 15); Tatooine was a frontier environment, with settlers under constant threat from nomadic indigenous peoples ('Tuskan Raiders' or 'Sand People'); Han Solo is an old fashioned gunslinger, kitted out in waistcoat, boots and low hanging gun-belt; Luke's uncle Owen and aunt Beru are farmers living at the edge of civilisation; and the gun and the gangs (the Hutts, with their hired hands, bounty hunters), are the 'law'.

There are also references to, among other things, Isaac Asimov's *Foundation* stories' 'The Empire'; to the histories of imperial Rome, Britain, and Nazi Germany; to Fritz Lang's 1926 masterpiece, *Metropolis* (Lucas' C3PO); and Carlos Castaneda's *Tales of Power*.

But while *SW* involves something of a pastiche of genres its eclecticism is not simple homage. Instead, its referential diversity suggests that here we have something that *sums* up all others in a single instance, and consequently it becomes a *representative* narrative. This has much to do with its appeal to 'myth', and the kind of myth it is largely predicated on.

George Lucas and Myth

According to Lucas, "being a student in the Sixties, I wanted to make socially relevant films.... But then I got this great idea for a rock & roll movie, with cars and all the stuff I knew about as a kid" (Lucas, in Kline 1999: 89). As he was completing *American Graffiti* (1973), he began slowly designing his space-adventure. *THX 1138* (1971) had been a financial disaster two years before, and he was having problems selling the idea of *Apocalypse Now*, on which he had spent some of the past four years developing – Vietnam movies were too controversial film studios and audiences at that stage.

SW was conceived against a backdrop of cultural turmoil in America – the Vietnam War limped to its ignominious end, and many in the nation suffered traumatic introspection; President Richard Nixon was implicated in the Watergate scandal (1974); and economic misery loomed on the horizon. Francis Ford Coppola had challenged his friend Lucas to make "a happier kind of film" (Rinzler 2008: 4). In response, *SW* was supposedly created to encourage wonder, an enjoyment of stories, and a fantasy imagination among the youth after Vietnam. More specifically Lucas hopes to *re-educate* young people.

To many critics Lucas' *SW*, and his claims concerning it, look like a return to the older American hero-myths, and thus like a simple escapism that both emotionally comforts the traumatised American psyche and politically mitigates the possibility of learning from the mistakes that resulted in Vietnam in the first place. For instance, the Empire's Nazi-look resonates for American audiences with less morally complex wars, and thus re-romanticises American involvement in conflict. So influential film critic Pauline Kael even describes *SW* (and Spielberg's *Jaws*, 1975) as infantilising the cinema, reconstituting the spectator as child, and then overwhelming her with sound and spectacle, obliterating irony, aesthetic self-consciousness and critical reflection (Biskind 1998: 344). Other critics have claimed that

SW responds to the need for Americans to renew faith in themselves as the 'good guys' on the world scene (e.g. Gordon 1978).

That reading, however, should be contested. Firstly, Lucas' politico-cultural dystopian *THX 1138*, adapted from his Samuel Warner Memorial Scholarship-winning student film *THX 1138.4EB/Electronic Labyrinth* (1967), is a critical observation on the United States of the late 1960s and early 70s, accusing it of promoting a dehumanising capitalism that makes conformist 'masses' no less than does the Communism it was fighting against. Secondly, when Lucas' significant involvement in originally conceiving of the politically subversive *Apocalypse Now* ended, he admits migrating several of its broad themes into *SW*. "What we had in common is we grew up in the '60s, protesting the Vietnam War" (Lucas, in Biskind 1998: 317). Lucas claims that he dealt with many of the themes he had planned for his version of *Apocalyse Now* in *SW* (see Lucas, in Jones 2016: 179–180). In particular, *America* was acting in ways similar to the "evil Empire"; the Emperor Palpatine is like Nixon; and the Rebel Alliance's guerrilla-fighters reflect the Vietcong (even if they had an all-American cast). The subtext of the technologically inferior Vietcong versus the might of 'imperial' America is played out again in *Return of the Jedi* (Biskind 1998: 342).

Thirdly, it is important to observe that *American Graffiti* produced the kind of fan-mail that convinced Lucas that an upbeat mood movie could be more transformative of young people's increasingly fractured lives. "Traditionally we get … [moral values] from the church, the family, and in the modern world we get them form the media – from movies" (Lucas, in Kline, 53). In response, among other things, he lightened the serious tone by introducing more humour into *SW*'s third script-draft (1 Aug 1975). It consequently makes sense to understand Lucas' claims concerning challenging the post-Vietnam mood as an attempt to encourage a *new hope*: not a wallowing in self-pity or pacifying introspection, but a learning to be *moral* agents.

As early as 1977 (the month *before SW*'s theatrical release) Lucas declares: "I wanted to do a modern fairy tale, a myth" (Lucas, in Kline 1999: 53). What does Lucas understand by 'myth' and by *SW* as updating "ancient mythological motifs" (Lucas, in Rinzler 2008: 5–6)? What has been discussed above provides several clues.

The first is the connection with moral truths and myths. Most commonly the 'journalistic' use of the term 'myth' operates in contrast to the terms 'truth' or 'fact'. This is largely a hangover from late nineteenth-century studies. So, for E.B. Tyler (1832–1917) myths are primitive pre-scientific explorations of the world that have to be read as literal, and accordingly scientifically redundant, explanations of states of affairs. In contrast, Lucas attempts to provide what he considers to be truthful insight into the nature of things and persons, and thereby provide a context for moral reflection and education through a particular visual narrative form. In this he builds more on twentieth-century scholarly developments.

The second is Lucas' reference to the updating of "*ancient* mythological motifs". The idea is not to generate a 'new myth', since such a thing is, by the very *cultural* nature of myths, not possible anyway. Myths are stories that *cultures* tell about themselves, and expressions of what cultures deem to be valuable and meaningful (morally and spiritually) – not narratives that flow simply from a single visionary.

The third is Lucas' reference to "ancient mythological *motifs*", suggesting that myths are largely alike. In this approach Lucas had learned from the likes of Joseph Campbell's (1903–1987). The connection of *Star Wars* more concretely with Joseph Campbell's *Hero of a Thousand Faces* was first mooted, albeit rather briefly, by Robert Collins (Collins 1977: 1–10). This is a connection that has been spoken of by Lucas on several occasions. The filmmaker explains that he had studied anthropology in college for a couple of years, and that there he encountered Campbell's *Hero of a Thousand Faces*. When writing *SW*

> I was going along on my own story, I was trying to write whatever I felt. And then I would go back once I'd written a script … and check it against the classic model of the hero's journey … to see if I had gone off the deep end, and simply by following my own inspiration … it was very close to the model.
>
> (Lucas, in Kaminski 2008: 215)

Here Lucas explicitly admits using the hero-myth as a touchstone for *SW*, checking his writing against the "classical model" (or, rather, Campbell's version), and discovering that he was already working in these terms. Consequently, when Lucas shows Campbell the 'classic trilogy' at Skywalker Ranch in 1983, the myth-scholar grandiosely remarks, "I thought real art stopped with Picasso, Joyce and Mann. Now I know it hasn't" (Campbell, in Larsen and Larsen 1991: 543).

Campbell's own approach largely built on the foundations laid in 1876 by Austrian scholar Johann Georg von Hahn on the 'Aryan' hero tales, and Lord Raglan's 1936 linking of the myth of the hero (the god) with ritual (following J.G. Frazer) with his patterning of 'mythic narrative'. Campbell compares the myths of various cultures and controversially argues, following Carl Jung's theory of archetypes, that they are all the same 'monomyth'. Ignoring the cultural specificities of each 'myth', he generalisingly claims there is broadly the same hero in each one, only with this essence being displayed under different, and culturally specific, guises (Campbell 1949: 4). Campbell's failure to pay sufficiently deep attention to the particularities of myths and their various concrete contexts is what produces the notion of the archetypes. In fact, "He is interested less in analyzing myths than in using myths to analyze human nature" (Segal 1987: 137–138). What emerges is not the interest in the many creation, fertility or deliverance myths, but rather in the myth of hero's journey, particularly the psychological one from childhood to adulthood – a journey of 'self-discovery'.

Through Campbell, Lucas is able to draw from a well-stocked store of ancient possibilities for characterisation and plot structuring when shaping the journey or 'adventures of Luke Skywalker'.

Case Study

Identifying a mythic resonance in any text is far from being the end of the process of myth-study, however, even though much of the scholarship continues to perpetuate a simplistic approach as if myths are timeless and monochromatic (for a recent example, see Guitton 2019). In fact, without a more contextual approach, myth-study may even be a distraction from asking crucial questions of the text (see Desloge 2012). According to Roland Barthes, "one can conceive of very ancient myths, but there are no eternal ones for it is human history which converts reality into speech and it alone rules the life and death of mythical language" (Barthes 1972: 108). Barthes' work in *Mythologies*, for instance, opens up questions about what values are being assumed and presented in myths, about "the complicity of myth in establishing and maintaining social dominance and power structures" (Wetmore 2005: 95). After all, "Storytelling … is never neutral. … [E]ach narrative carries its own weightings regarding the moral worth of its characters, and dramatises the moral relationship between certain actions and their consequences" (Kearney 2002: 155).

There are politically and ethically significant questions about the largely hidden and otherwise unquestioned cultural assumptions/myths that shape *SW* as well as give it an audience. These need to be exposed in order to be tested and possibly contested. So, for instance, does it express, assume and reinforce 1970s' American patriarchalism, racism, homophobia, individualism, or American supremacism (see McDowell 2016; Charbel 2016; Howe 2012)?

Among these debated issues, the one that will be the case study for the remainder of this chapter is announced in the title of the *SW* movies: it is a story of violence, of war! With the US's moon landings eight years earlier, "a triumph of the spirit and will as well as a major technological feat" (Henderson 1997: 136), for a moment Americans forgot the 'Cold War' troubles and celebrated optimistically. Yet Lucas' 'war' theme is not only references *Flash Gordon* space-serials, Kurosawa's *The Hidden Fortress*, and Vietnam, but suggests that even the new frontier (space) is not free from human conflict. After all, the 'space race' was itself the fruit of the Cold 'War'. By setting the audience in the 'middle' of war does *SW* invite the audience to see violent conflict as being originless, as being the way things are?

'You Don't Know the Power of the Dark Side' (Vader)

Biblical scholar Walter Wink has grandly identified the "myth of redemptive violence" as "the real religion of America" (Wink 1992: 13). This enshrines the belief that violence saves, that war brings peace, that might makes right. ... Violence simply appears to be the nature of the things. It's what works. It seems inevitable, the last and often, the first resort in conflicts.

(Wink 1998: 42)

A number of scholars have discovered just such a myth underlying *SW*. The critique is not about the *amount* of violence in *SW* – after all, anti-war movies like *Apocalypse Now* (dir. Coppola, 1979) are full of violence. Rather, the question concerns the *purpose* of the violence, whether it portrays a violence that disturbs us into moral reflection and vigilance against pressures to violate other people in our own contexts.

SW's final scene, the medal-ceremony set in the throne room of the Rebel base at an ancient Massassi temple on the fourth moon of Yavin, is instructive and emotionally climactic. Its temper is an entirely jubilant one, one of resolution achieved (Of course, Vader's escape has notably left enough unresolved to support a sequel.). While this may reflect historic moments like those in Trafalgar Square and Times Square after the Victories in Europe and Victories over Japan (1945), it ignores the cost and traumatic loss. For instance, while Luke's good childhood friend, Biggs Darklighter, has recently been killed in the battle, not only is there no mention of this but Luke's mood on returning is an unreservedly euphoric one. Rubey sees this as romanticising war as "tidy and uncannily bloodless" (Rubey 1978: 9), presenting it as thrilling and entertaining. Moreover, the sensibility of 'good' victorious, 'evil' defeated, leads critics to detect in *SW* a morally simplistic Manichaean sensibility (e.g. Biskind 1998: 342–343; Henderson 1997: 117; Wetmore 2005: 96; Lee 2016). This is reinforced by the suggestion that *SW*'s evil is rather obvious, and has its personification in flatly dark characters such as Darth Vader, and later Darth Sidious (*Return of the Jedi*, dir. Richard Marquand, 1983) and Darth Maul (*The Phantom Menace*, dir. Lucas, 1999). In *SW*'s second draft (1975) there was no backstory granting Vader a more complex psychology. Even when he does finally appear in the final movie, he, with his visual allusion to Nazism and black knight malevolence, exhibits nothing but power and the iconic presence of menace. Vader's costume is symbolic – a combination of Nazism (the helmet, and even the SS black), medieval monastic robes, a samurai girdle (and, again, the helmet as well, reminiscent in shape of the Japanese *kabuto*), and the black knight (the black armour), and Jack Kirby's Darkseid and Doctor Doom (see Rinzler 2008: 131). Only the smallest glimmer of something more complex appears in Obi-Wan's revelation that Vader had been "a young Jedi Knight".

Understanding a movie involves appreciating the whole *mise-en-scène*, and the images of this particular scene are full of significance. Firstly, Han's western gunslinger style costume refers to the violent American frontier myth that, among other things, skirts over the moral problems with the late nineteenth-century appeal to 'Manifest Destiny' in settling the West. *SW*, critics argue, displays a vigilantist suspiciousness of authority, and thus the gunslinger's being a law-unto-himself. "The ultimate victory of good over evil finally boils down to firing laser-blasters, detonating bombs, or slicing through one's enemies with a light saber" (Stone 2000: 139).

The battle of Yavin had involved the *mass* destruction of all those on the Death Star. Is this any different in scope from the Imperial destruction of Alderaan? The difference in the two is simply one of mood and attitude, so that the latter is to be seen as an aggressive and wicked act of those who are 'evil', whereas the former is a necessary act of moral virtue and heroism. *SW*, therefore, becomes as much a 'revenge narrative' as a quest and rescue story. According to Lawrence, when Luke, "with an utterly clear conscience", destroys the Death Star *SW* helps "restore a nuclear pleasure earlier dampened by the grim awareness that hundreds of thousands of Japanese were incinerated at Hiroshima and Nagasaki" (Lawrence 2006: 85).

Secondly, does this religious setting in the ancient Massassi temple provide religious justification for the preceding violent action against 'evil'? Critics often point to the 'religious' concept of 'the Force' as dividing reality into *both* good *and* evil. Luke may have used 'the Force' to help him select the appropriate moment to fire his proton torpedo into the Death Star's reactor shaft, but the first occasion in the movie that 'the Force' is mentioned is quite different. Vader in the Death Star Conference Room threatens the life of the religious scoffer, Admiral Motti, with the *power* of 'the Force'.

Thirdly, the visual imagery substantially echoes two moments from Leni Riefenstahl's Nazi propaganda movie *The Triumph of the Will* (1934). The first is when three figures silently march between two mass ranks of troops at Nurnberg, while the other, significantly, is the concluding, triumphant scene. According to Lucas, the visual overlaps were entirely unintentional, and that he had planned instead to use a set of images from Riefenstahl for "the Emperor on the Empire planet" (Lucas, in Rinzler 2008: 325). Critics remain unconvinced!

'Don't Make Me Destroy You' (Vader): Defensive Violence

The main difficulty with this reading is that it abstracts *SW* from its historical context (the questioning of American empire), and, crucially, from the succeeding movies in the saga. The succeeding movies subvert several of the frequently offered critiques (Manichaeism, and the 'myth of redemptive violence').

By *The Empire Strikes Back* (dir. Irvin Kershner, 1980), Luke, the heroic destroyer of the Death Star, has become a Rebel commander; and his 'Force-consciousness' has significantly improved (he 'Force-grabs' his lightsaber in the Wampa's cave on Hoth). Early in the movie a ghostly Obi-Wan Kenobi instructs Luke to go to Dagobah and be trained by Jedi Master Yoda. But what the young man finds on Dagobah is far from what he had expected.

The planet itself is a murky and swampy world, wholly uncivilised in a way that makes his former home-world, gangster-run Tatooine, appear cultured and sophisticated. It is not the place from which to expect a great Jedi Master.

On feeling he is being watched he swings around with blaster drawn only to see something apparently unthreatening – an unarmed diminutive green being with protruding ears. This character acts like a scavenger, uses strange grammatical syntax, is physically unimpressive, and appears more fool or jester than Jedi Master.

Later, however, he is unexpectedly revealed to be precisely the one the youth has been seeking. The problem for Luke, with his obviously militaristic notions of 'power' simply is that the reality did not fit the expectation of what "a great warrior" should look like. Yoda's initial appearance could not be more contrasting with that of Vader. The masked Sith Lord arrives striding over recently slain bodies, exuding a cool and power-full arrogance, distinguished by his menacing warrior dress and with his cape flowing behind him that impressively adds to the threat of his presence. His voice and manner reveal that he is one to be obeyed because, imposing in form and character, he is eminently fearsome. Soon after he is seen holding a Rebel commander by the neck a few feet off the ground before the sound of breaking bones can be heard. *The difference between Yoda and Vader has to do with different conceptions of power and understandings of the self –* for Vader, power is the power of force and the right of might; for Yoda, power has to do with the virtues of wisdom, self-control, and just living; for Vader, the self is to be exalted, and that at others' expense; while Yoda is a servant of 'the Force', and correspondingly a servant of all living things. The Luke who *begins* in *SW* with a macho sense of the hero-myth has to be brought up short by Yoda. The fact that he can ask "Is the dark-side stronger?" indicates just how difficult it is for him to move away from thinking in terms of sheer power, echoing Vader's response to Admiral Motti earlier in *SW* over "the power of the Force". Luke's sense of the Jedi way, of 'the Force', is to be radically purged of inappropriate conceptions and valuations. He is forced to *unlearn* what he has learnt, to face his prejudices and misunderstandings about life. This is why Yoda later challenges him with the rhetorical question: "Judge me by my size do you?"

So, Yoda responds to Luke's talk of a "great warrior" by claiming that "wars not make one great", and later instructs, "A Jedi uses the Force for knowledge and defence, never for attack." Anger, fear, hate, aggression, all those traits that are conducive to generating violence, characterise the dark-side. This is why the Jedi who resort to such unrestrained belligerence suffer for their actions. Luke's aggressiveness, for instance, in later cutting his training short in order to rush off to face Vader and save his friends culminates in his losing his right hand in his defeat. In this way the saga begins to seriously expose the problems of appealing to 'necessary violence'. Lucas had originally planned to name his central protagonist Luke Star*killer* and the change to Skywalker a month into shooting *SW* in 1976 itself is a significant nod towards the Jedi philosophy. The filmmaker too seems to be demonstrating an unlearning of what he had learned!

'I Will Not Turn and You'll Be Forced to Kill Me' (Luke Skywalker): Pacifism?

In many ways the mood of the third movie to bear the name of the *SW* brand, *Return of the Jedi*, echoes that of the first one. Lucas appointed Marquand to direct partly to be guaranteed more control at all levels in a way he was not with Kershner, director of *The Empire Strikes Back*. It involves a high-octane race to destroy a newly operational Death Star, has a climactic battle scene, and a celebratory end.

The climatic conflict is cast, though, in three different settings: a Rebel team on the forest moon of Endor, supported by the indigenous Ewok peoples, battles to destroy the shield generator that is protecting the incomplete Second Death Star; the Rebel fleet fights to destroy that super-weapon; and on the Second Death Star Luke clashes with Darth Vader in front of the Emperor.

Lucas comments that Luke "has the capacity to become Darth Vader simply by using hate and fear and using weapons as opposed to using compassion and caring and kindness" (Lucas 2004). The visual imagery is striking – Luke's Jedi clothing is now black, and his prosthetic right hand is an early reflection of his father's mechanised state. He is being urged by the Emperor to succumb to the values of the "dark side" (hate, anger, revenge and self-assertiveness), take revenge on Vader, and replace his nemesis at the Emperor's side.

This is a movie that for some time seems to have been heading for the title *Revenge of the Jedi*. Yet with the release date looming, the movie was renamed to *Return*... One of the reasons given, recounted by producer Howard Kazanjian and actor Mark Hamill, is that 'revenge' is not the business of Jedi (see Kaminski 2008: 282–284, 460). So, Luke finally refuses to succumb to the Emperor's temptation to kill his most bitter of foes in a fit of angry aggression when he has the chance, and discards his lightsaber, thereby leaving himself defenceless against the Emperor's own destructive rage. He is prepared to sacrifice himself rather than do evil.

In his spiritual journey into a "larger world" (Obi-Wan) Luke's whole value system has to be deconstructed (or "unlearned", in Yoda's terms) and replaced with a whole new way of seeing the life and interrelations of all things. Towards the end, then, his journey seems to have brought him closer to a 'pacifism' that is an active 'non-violence', a purposeful action that is beyond a 'bare peace'. His heroic journey is into a type of 'sainthood' rather than into 'warrior-heroism'. Of course, the Empire is defeated only through the violent act (albeit defence-of-another) of Vader/Anakin, the commando attack on the imperial shield bunker, and the torpedo from Lando Calrissian in the Millennium Falcon. Luke's action is just a hint of peace, a moment, but not any less significant for that!

Conclusion

"The films visually and through narrative are lengthy ruminations on violence and power" (Wetmore 2005: 20). But what kind of ruminations? The critics' discovery of the 'myth of redemptive violence' is too simple. Certain contextualising features must be borne in mind: for instance, Lucas' critical response of the Vietnam War, and his claims that Nixon's America embodies oppressive empire as much as the rebellion for freedom. Lucas may have himself come from a politically conservative home, but he broke with his father's wishes, headed off to what father George Lucas Sr. considered to be 'sin city' – Los Angeles and the University of Southern California – became engaged in avant-garde filmmaking, and disagreed with the Vietnam War. Moreover, the post-1977 movies in the saga crucially indicate that the various features that make *SW*'s violence look like a politics of revenge against the 'evil them' need understood differently. Taking these detailed steps enables a deeper reading of *SW* than ones often heard, and we have not even discussed the considerably more complex prequel trilogy in which the story-arc of the 'classic trilogy' ('the adventures of Luke Skywalker') moves in a thematically different direction ('the tragedy of Anakin Skywalker').

And yet despite the trajectory of this deeper reading and the cautionary message about violence, there still remains a concern: *SW*'s violence is insufficiently horrifying and emotionally involving, at least not until *Revenge of the Sith* (dir. Lucas 2005). Its form in this space action-adventure still looks too exhilarating, and children may not be dissuaded from engaging their 'enemies' with a lightsaber or a blaster pistol in conscious mimicking of their swashbuckling heroes. As they mature the question remains: will they begin to learn the lessons of Jedi compassion, self-giving and other-interestedness, or will they feel the pressure of *SW*'s ambiguity in the direction of reducing moral issues to simple affairs, and settling conflicts with 'alien' others with violence?

Summary

- George Lucas conceives of *SW* as a kind of *Flash Gordon* adventure serial and space opera.
- The real-world background was the Vietnam War, and *SW* is supposedly Lucas' attempt to morally *re-educate* young people.
- The ideas for *SW* slowly emerged through the influence of, among other things, Akira Kurosawa, John Ford, and especially Joseph Campbell.
- *SW* was influenced by other cultural myths, and many critics see it reflecting the American "myth of redemptive violence."
- However, *SW* needs to be read in its political and social context, and in the context of the other five movies that make up Lucas' *SW* saga.
- The saga displays various understandings of the social role of violence, from defensive violence to even a pacifist instinct.

Discussion Questions

- What are 'myths'?
- Do 'myths' help us understand *SW*?
- What, if any, resources does *SW* have for (a) supporting and/or (b) resisting the 'myth of redemptive violence'?
- What modern mythologies shape *SW*?

Glossary

Archetype An original image or paradigmatic character. According to Carl Jung the archetypes are to be found in all humanity.

Classic Trilogy *Star Wars* movies Episodes IV-VI, released 1977–1983 (*Star Wars* [later known as *A New Hope*], *The Empire Strikes Back*, and *Return of the Jedi*). Differentiated from the 'prequel trilogy', Episodes I–III released 1999–2005 (*The Phantom Menace, Attack of the Clones, Revenge of the Sith*).

Dystopia From the Greek literally meaning 'bad place'. A view of a degraded society, for instance where the government is repressive.

Ideology A set of beliefs which reflects the beliefs and interests of a nation, political or cultural system, or groups within society and shapes the way persons in that society understand themselves and how they should act.

Manichaeism The religious teachings of third-century Persian prophet, Mani. Associated with cosmic dualism – a primordial conflict between light and darkness, good and evil.

Manifest Destiny Nineteenth-century belief that America is God's chosen land that has been allotted the whole of North America, and thus could rightfully spread west across the continent.

Mise-en-scène Adapted from theatrical studies, literally meaning 'to put onto stage'. It refers to everything that can be seen inside the frame of the film: the characters and their positioning, the props, the lighting, the costumes, as well as how the framed image is established through camera angles, and so on.

Myth The Greek term *mythos*, meaning 'speech' or 'word'. In early Greek literature its reference ranged from 'a true story', 'an account of facts', and so 'fact' itself, to an invented story, a legend, fairy story, fable or poetic creation.

Mythology The body of inherited myths of any culture.

Screen-Crawl Provides information at the opening of the *Star Wars* movies as a time-saving plot device to fill in background matters. A visual nod back to the 1930s' *Flash Gordon* adventure serials.

Further Reading

Kapell, M.W., and Lawrence, J.S. (eds.) (2006), *Finding the Force of the Star Wars Franchise: Fans, Merchandise, and Critics*, New York, et al.: Peter Lang.

Moves away from myth-based criticism to ideology criticism, and critically evaluates *SW* as a cultural set of texts that demand deep critiques of its approach to issues of race, gender and sexuality, politics, economics, and religion. Also discusses issues of *SW*'s fandom.

Lucas, G. (Apr. 26, 1999), 'Of Myth and Men: A Conversation Between Bill Moyers and George Lucas on the Meaning of the Force and the True Theology of Star Wars', *Time* 153.16, 90–94. http://www.time.com/time/magazine/article/0,9171, 990820,00.html, accessed 4/4/06.

SW's creator discusses issues of myth, spirituality and religion in relation to his saga.

McDowell, J.C. (2016), *Identity Politics in George Lucas' Star Wars*, Jefferson, NC: McFarland Press.

Addresses issues of the violence of war, patriarchy, and white supremacism in *SW* by reading the saga in its historical context.

McDowell, J.C. (2017), *The Gospel According to Star Wars: Feeling the Force of God and the Good*, 2nd edn. Louisville: Westminster John Knox Press.

A critical theological treatment that reads *SW* contextually and attempts to understand the mythologies that shape it, from Joseph Campbell, and tragic drama, to contemporary American myths. Argues that *Star Wars*' ethical values do not easily succumb to violent, racist, sexist, and politically conservative myths as critics claim.

Rinzler, J.W. (2008), *The Making of Star Wars: The Definitive Story Behind the Original Film*, Ebury Press.

A detailed exploration of the making of *Star Wars* from archived interviews with George Lucas and key cast and crew.

Sweet, D.R. (2016), Star Wars *in the Public Square*: The Clone Wars *as Political Dialogue*, Jefferson: McFarland Press.

Reveals the ways in which *The Clone Wars*, following the trajectory of Lucas' *SW*, complicates and challenges the dominant political myths of American identity that contribute to the violence of national war-efforts.

Bibliography

Barthes, R. (1972), *Mythologies*, trans. Anette Lavers, New York: Hill and Wang.

Biskind, P. (1998), *Easy Riders, Raging Bulls: Sex-Drugs-and-Rock 'n' Roll Generation Saved Hollywood*, New York: Touchstone.

Campbell, J. (1949), *The Hero With a Thousand Faces*, New York: Princeton University Press.

Charbel, P. (2016), 'Deconstructing the Desert: The Bedouin Ideal and the True Children of Tatooine', in Peter W. Lee (ed.), *A Galaxy Here and Now: Historical and Cultural Readings of Star Wars*, Jefferson: McFarland: 138–161.

Cherry, C. (1998), *God's New Israel: Religious Interpretations of American Destiny*, rev. edn., University of North Carolina Press.

Collins, R.G. (1977), '*Star Wars*: The Pastiche of Myth and the Yearning for a Past Future', *The Journal of Popular Culture* 11.1: 1–10.

Desloge, N. (2012), '*Star Wars*: An Exhibition in cold War Politics', in Douglas Brode and Leah Deyneka (eds.), *Sex, Politics, and Religion in Star Wars: An Anthology*, Lanham, Toronto, Plymouth: The Scarecrow Press: 55–62.

Eagleton, T. (2003), *After Theory*, London and New York: Penguin Books.

Gordon, A. (1978), '*Star Wars*: A Myth for Our Time', *Literature/Film Quarterly* 6.4: 314–326.

Guitton, M.J. (2019), 'The Underwater Quest of Prince Lee-Char: Renewing the Hero Archetype in Star Wars', *Journal of Religion and Popular Culture* 31.1: 44–58.

Henderson, M. (1997), *Star Wars: The Magic of Myth*, New York: Bantam Books.

Howe, A. (2012), '*Star Wars* in Black and White: Race and Racism in a Galaxy Not So Far Away', in Douglas Brode and Leah Deyneka (eds.), *Sex, Politics, and Religion in Star Wars: An Anthology*, Lanham, Toronto, Plymouth: The Scarecrow Press: 11–23.

Jones, B.J. (2016), *George Lucas: A Life*, London: Headline.

Kaminski, M. (2008), *The Secret History of Star Wars: The Art of Storytelling and the Making of a Modern Epic*, Kingston, Ontario: Legacy Books Press.

Kearney, R. (2002), *On Stories*, London: Routledge.

Kline, S. (ed.) (1999), *George Lucas: Interviews*, Jackson: University Press of Mississippi.

Larsen, S. and Larsen, R. (1991), *A Fire in the Wind: The Life of Joseph Campbell*, New York: Doubleday.

Lawrence, J.S. (2006), 'Joseph Campbell, George Lucas, and the Monomyth', in Matthew Wilhelm Kapell and John Shelton Lawrence (eds.), *Finding the Force of the Star Wars Franchise: Fans, Merchandise, and Critics*, New York, et al.: Peter Lang: 21–33.

Lee, P.W. (2016), 'Periodizing a Civil War: Reaffirming an American Empire of Dreams', in Peter W. Lee (ed.), *A Galaxy Here and Now: Historical and Cultural Readings of* Star Wars, Jefferson: McFarland: 162–188.

Lucas, G. (Apr. 26, 1999), 'Of Myth and Men: A Conversation Between Bill Moyers and George Lucas on the Meaning of the Force and the True Theology of Star Wars', *Time* 153.16, 90–94 http://www.time.com/time/magazine/article/0,9171,990820,00.html, accessed 4/4/06.

Lucas, G. (2004), 'Commentary', DVD of *The Empire Strikes Back*.

McDowell, J.C. (2016), *Identity Politics in George Lucas' Star Wars*, Jefferson, NC: McFarland Press.

McDowell, J.C. (2017), *The Gospel According to Star Wars: Feeling the Force of God and the Good*, 2nd edn. Louisville: Westminster John Knox Press.

McVeigh, S.P. (2006), 'The Galactic Way of Warfare', in Matthew Wilhelm Kapell and John Shelton Lawrence (eds.), *Finding the Force of Star Wars: Fans, Merchandise, and Critics*. New York, et al.: Peter Lang: 35–58.

Miles, M.R. and Plate, S.B. (2004), 'Hospitable Vision: Some Notes on the Ethics of Seeing Film', *Crosscurrents*: 22–31.

Plate, S.B. (2008), 'Filmmaking and World Making: Re-Creating Time and Space in Myth and Film', in Gregory J. Watkins (ed.), *Teaching Religion and Film*, Oxford: Oxford University Press: 219–231.

Rinzler, J.W. (2008), *The Making of Star Wars: The Definitive Story Behind the Original Film*, Ebury Press.

Rubey, D. (1978), 'Not So Far Away', *Jump Cut* 18: 8–14.

Segal, R.A. (1987), *Joseph Campbell: An Introduction*, New York: Garland.

Silvio, C., and Vinci, T.M. (2007), 'Introduction: Moving Away From Myth: *Star Wars* as Cultural Artifact', in Carl Silvio and Tony M. Vinci (eds.), *Culture, Identities and Technology in the* Star Wars *Films: Essays on the Two Trilogies*, Jefferson, NC: McFarland and Company Inc.: 1–8.

Stone, B.P. (2000), *Faith and the Film: Theological Themes at the Cinema*, St. Louis, Miss.: Chalice Press.

Sweet, D.R. (2016), Star Wars *in the Public Square*: The Clone Wars *as Political Dialogue*, Jefferson, NC: McFarland Press.

Wetmore Jr., K.J. (2005), *The Empire Triumphant: Race, Religion and Rebellion in the Star Wars Films*, Jefferson, NC, and London: McFarland & Company, Inc.

Wink, W. (1992), *Engaging the Powers: Discernment and Resistance in a World of Domination*, Minneapolis: Fortress.

Wink, W. (1998), *The Powers That Be: Theology for a New Millennium*, New York: Doubleday.

Žižek, S. (2008), *Violence: Six Sideways Reflections*, New York: Picador.

Filmography

American Graffiti, George Lucas, dir. (1973)

Apocalypse Now, Francis Ford Coppola, dir. (1979)

Attack of the Clones, George Lucas, dir. (2002)

Electronic Labyrinth: THX1138.4EB, George Lucas, dir. (1967)

Flash Gordon, Wallace Worsley, Jr. and Gunther von Fritsch, dir. (1954–1955)

Jaws, Stephen Spielberg, dir. (1975)

Metropolis, Fritz Lang, dir. (1926/1927)

Return of the Jedi, George Lucas, dir. (1983)

Revenge of the Sith, George Lucas, dir. (2005)

Star Wars, George Lucas, dir. (1977)

The Empire Strikes Back, Irvin Kershner, dir. (1980)

The Hidden Fortress, Akira Kurosawa, dir. (1958)

The Phantom Menace, George Lucas, dir. (1999)

The Searchers, John Ford, dir. (1956)

THX 1138, George Lucas, dir. (1971)

Triumph of the Will, Leni Riefenstahl, dir. (1934)

4 On the Sacred Power of Violence in Popular Culture

American Football and the Films of Tarantino

Eric Bain-Selbo

Introduction

Religions are made up of human beings, and human beings are violent. While most religions teach non-violence to some degree, such teachings have not prevented many of their adherents from engaging in violence either individually or collectively. One might study religion and violence by looking at how religious people can engage in violence in spite of religious beliefs and attitudes. But, many contemporary theorists have focused on the *violence that is constitutive of religion*. In other words, religions are not institutions that may or may not engage in violence. They are institutions that are inherently violent. Religion and violence are intertwined. While all violence is not religious, much of it is.

Violence is ubiquitous in popular culture. As someone who is an American football fan and a bit of a film geek, I certainly have experienced the ubiquity of violence in both forms of popular culture. I enjoy it. But I am opposed to the kind of violence that brings (or should bring) criminal charges and I am mostly opposed to the violence of war. I generally consider myself a pacifist. Many critics of popular culture lament the role or even the glorification of violence that they claim can be found in various phenomena—from graphic novels to sport, from song lyrics to films, and much more. I have always been suspicious of such critics, particularly regarding their concerns that violence in popular culture leads to violent behavior or that it represents some moral decline in contemporary culture—as if our ancestors were not as violent as we are today (in fact, they were more so). At the same time, I believe that violence in popular culture is worth thinking about—that it does tell us something about human beings and contemporary culture. While it is easy to condemn violence (either real or fictional), there is a way to better understand how it functions psychologically and/or sociologically for human cultures. An understanding of the relationship of religion and violence can help shed light on the meaning and purpose of violence in American popular culture. And in this chapter, I will review some approaches to religion and violence and utilize them to interpret violence in popular culture, particularly in the sport of American football and the films of Quentin Tarantino.

DOI: 10.4324/9781003079729-5

In the end we will see that violence functions in popular culture in some of the same ways that it does in religion—gaining a better understanding of popular culture, religion, and violence in the process.

Theory and Method

Violence by people in religious communities on the basis of and in the service of religious beliefs or institutions often has been seen as something that happened only in 'primitive' or tribal religions and cultures. But even the major religious traditions in more 'civilized' areas of the world have been bound with violence. Krishna encourages the warrior Arjuna to engage in warfare in the Hindu *Bhagavad Gita*. Krishna argues it is Arjuna's sacred duty (see chapter two "Sānkhya Yog," in particular). The Abrahamic traditions are punctuated with acts of violence, often by God. Whether it is Yahweh's wrath against the Egyptians (the story of the Exodus) or his own people (Exodus 32.25–35 describes the plague that the Lord inflicts on his people, even after his servants—the Levites—had slaughtered about 3,000 of them); God's brutal sacrifice of his own son in the Christian New Testament (not to mention the apocalyptic violence in the book of Revelation); or Allah's legitimation of military force and conquest against unbelievers (see surah 9.73 in the *Qur'ān*), violence is central to the histories and narratives of the Abrahamic traditions. Today, religious adherents often turn to violence as a means of protecting or forwarding explicitly or implicitly religious objectives. In the following sections I explain three functions of violence in religious contexts. All three are interrelated. We then will see how these perspectives or functions can be used to interpret violence in seemingly secular contexts.

Cosmological Function: The Holy and the Damned

Central to understanding religious violence perpetrated between groups is to understand the dichotomy of 'us versus them' in religious thinking. This dichotomy is part of a larger dualistic worldview in which there is good and evil. In such a Manichean worldview, 'we' are good and 'they' are evil. Regina Schwartz brilliantly illustrates the 'us versus them' dichotomy that is central to the Biblical traditions. Central to her argument are the ideas of identity and scarcity (Schwartz 1997: 3–6).

All groups, by definition, go through a process of identity formation. There has to be some process by which those included in the group are conceptually and physically separated from those outside the group. But identity formation is not something that simply happens at the initial formation of a group. It must continue for as long as the group exists. The parameters and rules of the group must be affirmed continuously to distinguish the group from others. For example, the ancient Israelites formed a group characterized by physical marking (circumcision for the men), particular religious beliefs (e.g., belief in one God), and dietary restrictions (e.g., prohibitions against eating pork). This process of identity formation means that religion by definition *is* violent. It is not just that religion, through identity formation, *can* lead to violence. It is that religion, as a form of identity formation, always already is violent—if nothing else symbolically, in that it *cuts* one group off from another (in this case, the cutting literally of the male foreskin).

Schwartz also draws our attention to the fact that the physical world and human social structures are characterized by a scarcity of resources. Scarcity is a fundamental condition of group life, and it dramatically shapes relations among groups. There is only so much land or food or other resources to go around. Each group is in competition with other groups for limited resources. But there also are psychological or theological scarcities. God or the gods only can provide for some groups, not all. Only some groups will receive divine blessings. We see this most starkly in the identification of Jews as God's 'chosen people.' But the idea persists in Christianity and Islam. What complicates the matter even more is when the psychological or theological blessings are intertwined with tangible goods like land or food or other resources. So, for example, God's blessing on his people (Jews) entails their possession of the Holy Land (Israel).

When the 'us versus them' conflict over scarce resources is understood in the context of a greater, transcendent battle between the forces of good and the forces of evil, then we have the makings for a cosmic war. Reza Aslan identifies a cosmic war as "a conflict in which God is believed to be directly engaged on one side over the other" (Aslan 2009: 5). Of course, both sides believe God is on their side.

An important aspect of cosmic war is the demonizing of the other—the opponent or combatant. Mark Juergensmeyer describes this as satanization. "The process of satanization is aimed at reducing the power of one's opponents and discrediting them," he writes. "By belittling and humiliating them—by making them subhuman—one is asserting one's own superior moral power" (Juergensmeyer 2003: 186). Satanization is part of the Manichean dualism that is central to cosmic war. In a cosmic war there is no room for compromise. As Bruce Lincoln notes, in cosmic war "Sons of Light confront Sons of Darkness, and all must enlist on one side or another, without possibility of neutrality, hesitation, or middle ground" (Lincoln 2006: 20). Thus, "the stage is set for prolonged, ferocious, and enormously destructive combat" (Lincoln 2006: 95). Even someone who suggests a compromise then is considered an enemy by his own side (Juergensmeyer 2003: 157). Ultimately, this mindset results in apocalyptic thinking—the final confrontation of good versus evil, with good prevailing in the end (Selengut 2008: 88).

Juergensmeyer notes that putting conflicts into a religious context ultimately is about meaning. Opposing the chaos and violence of the world (even with violence) is the *raison d'etre* of religion—and through religion that chaos and violence is given meaning.

Ethical Function: Justice, Order, and Vengeance

Combating the chaos and evil that the other represents is not just about restoring order for the sake of restoring order. The restoration of order is a matter of justice—divine justice to be exact. The universe is characterized by a moral order established by God—an order that occasionally can get 'out of whack' and that requires the righteous actions of God's soldiers to restore it.

Individuals act justly or righteously when they use violence to establish or reestablish divine order. Such violence often is in response to previous violence, the latter being the source of the creation of disorder. Thus, the use of righteous violence to combat evil violence frequently is a matter of revenge—the revenge of the good (us) against the evil (them). It is an effort to strike back upon those who do harm to others and who disrupt the harmony of the divine order. So, the violence is not simply a matter of retaliating against those who perpetrate evil (though such revenge can be sweet); it is a matter of serving a greater divine purpose. Ultimately, that divine purpose makes the use of violence a moral (because commanded—implicitly or explicitly—by God) action. In fact, we can take it a step further and insist that one is obligated morally to perform acts of violence in the service of a greater purpose or order. For example, Christian radicals who blow up abortion clinics or kill abortion providers frequently feel it is their moral and religious duty to engage in such acts. While this perspective is best represented in the Abrahamic traditions (i.e., Judaism, Christianity, and Islam), it also can be found in those major traditions from India (Hinduism and Buddhism) that are based on the karmic system. In the *Bhagavad Gita* the violence of the warrior Arjuna is justified both in terms of restoring divine order and by the fact that those who will die in battle are paying their karmic debt.

Social-Psychological Function: Sacrifice

Violence in religion is more than simply the acts of God or divinely ordained warfare. It includes that violence that we do to ourselves—self-imposed privations or sacrifices done for religious reasons. Emile Durkheim, the early 20th-century sociologist, provides examples of sacrifice in his analysis of aboriginal totemic religions in Australia (Durkheim 1995: 84–95). According to Durkheim, the totem, ancestor, or god for whom sacrifices are made ultimately are expressions of the collective. Thus, the sacrifices made symbolically for the totem, ancestor, or god reflect the real sacrifices that must be made by the individual for the good of the collective. We sacrifice something of ourselves (our freedom, our selfishness) and/or something that is good for us (an animal given for slaughter on the altar or part of our harvest burned to the gods) to affirm our commitment to the group—a commitment that requires continual self-sacrifice, especially in times of intergroup conflict.

Sacrifices raise us toward something that transcends our individual ego, but that transcendent thing is the collective itself. In this light, the sacrifices made by 'primitives' may not seem so strange to us when we consider our own sacrifices (e.g., in war) that we are willing to make for the good of the collective. In this sense, the fundamental nature of sacrifice has not changed for millennia (Durkheim 1995: 330–354).

A more contemporary scholar like René Girard also tries to make connections between the violence we find in religion (particularly ancient) and events and structures in the world today. Girard is interested especially in the sacrifice of the other, whether that be of animal or human. His hypothesis is that "society is seeking to deflect upon a relatively indifferent victim, a 'sacrificeable' victim, the violence that would otherwise be vented on its own members, the people it most desires to protect" (Girard 1977: 4). How does sacrifice do this? "The sacrifice serves to protect the entire community from *its own* violence," Girard writes, "it prompts the entire community to choose victims outside itself. The elements of dissension scattered throughout the community are drawn to the person of the sacrificial victim and eliminated, at least temporarily, by its sacrifice" (Girard 1977: 8). Any community necessarily will have tensions as individuals vie with one another for a limited amount of goods. By directing negative emotions and energy onto the shoulders of the sacrificial victim—the 'scapegoat'—members of the community are able to overcome those negative emotions and energy through the ritualized killing of the victim.

For Girard, violence and the sacred are "inseparable" (Girard 1977: 19). Put more strongly, "the operations of violence and the sacred are ultimately the same process" (Girard 1977: 258). The purpose of religion is to prevent "reciprocal violence" (Girard 1977: 55). This continuous retaliation or revenge—fueled by the frustration of the necessary curbing of our egoism or selfishness and our competition for scarce resources—is the never-ending cycle of violence that eventually will destroy a society. Thus, instead of providing an unending cycle of revenge that produces real victims of violence, societies develop religions with sacrificial rituals in which surrogate victims suffer the violence of the community. As Girard concludes, there is no society without religion because without religion society cannot exist (Girard 1977: 221).

The function of ritual is "to 'purify' violence; that is, to 'trick' violence into spending itself on victims whose death will provoke no reprisals" (Girard 1977: 36)—"that is, to keep violence *outside* the community" (Girard 1977: 92). Girard looks across time and cultures to find ritualized behavior that supports his thesis. One of the most common rituals in which the surrogate-victim mechanism is operative is the festival (Girard 1977: 119). The festival will include a variety of behaviors that affirm the social norms via the ritualized practice of breaking those norms. In other words, by permitting *only through ritual practice* what is otherwise prohibited (e.g., sexual promiscuity), the norms of the society during everyday or profane times are affirmed for the members of the community. Festivals also are the events in which the surrogate-victim mechanism is operative.

While killing is normally prohibited, during the festival it is permitted—either literally or symbolically.

While most of the examples that Girard uses are from more ancient times, he nevertheless affirms the role of sacrificial rituals in the formation of all societies and the continuing need for them. Girard believes that we more often than not are in a state of "sacrificial crisis" (Girard 1977: 39–67). This crisis is a consequence of the disappearance of sacrificial rituals, preventing society's ability to find or create a surrogate-victim and perpetrate its violence against that victim. Girard argues that

> *sacrificial crisis*, that is, the disappearance of the sacrificial rites, coincides with the disappearance of the difference between impure violence and purifying violence. When this difference has been effaced, purification is no longer possible and impure, contagious, reciprocal violence spreads throughout the community.
>
> (Girard 1977: 49, italics in original)

When all violence is condemned, then we are incapable of ritually affirming violence through the surrogate-victim mechanism. The consequence, ironically, is an increase in non-ritualized violence (including vendetta) throughout society. This is why Girard writes:

> Sacrifice is the boon worthy above all others of being preserved, celebrated and memorialized, reiterated and reenacted in a thousand different forms, for it alone can prevent transcendental violence from turning back into reciprocal violence, the violence that really hurts, setting man against man and threatening the total destruction of the community.
>
> (Girard 1977: 124–125)

Sacrificial rituals are an effective way to prevent sacrificial crises and thus guard societies against excessive violence.

While sacrifice and promiscuity may be stereotypical aspects of festivals, so too is play. Durkheim argues that games originated in a religious context (Durkheim 1995: 385). Games or play also give rise to collective effervescence—the ecstatic bonding of individuals into a collective (Durkheim 1995: 385). Play, for Girard, is an expression of the sacred. It is another means by which genuine violence is avoided by virtue of the ritualized nature of the play itself.

> [W]e must subordinate play to religion, and in particular to the sacrificial crisis. Play has a religious origin, to be sure, insofar as it reproduces certain aspects of the sacrificial crisis. The arbitrary nature of the prize makes it clear that the contest has no other objective than itself, but this contest is regulated in such a manner that, in principle at least, it can never degenerate into a brutal fight to the finish.
>
> (Girard 1977: 154)

The play may be rough and even violent at times. There even is a victim in the form of the loser. But play never gives itself over to unwarranted violence or reciprocal violence. The rules of the ritual prohibit this possibility.

Case Studies

Play, Ritual, and Violence in American Football

American football is an exemplary intersection of religion, play, and violence. Michael Oriard recognizes the integral role that violence plays in the sport:

> [Football is] the dramatic confrontation of artistry with violence, both equally necessary. The receiver's balletic moves and catch would not impress us nearly as much if the possibility of annihilation were not real; the violence of the collision would be gratuitous, pointless, if it did not threaten something valuable and important. The violence, in fact, partially creates the artistry: the simple act of catching a thrown ball becomes a marvelous achievement only in defiance of the brutal blow. Football becomes contact ballet.
>
> (Oriard 1993: 1–2)

Violence is central to the beauty and power of the game. American football is ritualized violence—it is composed of prescribed and proscribed acts that serve a collective purpose and provide shared meaning. In this way it is religious in character.

In many locales, particularly university campuses, the ritual of American football is performed in the context of a festival, one characterized by the violation of norms that in turn affirms those norms for more profane times. For example, while many people on game day drink alcoholic beverages (sometimes to great excess) on the grounds of the university, they would be escorted off campus or even arrested if they consumed alcohol in the same place at other times. In this case, the exception (being allowed to drink publicly on campus) affirms the rule (no public consumption of alcohol on campus). The festival context sets the stage for the ritual violence.

Football certainly entails violent confrontations between players, but it is controlled violence nonetheless. Philosopher and theologian Michael Novak argues that the controlled conflict "ventilates" our rage (Novak 1994: 84). "The human animal suffers enormous daily violence," he adds, echoing both Durkheim and Girard. "Football is an attempt to harness violence, to formalize it, to confine it within certain canonical limits, and then to release it in order to wrest from it a measure of wit, beauty, and redemption" (Novak 1994: 94).

Sacrifice is a necessary element in football. This sacrifice is not only the "surrogate" or loser of the contest, but all the players. As Novak notes:

> Once an athlete accepts the uniform, he is in effect donning priestly vestments. It is the function of priests to offer sacrifices ... Often the

sacrifice is literal: smashed knees, torn muscles, injury-abbreviated careers. Always the sacrifice is ritual: the athlete bears the burden of identification. He is no longer living his own life only.

(Novak 1994: 141)

Examples of sacrifices abound. Whether it is broken bones or concussions or even death, American football players sacrifice themselves in the performance of the ritual. Novak concludes "football dramatizes the sacrifice, discipline, and inner rage of collective behavior" (Novak 1994: 207)—sacrifice, discipline, and rage that Durkheim and Girard would find to be fundamentally religious.

Football is a "revelatory liturgy," Novak explains. "It externalizes the warfare in our hearts and offers us a means of knowing ourselves and wresting some grace from our true natures" (Novak 1994: 96). We might not always want to know of our violent and aggressive selves, but at least some cultural creations can turn that violence and aggression into something that has some merit and beauty. American football perhaps is such a thing. It is, as Oriard describes it, "contact ballet."

"Since the earliest times," Michael Mandelbaum writes,

from gladiatorial contests in ancient Rome to public hangings in early modern England to boxing in the nineteenth and twentieth centuries—not to mention Hollywood movies of the twenty-first—staged events with violence at their core have commanded public attention.

(Mandelbaum 2004: 176–177)

Several questions emerge in our recognition of this historical fact of life. What does it tell us about sport? Is the "staged violence" of sports like American football what gives them their vast appeal? And what is it precisely that the spectator gets from witnessing such a violent spectacle?

Everyone seems to be in agreement that the catharsis theory of sports violence is not sufficient. The catharsis theory suggests that the violence we engage in or watch in sports relieves us of our excessive violent urges and thus allows us to function better psychologically and certainly socially. Robert J. Higgs argues that explanations like the catharsis theory may help to explain the "ubiquity" of sports, but they do not explain "the reverence paid to them" (Higgs 1995: 97). Michael Oriard insists that the catharsis theory may not be wrong, but it at least is "oversimplified" (Oriard 1993: 6). Higgs and Oriard are not social scientists, nor psychologists, but their conclusions are supported by such researchers. Daniel L. Wann and his collaborators note that "there is virtually no empirical evidence validating the existence of catharsis in sport ... The 'blowing off steam' theory of sport spectating may be attractive, but it is quite inaccurate" (Wann et al. 2001: 198). John H. Kerr likewise is suspicious of a catharsis theory of sports violence, insisting that there is little experimental evidence to support it (Kerr 2005: 124).

These perspectives (especially those from Wann et al. and Kerr) would seem to contradict Girard and the application of his theory to sport. Girard's work seems to rely upon some notion of a catharsis theory—the sacrificial victim relieving us of the violence that we otherwise would commit against one another. But note that the catharsis theory is not completely and conclusively discredited. It may be necessary for the full explanation of the appeal of violence, but it is not sufficient.

Kerr argues for a more comprehensive psychological understanding of sports violence than simply a catharsis theory. He notes that contemporary life (at least in Europe and the United States) is not very exciting. The range of emotions, especially at the highest or most pleasant end, is fairly narrow (little wonder then that many Western cultures seem fixated on sex, particularly orgasms). Consequently, "people have to actively seek out thrills and vicarious risk-taking through, for example, watching sports" (Kerr 2005: 118). Anyone watching a crowd at a major sporting event can witness the intensity of the emotions that many fans experience. Fans attain high levels of arousal (akin to Durkheim's notion of collective effervescence), and this intense experience is a "pleasant excitement" (Kerr 2005: 98). This experience is particularly prevalent with violent sports like American football and ice hockey. Kerr concludes that "watching violent sports produces increases in levels of arousal, and … people deliberately watch to achieve elevated arousal" (Kerr 2005: 118). Here then we might have an explanation not only of the social-psychological appeal of violent sports, but of certain stereotypical religious rituals (e.g., sacrifices) as well.

Is such arousal good or bad for us? The flip side of the catharsis theory is that participating in or watching violent sports spurs people to act violently in other contexts. This argument is similar to ones made about violence on television or in the movies—that such violence encourages others (especially children) to act violently. Higgs, for example, tries to connect violence in sports with aggression or violence towards women in America (Higgs 1995: 320–322). He and Michael C. Braswell argue that sports initiate a cycle of violence or aggression. "[I]nstead of ventilating aggression," they claim, sports

> refuel it so that a loss or setback in sports as in war is a call for stronger retaliation. In the Church of Sports, there is no answer to this that we can see, only rivalry, revenge, and redemption from season to season.
>
> (Higgs and Braswell 2004: 107)

We then have exactly the kind of violence that Girard claims religion helps to avoid. While such retaliatory violence usually is contained within the context of the rules of the game, there are instances in which the violence of a sport spills into the stands—leading to physical confrontations between players and fans or between rival fans. Kerr's work recounts many of these instances, including some (such as soccer hooliganism in Europe) that led to the deaths of non-participants (2005: 94–113).

Kerr notes that the research is split on the issue of the connection between violence in various forms of popular culture and among those who participate in or view them. He concludes that the "popular wisdom which suggests media violence and media sports violence has harmful effects on people, especially where those viewers are young children, may not be correct" (Kerr 2005: 130). So, if sports violence perhaps does us no harm, does it do any good? The answer, for Kerr, is affirmative. The "pleasant excitement" of violent sports can be an important part of our overall psychological health. He concludes,

> there are situations where certain types of aggressive and violent acts are central to people's enjoyment of activities. These activities range from athletic contests to viewing violent sports as a spectator, or watching violent sports movies. Being a part of these activities does no psychological harm to the vast majority of those who participate and may actually benefit their psychological health.
>
> (Kerr 2005: 148)

The argument that participating in or watching violence produces a psychological good may go a long way to explaining why violence has been such an integral part of our games and sports and religion through the centuries—perhaps redeeming (in some way) Girard's theory as well. The argument, in short, helps explain the pervasiveness of violence in popular culture and why we seem to like it so much (despite our occasional protestations to the contrary)—something we should keep in mind when interpreting Tarantino films.

In addition to the social-psychological function, sports also facilitate 'us versus them' thinking. In short, sports can function cosmologically. 'Our' team is better than 'yours.' Rivalries run across the athletic landscape—and perhaps none are more heated than those in American football. Only one team can win. Even more, only one team can earn the honor and adulation that comes with victory. Only one team can have 'bragging rights' after the game. In other words, there is a scarcity of goods (victory, honor, etc.) to go around. This situation undoubtedly contributes to the fervor and even violence of the game (and, very occasionally, among fans). Thus, American football is an exemplary model of how sports reflect a 'cosmic war' perspective in which no compromise is possible, and it is 'winner take all.' This 'cosmic war' perspective also has an ethical function. Fans not only are delighted when their team wins, but there is a sense in which the victory is just or merited. Winning a game (and, in American football, that entails the use of violence) also can be experienced as a type of revenge—a restoring of proper order—when it succeeds a previous loss.

From its sacrifice and play to its 'cosmic war' framework, it is little wonder why sports are such an important part of popular culture. And no major sport in the United States is more popular or more violent than football. While this case study has focused on the social-psychological function of violence in football, the cosmological and ethical functions also are integral to the experience of the game. Indeed, what makes football so popular is that the violence of the game can function in all three ways for the fans. Thus, the example of American football shows not only how sports can function religiously, but how violence is part of why that may be the case.

Violence in Film: Quentin Tarantino

With American football and many other sports, violence is ritualized in ways similar to religion. The ritualizing of violence may be a way of coping with the everyday self-sacrifice and mundane character of contemporary society. The contesting of American football games and the violence that ensues also replicates a fundamental religious perspective (the Manichean divide between good and evil, 'us and them,' the prerequisite for a cosmic war). Another place where we see the ritualizing of violence is in film, and perhaps no contemporary filmmaker is as noted for his treatment of violence than Quentin Tarantino. Joshua Mooney describes Tarantino's early films as

> ultra-violent crime stories [in which] almost everyone dies … And they do not, as the poet said, go gently. Usually, they have to be shot. Their blood doesn't spill so much as it gushes, spurts, splatters, soaks and coats. Sometimes it takes the stragglers an excruciatingly long time to die, but in the end, they get there too.
>
> (Peary 1998: 70)

Tarantino certainly is not afraid to take on religious themes or ideas in his movies. Take the example of *Pulp Fiction* (1994), a film written and directed by Tarantino. Hit man Jules (played by Samuel L. Jackson) not only quotes scripture before blowing away those who have wronged his boss, but he also claims to have experienced a miracle when he narrowly survives a shooting. In *From Dusk Till Dawn* (1996), written by Tarantino and directed by Richard Rodriguez, two dangerous criminals (played by George Clooney and Tarantino) hijack a family and its mobile home in order to escape into Mexico (where they end up at the infamous club The Titty Twister, fighting off vampires in a gory, graphic battle). The father (played by Harvey Keitel) is a preacher who, after his wife's death, has turned his back on God. Tarantino also directed and wrote both *Kill Bill* movies (2003, 2004), starring Uma Thurman and David Carradine. The films are extremely violent and contain extensive martial arts sequences. The plot draws on magical and philosophical elements of Eastern religions (we might assume Buddhism and Taoism in particular).

Whether or not Tarantino deals substantively with religious themes, all of his films include his trademark violence. The failed heist in *Reservoir Dogs* (his first film from 1992) not only has ample gunshot violence; it also has a torture scene in which one of the criminals cuts off the ear of a police officer, prancing around his bound-to-a-chair body to the music of the 1972 pop classic "Stuck in the Middle with You" (originally performed by the band Stealers Wheel). The scene has been described as "perhaps the single most cited moment of violence in all of the 1990s American cinema" (Gronstad 2008: 171). *Inglourious Basterds* (2009) features a renegade American military unit (made up mostly of Jews) that tracks down, kills, and scalps Nazis. It also features a young female survivor of a "Jew hunt" who plots the demise (in her Paris movie theatre nonetheless) of top Nazi brass (including, we find out, Hitler). Few viewers could possibly forget the brutal 'mandingo' fight scene in *Django Unchained* (2012)—where two slaves fight to the death (one eventually 'finishing off' the other with a hammer) for the amusement and profit of their owners. Even *Once Upon a Time in Hollywood* (2020), which probably has the least amount of violence in it, culminates with movie stunt man, Cliff, beating three members of Charles Manson's cult—one of them being finished off with a flamethrower by a fading television and movie star by the name of Rick Dalton.

Many scholars are concerned about the violence in television and film and what it says about American culture (e.g., see Hibbs 1999). There also is the added concern of the effects of television and film violence on children. Thus, it is little wonder that Tarantino has been denounced for the violence in his films. Johann Hari credits Tarantino for the realism of the violence in *Reservoir Dogs* but sees the use of violence in subsequent films to be morally dangerous. "I'm not saying it makes people violent," Hari argues,

> But it does leave the viewer just a millimeter more morally corroded. Laughing at simulated torture—and even cheering it on, as we are encouraged to through all of Tarantino's later films—leaves a moral muscle just a tiny bit more atrophied.
>
> (Hari 2009)

But what the critics miss is that the violence in Tarantino's movies is far from gratuitous or hollow. Aaron Anderson makes a compelling argument that violence in film, at least the kind of violence that Tarantino uses, is critical for creating meaning and developing the narrative and the characters. He argues that personal action

> necessarily involves a wide array of inner thoughts, both conscious and unconscious. Actions that affect other people—as violence does—therefore constitute a type of pragmatic ethics in which inner views about how one actually interacts with the world become outwardly embodied.
>
> (Anderson 2004)

One of the central meanings or themes of Tarantino's violence is revenge. In this regard, he certainly is not an unusual case in American popular culture.

As William D. Romanowski argues, "Violence has a central place in American mythology as a means of justice and retribution" (Romanowski 2007: 209). Romanowski consequently points us in an important direction. Revenge is never without meaning or a connection with the idea of justice. Thus, violence associated with vengeance or revenge—either in Tarantino films or as religious acts—serves a meaningful ethical function.

While Tarantino's films certainly reflect the idea of never-ending violence, that is not the message of the films. As Bence Nanay and Ian Schnee claim, "Tarantino's films are concerned with ways to end violence … the theme of the cycle of violence, and of breaking out of the cycle of violence, is perhaps strongest in *Pulp Fiction*" (Greene and Mohammad 2007: 185). In this regard, many of Tarantino films can be read effectively through a Girardian lens.

In *Pulp Fiction*, many of the occasions for violence involve revenge—the administering of punishment or retribution, the meting out of justice. Hit men Jules and Vincent kill several men who betrayed their boss. The boss likewise seeks revenge on a boxer who double-crossed him—failing to throw a fight as agreed. Later in the movie, the boss prepares for revenge on two rednecks who anally raped him. Early in the movie, there also is a conversation between Jules and Vincent in which they consider the moral dimensions of a story they had heard about the boss throwing an associate off a building because the associate had massaged the boss' wife's feet. In short, almost all the violence in the film involves revenge. In all cases, there is an implicit or explicit understanding of justice, and from that understanding of justice violence is demanded (perhaps even morally demanded). Justice is not treated as simply a human construct, but as a given in the universe. In other words, it has an implicit transcendent or religious dimension. While the characters may disagree about what constitutes justice, they certainly talk and act as if justice *does* exist.

An important plot development in the movie is the dramatic religious experience of Jules—an experience that leads to a conversion of sorts. Early in the film, Jules recites (as he regularly does before a killing) a passage from the Bible (the claim is that it is Ezekiel 25:17, though only the last two lines are close to the Biblical verse):

> The path of the righteous man is beset on all sides with the iniquities of the selfish and the tyranny of evil men. Blessed is he who in the name of charity and good will shepherds the weak through the valley of darkness, for he is truly his brother's keeper and the finder of lost children. And I will strike down upon those with great vengeance and with furious anger those who attempt to poison and destroy my brothers. And you will know that my name is the Lord when I lay my vengeance upon thee.

Given his murderous ways, the vengeful voice of God from this passage fits well with Jules's lifestyle. But after experiencing the 'miracle' (Vincent has doubts about this) of having been shot at but having every bullet miss him,

Jules identifies more with the first part of the passage—the part about shep-herding "the weak through the valley of darkness." Jules realizes perhaps that his lifestyle simply perpetuates the cycle of violence. In the last scene of the film, Jules does not use violence to end violence, he simply walks away. Vincent, as we already have learned from the temporally disjointed nature of *Pulp Fiction*, does not walk away and is killed.

"At the end of the movie," Tarantino reminds us,

> for all the talk about the film being violent and this, that and the other, the guy who actually becomes the lead character ... is a killer who has a religious epiphany! And it's played straight. It's not a big joke. That's supposed to be meaningful—and not in a sanctimonious way.
>
> (Peary 1998: 147)

It is meaningful (whether or not Tarantino meant it this way) because Jules moves beyond the cycle of violence. But the power of that movement comes from the violent context of the film. The violence was needed for the epiph-any to have any force.

David Kyle Johnson argues that "for a clear portrayal of revenge as mor-ally justified, one need look no further than *Kill Bill*" (Greene and Mohammad 2007: 59). Uma Thurman plays Beatrix Kiddo, a member of a company of assassins who decides to leave the business and marry a record store owner. Her boss and former lover Bill, played by David Carradine, feels betrayed upon discovering her plans (he initially thought she was dead). He seeks revenge for his hurt feelings, and his band of assassins kills the wedding party at the rehearsal and mercilessly beats Beatrix. Bill then shoots her in the head. Unbeknownst to Bill, however, Beatrix survives the gunshot and after a lengthy coma (during which she even gives birth to Bill's daughter) seeks her revenge on the assassins and finally on Bill.

In the case of *Kill Bill*, the audience most certainly sides with Beatrix in her rampage of vengeance. She has been wronged terribly, and justice demands retribution. In this regard, her violent acts are a way of achieving justice and restoring order out of chaos—typical functions of religious actions and narratives. Revenge thus becomes a religious exercise. As Beatrix tells us, "When fortune smiles on something as violent and ugly as revenge, it seems proof like no other that not only does God exist, you're doing his will." Revenge then is a moral duty. It is righteous action, for it restores the divine and just order.

Anderson notes that

> the film itself is not simply a revenge drama, but also a story of redemp-tion. The only way that Kiddo can deserve a normal life is to pay pen-ance for her own past life. This penance, however, takes the form of more violent actions, involving both Kiddo's ability to inflict harm upon others as well as her ability to endure pain and injury herself.
>
> (Anderson 2004)

In other words, she must make certain sacrifices (including sacrificing others) in order to re-enter the collective.

By the end of the second film, after coolly killing Bill with the Five Point Palm Exploding Heart Technique, Beatrix ends her rampage of revenge and drives off with her daughter. The hope, of course, is that the cycle of revenge is ended. Maybe. In the first film we watch as Beatrix kills Vernita. When confronted by Vernita's young daughter Nikki, Beatrix says

> It was not my intention to do this in front of you. For that I'm sorry. But you can take my word for it, your mother had it comin'. When you grow up, if you still feel raw about it, I'll be waiting.

Here we see the prospect of the never-ending cycle of violence.

In his review of *Inglourious Basterds*, Charles Taylor notes that "the director wants us to relish the revenge taken on the Nazis." In the culminating scene of Nazi destruction, "it's the lust for vengeance that powers the film's most delirious and daring passage" (Taylor 2010: 105). While Tarantino may suggest the moral ambiguity of some of his characters (even some of the most violent), Nazis are a stereotypical symbol for evil incarnate. They are the diabolical other against whom violence must be unleashed and is fully justified. The cosmological function of violence is certainly clear here. Their destruction brings justice to an otherwise chaotic and evil situation. The silver screen heroes of *Inglorious Basterds* (much like the football heroes on the gridiron) are warriors in contemporary cosmic wars—warriors who (hopefully?) judge the evildoers, destroy them, and restore order. In Tarantino's fictional account, he rewrites history so that we can see the physical demise of Hitler. He does not die unnoticed in a bunker, but very publicly in a theatre at the hands of Jews. Similarly, *Once Upon a Time in Hollywood* (2019) also rewrites history. Tarantino weaves together a number of storylines, but the culminating scene involves stuntman Cliff Booth (played by Brad Pitt) killing members of the "Manson Family" who unwittingly wander into the house of fading television and movie star Rick Dalton (played by Leonardo DiCaprio). While neither Booth nor Dalton is a historical figure, the "Manson Family" was real. The group was led by cult figure Charles Manson, and several members famously engaged in a killing spree in Los Angeles in 1969. Actress Sharon Tate was among the victims. In this historical revision, Cliff prevents the murder of real-life actress Sharon Tate and her friends by members of the "Manson Family" by killing the members first—preserving or achieving justice and protecting the innocence of Hollywood.

Two of Tarantino's films draw upon 'America's original sin' (slavery) and the subsequent Civil War as the context for (redemptive?) violence. *The Hateful Eight* (2015) begins with a carriage moving through a snow-covered mountainous landscape—led symbolically by a black horse and a white horse. The film is set in the post-Civil War West, and the basic plot is about Daisy Domergue's brother trying to rescue her from a bounty hunter who is taking her to her hanging. But the underlying tension of the movie very much revolves around the continuing animosities of the Civil War—particularly between black Union Major Marquis Warren (also played by Samuel L. Jackson, a regular in Tarantino films) and Confederates General Sandy Smithers and Sheriff Chris Mannix. As tensions reach a climax with Warren's telling of how he tortured and killed Smithers's son years before, Warren shoots Smithers and a bloodbath ensues. Warren and Mannix, however, end up on the same side of the conflict as they achieve some measure of revenge against the Domergue gang. But the film concludes with Warren and Mannix, the only ones left, possibly on their way to bleeding to death—a final indication of the destructiveness of cycles of violence.

In *Django Unchained*, this time set in the antebellum period and mostly in the South, a freed slave named Django (played by Jamie Foxx) gets revenge against white people by joining up with a German bounty-hunter. He even achieves revenge against his own tormenters. But the revenge is set within the larger context of his effort to liberate his wife, Broomhilda von Shaft (played by Kerry Washington), from the clutches of the truly evil Calvin Candie (played by Leonardo DiCaprio). Here we see love triumphing over the evil and violence of slavery. Once Django and Broomhilda are re-united, they ride off into the night and one is left assuming that Django's killing days are over.

So, in Tarantino films we see extensive use of violence—but not violence that is completely disconnected from a conception of justice and righteous order. The violence at least implies a sense of justice, and often the connection is made explicit. While Tarantino's films seem to include a never-ending cycle of violence, certain plot developments suggest ways of escaping that cycle (or, at least, the merits of doing so). In these ways, Tarantino's violence serves an ethical function.

Another way to think about the violence in Tarantino movies is related to the idea of sacrifice. As we saw with American football, fans vicariously experience the violence of games. This experience is one of sacrificing the victim ('scapegoat')—the loser, the one being tackled or hit, etc. Such violent sacrifice of the victim compensates for the internal violence we must do to ourselves as members of a society (e.g., repressing our instinctual desires). Through Tarantino films, we get to vicariously sacrifice victims—even victims who really deserve such sacrifice. We particularly relish the destruction of the bad or evil characters, such as those who sought to kill Beatrix Kiddo, the Nazis in *Inglourious Basterds*, or Calvin Candie in *Django Unchained*. In a sense, these characters represent all those who have wronged us as well, and their destruction at least provides some psychological reckoning in the context of the film and perhaps also in our lives. This reaffirmation of order helps to maintain the communal value system—a system that helps to distinguish between right and wrong, good and evil.

We also are drawn to the personal sacrifices that characters make as they pursue their aims through the narrative of the films. Beatrix literally risks life and limb in order to exact her revenge. Similarly, the "basterds" in *Inglourious Basterds* are willing to risk everything in order to destroy the Nazis. And Django seems particularly praiseworthy as he risks everything to get back his beloved Broomhilda. As Durkheim notes, such risk-taking and willingness to bear pain raise these characters (and vicariously raise us) above our meager and profane selves (Durkheim 1995: 317–321). And, as Kerr observes, such risk-taking provides audiences with the opportunity to vicariously participate in it and thus to elevate our emotional lives out of the doldrums of contemporary existence (Kerr 2005: 118). In these ways and others, Tarantino films provide psychological benefits akin to those provided in religious settings.

Conclusion

There is ample evidence that institutional religion has less influence on the majority of people in the West—particularly in Europe, but in the United States as well (Bain-Selbo 2022: 158–171). If at least one function of religion has been to ritualize and control violence, then my claim is that popular culture has come to be the place (for many people) where violence is ritualized and controlled. Whether we are watching violence in various sports or actors on television and film, violence continues to be central to our psychic and social lives. It is not gratuitous and barbaric; it is necessary and meaningful—whether that be in a religious or a secular context.

Summary

- There is a close relationship (some scholars claim it is inherent) between religion and violence.
- The violence in religion serves important cosmological, ethical, and social-psychological functions.
- The violence in sports functions in similar ways to the violence in religion.
- The violence in popular media (television, film, etc.) functions in similar ways to the violence in religion.
- Violence in popular culture may serve as a substitute for stereotypically religious violence in an increasingly secular society.

Discussion Questions

- Are human beings inherently violent?
- Is religion inherently violent?
- Is violence in sports like ice hockey or football an important reason for why they are so popular?
- Is violence the key to why many films are so popular?

- Is there a "gender gap" in regard to the importance and role of violence in popular culture?
- Is violence in popular culture *better* than violence in religion, since the former rarely leads to the harming or death of people as is the case with the latter?

Glossary

Asceticism   The practice or set of practices in which people deny themselves certain worldly pleasures (e.g., food, sex, etc.) as part of their spiritual path.

Bhagavad Gita   Literally "Song of the Lord"; an Indian religious text that is the sixth part of the *Mahabharata*; the text is approximately 2000 years old.

Karma   Literally meaning "action," it is the Indian law of cause and effect as these pertain to individual behavior and its consequences either in this lifetime or future ones.

Manichaenism   A view attributed to the Manichees (3rd century) in which the world is divided into the world of light and the world of darkness, good and evil, and history is the working out of the struggle between the two.

Ritual   Prescribed actions or behaviors that express communal and/or religious meanings.

Scapegoat   A surrogate victim that bears responsibility for the evil or ills faced by a community.

Totem   A natural object (typically an animal or plant) that represents the community and/or its gods.

Transcendent   Referring to that which is qualitatively different and separate from this world; for example, God is transcendent (other-worldly) even if he/she/it also works in the world.

Further Reading

Bain-Selbo, Eric (2017) *Violence in Southern Sport and Culture: Sacred Battles on the Gridiron*, Cham, Switzerland: Springer.
   A short introduction to religious violence and application to college football in the American South.

Girard, Rene (1977) *Violence and the Sacred*, trans. Patrick Gregory, Baltimore, MD: Johns Hopkins University Press.
   A classic theoretical work that has influenced numerous scholars in regard to theories of religion, ritual, and violence.

Juergensmeyer, Mark (2003) *Terror in the Mind of God: The Global Rise of Religious Violence*, 3rd edn, Berkeley, CA: University of California Press.
   Perhaps the most important and frequently cited book on contemporary religious violence. A standard in the field.

Lincoln, Bruce (2006) *Holy Terrors: Thinking About Religion After September 11*, 2nd edn, Chicago: University of Chicago Press.

A powerful critique of the discourse surrounding 9/11 and how it reflects upon the study of religion.

Schwartz, Regina (1997) *The Curse of Cain: The Violent Legacy of Monotheism*, Chicago: University of Chicago Press.

A powerful genealogy of violence in the Abrahamic traditions.

Selengut, Charles (2008) *Sacred Fury: Understanding Religious Violence*, Lanham, MD: Rowman & Littlefield.

An excellent introduction to various ways of interpreting religious violence, with ample historical examples.

Bibliography

Anderson, Aaron (2004) "Mindful Violence: The Visibility of Power and the Inner Life in *Kill Bill*," *Jump Cut: A Review of Contemporary Media*, no. 47. Online. Available http://www.ejumpcut.org/archive/jc47.2005/KillBill/ (accessed 19 May 2021).

Arendt, Hannah (1994) *Eichmann in Jerusalem: A Report on the Banality of Evil*, New York: Penguin Books.

Aslan, Reza (2009) *How to Win a Cosmic War: God, Globalization, and the End of the War on Terror*, New York: Random House.

Bain-Selbo, Eric (2022) *The End(s) of Religion: A History of How the Study of Religion Makes Religion Irrelevant*, New York: Bloomsbury.

Durkheim, Emile (1995) *The Elementary Forms of Religious Life*, trans. Karen E. Fields, New York: The Free Press.

Girard, Rene (1977) *Violence and the Sacred*, trans. Patrick Gregory, Baltimore, MD: Johns Hopkins University Press.

Greene, Richard, and Mohammad, K. Silem, eds. (2007) *Quentin Tarantino and Philosophy: How to Philosophize with a Pair of Pliers and a Blowtorch*, Chicago: Open Court.

Gronstad, Asbjorn (2008) *Transfigurations: Violence, Death, and Masculinity in American Cinema*, Amsterdam: Amsterdam University Press.

Hari, Johann (2009) "The Tragedy of Tarantino: He Has Proved His Critics Right," *The Independent* (London), 26 August.

Hibbs, Thomas S. (1999) *Shows about Nothing: Nihilism in Popular Culture from The Exorcist to Seinfeld*, Dallas, TX: Spence Publishing Group.

Higgs, Robert J. (1995) *God in the Stadium: Sports & Religion in America*, Lexington, KY: The University Press of Kentucky.

Higgs, Robert J. and Braswell, Michael C. (2004) *An Unholy Alliance: The Sacred and Modern Sports*, Macon, GA: Mercer University Press.

Juergensmeyer, Mark (2003) *Terror in the Mind of God: The Global Rise of Religious Violence*, 3rd edn., Berkeley, CA: University of California Press.

Kerr, John H. (2005) *Rethinking Aggression and Violence in Sport*, New York: Routledge.

Lincoln, Bruce (2006) *Holy Terrors: Thinking About Religion After September 11*. 2nd edn., Chicago: University of Chicago Press.

Mandelbaum, Michael (2004) *The Meaning of Sports: Why Americans Watch Baseball, Football, and Basketball and What They See When They Do*, Cambridge, MA: Perseus Books.

Novak, Michael (1994) *The Joy of Sports: Endzones, Bases, Baskets, Balls, and the Consecration of the American Spirit*, rev. edn., Lanham, MD: Madison Books.

Oriard, Michael (1993) *Reading Football: How the Popular Press Created an American Spectacle*, Chapel Hill, NC: The University of North Carolina Press.

Peary, Gerald (ed.) (1998) *Quentin Tarantino: Interviews*, Jackson, MS: The University Press of Mississippi.

Romanowski, William D. (2007) *Eyes Wide Open: Looking for God in Popular Culture*, rev. and exp. edn., Grand Rapids, MI: Brazos Press.

Schwartz, Regina (1997) *The Curse of Cain: The Violent Legacy of Monotheism*, Chicago: University of Chicago Press.

Selengut, Charles (2008) *Sacred Fury: Understanding Religious Violence*, Lanham, MD: Rowman & Littlefield.

Taylor, Charles (2010) "Violence as the Best Revenge: Fantasies of Dead Nazis," *Dissent*, Winter.

Wann, Daniel L., Melnick, Merrill J., Russell, Gordon W., and Pease, Dale G. (2001) *Sports Fans: The Psychology and Social Impact of Spectators*, New York: Routledge.

5 What Makes Music Religious?

Contemporary Christian Music and Secularization

Courtney Wilder and Jeremy Rehwaldt

Introduction

This chapter emerges from two somewhat different sets of interests and experiences: Jeremy's engagement with Christian megachurches and Courtney's work on popular culture and Christianity. Jeremy has a long-standing interest in how large churches have grown by using modern technology, employing contemporary business strategies, and incorporating contemporary cultural forms and practices—in this case, music. Courtney has studied Christianity and popular culture, particularly the emergence of religious meaning in secular cultural forms. These two sets of interests came together during a conversation the two of us had about how the concepts of the sacred and the secular function with respect to religious popular music and other categories. We wondered about the impact of "Christian" as a marketing term on religious and artistic expression. In the first edition of this book we focused specifically on Christian "hipsters," analyzing how the hipster aesthetic of the early 2000s (characterized by a particular aesthetic linked to clothes, music, and so on, as well as cynical detachment) interacted with Christian belief and practice. In this second edition, the focus has expanded, just as the use of religious symbolism in secular culture itself broadened.

Christians have always lived in particular cultural and social worlds, and this is reflected in many aspects of religious life: church architecture, worship practices, the attire and behavior of worshippers, and our focus here: Christian music, as it is written and performed both inside and outside of religious settings. Megachurches, for example, often have "praise bands" incorporating styles and instruments—such as drum and electric guitar—more often associated with secular music. Increasingly, explicitly religious themes are also common in decidedly secular music. Some artists perform songs that are played regularly on mainstream Christian radio and climb the Billboard Christian streaming charts, where they might remain year after year. Other artists draw on Christian images and symbols to create meaning outside the Christian tradition itself. What can the difference between these groups tell us about the relationship of religion and popular culture? In particular, what can the

DOI: 10.4324/9781003079729-6

relationship between groups popular in contemporary Christian music (CCM) and other artists using Christian symbolism tell us about processes of secularization?

For several centuries, scholars have predicted the **secularization** of society—that is, a diminishment of the importance of religion—and they have discussed and analyzed a range of theories about this process. Conrad Ostwalt argues that secularization is not a one-way street from religious to nonreligious, as early theories had contended, but can be best understood as a transformation of the relationship between religion and society in which "not only do we see religious institutions becoming more like the secular world, we also see secular forms of entertainment and culture carrying religious messages" (Ostwalt 2012: 50).

This chapter explores music as a cultural and religious phenomenon, specifically using the concept of secularization to focus on the way that the Christian tradition is used and reconfigured within contemporary music. We begin by laying out the history of secularization and Ostwalt's reformulation, then turn to an analysis of contemporary music. We will also define **evangelicalism** before turning to specific songs to demonstrate different approaches and their relevance for understanding secularization. We argue that the use of Christian symbols outside of self-identified "Christian" music functions in a way that illuminates the interaction between religious and nonreligious realms. In such situations, there is no sharp contrast between the religious and the secular; instead, the sacred and the secular simultaneously influence one another, in a **bidirectional** relationship, just as Ostwalt describes in his analysis of secularization.

Theory and Method

Questions about the relationship between the sacred, or the religious realm of human existence, and the secular, or the nonreligious realm, are long-standing within Christianity. For centuries, thinkers in the Western world—including Voltaire, Thomas Jefferson, August Comte, Frederick Engels, and Sigmund Freud—predicted the rise of secular society and the fall of religion (for a brief history, see Stark 1999: 249). Modern sociologists of religion offer a variety of analyses of the relationship between the sacred and the secular. Early forms of secularization theory, which have been very influential, argue that Western society is gradually and irreversibly becoming less religious. In response, some scholars have argued that societies move through cycles of religious decline and revival; others have argued that secularization moves with starts and stops, progress and reversals, in which "social movements in the direction of secularization spawn religious countermovements in the direction of sacralization" (Goldstein 2009: 175). Still others argue that the premise of most secularization theory, that the power and importance of religion is declining, is itself flawed, and that religious participation in previous historical periods tends to be overestimated and thus modern people are as religious as ever (Stark 1999). This argument presents serious problems for proponents of early secularization theory, as historical data appears to conflict strongly with the claim that religion is in decline (Berger 2008).

Conrad Ostwalt, in his book *Secular Steeples* (2003; 2nd edition in 2012), offers an analysis of the relationship between the sacred and the secular that accounts for the interaction between religious and nonreligious cultural expressions and does not rely on the premise that Western culture is in the process of religious decline. He argues that secularization is a bidirectional movement: many religious organizations take on aspects and approaches used in the secular world, and many religious ideas are expressed in secular culture (50). Thus, the broader world becomes the setting for spiritual experiences. Ostwalt's position contrasts most strongly with the understanding of secularization that prevailed in the 1960s, articulated prominently by Peter Berger in *The Sacred Canopy*. In this book, Berger argues for inevitable, one-directional religious decline and says that modern societies are becoming irreversibly less religious over time. In his more recent writing, Berger (2008) says that modernity generates not a loss of religion, but rather an increase in religious pluralism.

In contrast to Berger's position in *The Sacred Canopy*, Ostwalt says:

> Contemporary American culture witnesses secularization occurring in two directions: 1) the churches and religious organizations are becoming increasingly more attuned to the secular environment, particularly to popular culture, and are in some cases trying to emulate it in the effort to remain relevant; 2) popular culture forms, including literature, film, and music, are becoming increasingly more visible vehicles of religious images, symbols, and categories. These two directions of secularization demonstrate the blurred or malleable boundaries between religion and culture, the sacred and the secular, that define the relationship of religion and culture in the postmodern era.
>
> (48)

In other words, on Ostwalt's account, we should expect to see instances of religious communities drawing on secular forms to maintain people's interest in their message, while, at the same time, we ought to see the diffusion of religious ideas in the broader cultural environment. Popular Christian music, which Ostwalt does not analyze in his book, provides a test case for Ostwalt's theory, and we turn there next.

Setting Up the Case Study

The two modes of interaction between religion and popular culture that Ostwalt describes above are both visible in music. The first mode of interaction, in which religious institutions incorporate secular forms, practices, and approaches, is clearly visible in contemporary Christian music (CCM), an enormous industry that reaches large swaths of the American public, though its listenership has declined over the past decade. For example, in 2014, more than 60 percent of people in the United States had listened to Christian music within the previous month, and Christian music made up 3.1 of total music consumption in the United States (Gospel Music Association 2015; Nielsen 2014: 2). In the following years, Christian music consumption slowly decreased; by 2021, it made up 1.8 percent of total music consumption (MRC Data 2022: 50). It is not clear that this trend will continue, as a 2022 CBS News poll showed that young people aged 18–29 were just as likely as people overall to identify Christian/Gospel music as their favorite genre (Backus 2022).

The second form of secularization—in which religious ideas are used in popular culture and popular culture is used for religious functions—can be seen in a variety of popular music that features Christian symbols used in new ways. In order to lay out the relationship between these two approaches, we will begin by explaining who evangelicals are and what contemporary Christian music is. Following these brief definitional sketches, we will analyze the particular features of the music in light of Ostwalt's concept.

What Is an Evangelical?

There is significant overlap between consumers of contemporary Christian music (CCM) and evangelical Christians. The latter term is by no means a straightforward or clear-cut descriptor; Robert Johnston offers an analysis of evangelicalism among Christians in the United States that serves both to illuminate the concept and to explain many recurring features of CCM. Johnston argues that the word "evangelical" has many different, sometimes competing, definitions, often employed by evangelicals themselves (Johnston 1991: 253). Johnston offers a solution: he argues that the term "evangelical" ought to be understood as describing a set of **family resemblances,** or shared qualities and characteristics. For instance, you might resemble your parents, siblings, cousins, aunts and uncles, and grandparents by virtue of shared physical traits, shared family names, traditions, and cultural practices. According to Johnston, evangelical churches and denominations are similar in that they resemble each other without being identical.

What are these shared features of evangelicals? And how do they influence popular Christian music? A combination of doctrines and practices, including methods of reading the Bible, make up the features that form this family resemblance (260). Johnston sums them up: "An emphasis on personal religious experience, an insistence upon witness and mission, a loyalty to biblical authority, an understanding of salvation by grace through faith" (259). We can add to this summary an emphasis on living a life of personal piety and holiness, accepting Jesus as one's Savior, and being born again. All of the above features are visible within the CCM genre.

What Is Contemporary Christian Music?

If evangelicals can be understood as a family of Christians emphasizing an overlapping set of doctrines and perspectives, what kind of music do they listen to? Christian rock music emerged as a distinctive genre in the 1960s, and Christian popular music rapidly expanded into other musical genres as well. As Ostwalt observes,

> From light rock to rap to punk to hard rock—these forms have been adopted by the contemporary Christian music scene. The popularization of Christian rock/pop music witnesses to a purposeful adaptation of a secular medium for the propagation of the Christian message. The strategy is to tap into youth culture and Christianize it.
>
> (249)

In other words, CCM developed in order to provide a "safe" alternative for Christian youth, on the one hand, and to spread the gospel to the "unsaved," on the other. Contemporary Christian music was thus born of a desire by some Christians to avoid "worldliness" and to create an alternative set of cultural products that would be attractive to young people while maintaining a separation from the mainstream, just as Ostwalt describes.

To make the boundaries of its genre clearer, in 1998 the Gospel Music Association defined Christian music, for the purposes of its Dove Awards—a significant means of recognition for CCM artists (www.gospelmusic.org)—as follows:

> Music in any style whose lyric is substantially based upon historically orthodox Christian truth contained in or derived from the Holy Bible; and/or an expression of worship of God or praise for his works; and/or testimony of relationship with God through Christ; and/or obviously prompted and informed by a Christian worldview.
>
> (Beaujon 2006: 177)

While this definition was later changed to be less restrictive (see Gospel Music Association 2016: 3), it provides important information about the perspective of the CCM industry and its associated radio stations.

Case Study

Having set out definitions of the key concepts in our analysis, we turn to the music itself. At issue is the relationship between the sacred and the secular in both CCM and popular music more generally. We argue below that CCM, as a genre, is an attempt to use popular cultural forms to remain relevant in the face of what seems to be widespread secularization, and that outside of that genre, artists of all stripes use popular culture to engage in religious reflection, often in a way that questions and critiques Christian norms.

Analyzing Contemporary Christian Music

In order to get a handle on the content and style of recent CCM music, we examined the top ten Christian streaming songs on Spotify during 2019, the 2020 Billboard list of top 50 Christian streaming songs, and the top 40 Christian songs on iTunes in August 2021. We found substantial overlap among the three lists, with three songs on all three lists and eight more songs on both the 2020 Billboard and 2021 iTunes lists, illustrating the longevity and popularity of particular artists and songs.

We first noticed this trend during our analysis of CCM music in 2009 for the first edition of this book. At that time, we selected one week at random from June through October 2009 and looked at the "top 19" song lists for K-LOVE, a national Christian radio network (www.klove.com). Those five "top 19" lists had a total of only 28 artists represented, all of whom had had songs in the top 25 of the Billboard Christian charts, based on "radio airplay audience impressions" (www.billboard.com). Moreover, all but four had been nominated for the Dove awards.

We see something similar in the data from 2019 to 2021. Of the 11 songs we identified, eight of the songs or the artists who recorded them were nominated for a 2020 Gospel Music Association Dove Award, and all of the artists associated with the 11 songs (except We the Kingdom, which was a new artist in 2020) were nominees, performers, or presenters at the 2019 Dove Awards ceremony. From this data we note that there is wide overlap among key indicators of popularity for CCM, such as play on major streaming services and awards from the Gospel Music Association. Moreover, those artists that make it big are also those that fit the narrow criteria set out by the GMA, as described earlier, and are supported by the GMA itself through award nominations. Do these artists have anything else in common beyond receiving the blessing of the CCM industry? We focused on the 11 songs that crossed the 2019, 2020, and 2021 lists for the purpose of analyzing their lyrics, musical styles, and theological content.

Many of the songs found on Christian radio and popular on streaming services have an identifiable "adult contemporary" style; all 11 of the songs in this longest-on-the-charts group fall into that stylistic range: highly "produced," slow to mid-tempo, with guitars, background strings, and swelling choruses. Lyrically, the songs also fall into a relatively narrow range of topics and approaches, with a couple of exceptions. All are explicitly about God. Six have lyrics aimed toward God, emphasizing God's presence in one's life. The doctrinal tropes emerge in lyrical content that is simple, repetitive, and often in the second person. For instance, in "Oceans (Where Feet May Fail)," released in 2013 and still on the charts nearly a decade later, the singer from Hillsong United, an Australian worship group, exclaims, "Your sovereign hand/Will be my guide/Where feet may fail and fear surrounds me/You've never failed/And You won't start now" (Crocker, Houston, and Ligthelm 2013). These songs often make declarations about the nature of Christian faith posited as simple propositions that the listeners are implicitly encouraged to accept.

Other songs are exhortative, providing a narrow range of theological instruction, many focusing on God's presence in difficult times. For example, Zach Williams and Dolly Parton's "There was Jesus" notes the presence of Jesus "when the life I built came crashing to the ground/when the friends I had were nowhere to be found" (Williams, Beathard, and Smith 2019). Similarly, Lauren Daigle takes on the voice of God, explaining that "there's never been a moment/you were forgotten./You are not hopeless … In the middle of the darkest night/It's true, I will rescue you" (Daigle, Mabury, and Ingram 2019). This song highlights a message repeated again and again in CCM songs: Life is difficult, but God is with you in difficult times.

"Holy Water," by We the Kingdom, winner of the Dove Award for New Artist of the Year in 2020, focuses on another common message: Jesus has died for you, healing your brokenness, and because of this, some day you will be in heaven. The song explains, "Dead man walking, slave to sin/I wanna know about being born again/I need you/Oh, God, I need you" (Cash et al. 2020). The message of the song is clear and to the point, matching what one CCM fan describes as the typical lyrical style:

> If they're really a Christian band, and they're trying to win people over to Christ, there's no blurry lines…. The truth is bold. I don't think people who hear a song should have to *do something* to find out what it means…. Irony in Christian music would not be good.
>
> (Radosh 2010: 4–5)

The usual means of establishing who is "really a Christian band" within the CCM industry is to draw sharp lines between what is Christian and what is too worldly, and then market the former as affirming of faith and safe for children. Music that gets airplay on Christian stations tends to be explicitly religious, invoking the name of Jesus and affirming the most basic form of the Christian relationship to God: Jesus loves me, Jesus died for my sins, I love Jesus. Artists who are popular on the CCM charts affirm this style of sharing their faith, and the public identity of CCM artists tends to emphasize strongly their personal virtue, pursuit of holiness, and, often, adherence to conservative political positions. For example, Matthew Paul Turner, then-editor of *CCM*, a magazine covering Christian music, relates a story of being forced by his publisher to ask Amy Grant to apologize several years after the fact to the readers of *CCM* for her 1999 divorce. When his story did not portray Grant as sufficiently apologetic, he says, it was rewritten with fabricated apologetic quotes to placate *CCM*'s publisher, and, presumably, its readers (Turner 2010).

That same tension persists today. Artists participating in the Christian music scene sometimes chafe against the norms and expectations of CCM, much to the chagrin of the industry and some fans. This appears most evident when artists push back against homophobia or are perceived to have doubts about their faith. For an example of the first, Lauren Daigle, whose tracks have been, year after year, among the most streamed Christian songs, recently performed on *Ellen*, which led to substantial criticism from some of her fans, who were upset that Daigle performed on a show with an openly lesbian host (Merritt 2018). Years earlier, Dan Haseltine, lead singer for the multiplatinum Christian group Jars of Clay, tweeted a series of questions in support of marriage equality, creating a "mini firestorm" among his fans (Ohlheiser 2014). As a result, stores pulled the group's albums off the shelves, Christian radio stations stopped playing Jars of Clay, and the group was disinvited from a number of festivals where they had been scheduled to play (Baldridge 2020). In Daigle's case, she has reframed her own participation in the industry by labeling herself an "artist" rather than a "Christian artist" ("Lauren Daigle" 2019).

Bringing Religious Ideas into Secular Culture

While artists like Lauren Daigle are constrained by the expectations of the CCM industry and of their fans—expectations that often result in censure when they are transgressed—other artists have more latitude to integrate religious symbols and imagery in their songs and performances in order to generate deeply religious art that simultaneously critiques Christian social norms and seeks to develop healthier and more inclusive theological positions. Such artists often demonstrate an understanding of the sacred/secular relationship that reflects Ostwalt's second mode of secularization; that is, while the CCM industry sees secularization as a one-way eroding of the power of religion and religious institutions, other artists and their listeners affirm a model of musical self-expression, and especially songwriting that speaks deeply to religious problems and questions using secular modes of expression.

Semler's "Jesus from Texas"

Some such artists have found a new opportunity in the shift from album sales to streaming services, permitting them to enter the Christian music charts from outside of the CCM industry and its constraints. One such artist is Grace Selmer Baldridge, who performs under the name Semler and is using Christian symbols, images, and theology to explore queer identity. Semler meditates on creation in their song "Jesus from Texas." The song, which speaks directly to younger queer people, provides images of family created by choice. Semler's religious point of view was shaped by overt hostility from Christians, as they explain in an interview:

> I remember when Young Life started kind of loitering around our school when I was in high school, and I remember being introduced to a very different Christian doctrine [from my family's Episcopal practice] that was quite confusing for me and that made it pretty clear that my sexuality and my identity was something to hide and potentially something to be ashamed of…. You know, I remember praying over someone at, like, a church camp because they were gay and thinking in the back of my head, like, oh, my gosh…. I recognized we're praying that she isn't what I am, and I'm gay. And now that's a little thing of, like, better keep this secret. I don't want people praying over me. I don't

want to be crying and having strangers—because I don't know this girl. Like, I still don't know her last name. I have this vivid memory of her that came rushing back now that I'm 30 years old, and I don't know her name, and I don't know if she's OK.

(Martin 2021)

"Jesus from Texas" begins, "My Mom turned eighteen in the 1960s and she doesn't remember **Stonewall**/To be fair, she can't have known that I'd be her kid/That the bricks launched at police would compel me to exist." This juxtaposition of her mother's relative ignorance at 18 with the claim that bricks thrown in defiance and self-assertion brought her into being introduces the image of a dual **origin story**. Semler is their parents' child, but they are also the child of queer people who preceded them. The album title, *Preacher's Kid: Unholy Demos*, underlines this tension.

The album reached number 1 on Christian music charts shortly after its release (Hunt 2021), despite Semler's clear identity as a queer person, which puts them outside the boundaries the industry has established for Christian artists. Semler says candidly,

As a queer person, something I've done for self-defense is if someone is explicitly Christian, I assume they will not accept me—it's easier to be proven wrong, because I've been so hurt by assuming people would accept me, and then they don't. So then if I'm surprised, it's a pleasant surprise rather than a heartbreaking one, and the reception of this album has been such a pleasant surprise.

(Hunt 2021)

"Jesus from Texas" highlights the transmission of identity from elder to younger queer person: "And I think about that now down the ballot/of the ones I love and don't know yet/I voted for you" (Baldridge 2021). This situates Semler as parent or elder sibling to as-yet-unknown young people. The role sits uneasily on their shoulders: "Oh what a terrible honor it is/to watch the sky fall as a character witness/I spent the rest of the night freaking out/I had to get high just to put myself down." While the song does not provide particulars, it is not difficult in 2021 to imagine the recent political or social events that might qualify as earth-shattering for any young queer person in the United States.

Semler is attuned to the isolation of younger queer people and proactively engages in creating space for and connections among other queer people. A few lines later, Semler sings, "I grew up a preacher's kid cleaning up after communion/So I know that church is not a way to live/It's a weekly reunion." Here the dual origin stories are reconfigured and reunited: like queer families by choice, church can, in its healthiest and most loving form, create a family with whom one reunites each week. Semler extends their own background and firm rooting in Christianity out into the queer community. Church is not a set of rules, but a means of creation.

The next verse is breathtakingly sad. Semler recounts in an interview,

> State of Grace [their docuseries] got started about 2 years ago. I had just experienced a sudden rejection from someone very close to me, one of my oldest and best friends. I asked her to be a bridesmaid for my wedding, and that was the time she sort of revealed how she felt. That was wild because I've known this person since I was two—it was sudden.
>
> (Hunt 2021)

Semler transformed this experience into art, singing, "My best friend found God so we lost touch/I guess a savior beats a friend who thinks you're good enough/I hope she finds love and peace/and if her kid comes out I hope that she calls me" (Baldridge 2021). The pronoun is ambiguous, leaving the listener to decide whether it is the mother or the child whom Semler hopes to hear from. The story serves as a microcosm of Semler's work: "I was told point blank by a Christian music executive that there was no space and no audience for a story like mine, and I want to show that the opposite is true. That's something I'm really hopeful for" (Hunt 2021). In the face of rejection, they remain steadfast witnesses to the state of the world and to their own experience.

The song concludes, "Oh what a terrible honor it's been/To learn that my blessings are things you call sins/I'll spend the rest of my life tearing down/The Jesus from Texas you put in a crown/But I won't give up on you" (Baldridge 2021). This conviction illustrates Semler's faith, their gift for writing lyrics, their rejection of a distorted Christianity, and the promise to remain a witness to love and a creator of families outside that distortion. Again, the "you" of this last line is ambiguous: is it the friend, addressed directly? Is it Semler's own chosen family? Is it the broad community of queer people seeking something better and truer than the Christianity that has excluded them? Is it all of the above? In any of these cases, this is a profoundly loving and religious message. As Ostwalt notes, "Religion is everywhere in popular music and videos, and it is not coming from religious bodies or from any recognizable religious community" (252).

Lil Nas X's "Montero (Call Me by Your Name)"

While Semler's compelling use of Christian images propelled *Preacher's Kid* to the top of the Christian charts, other artists are using Christian religious imagery in more decidedly secular music. As Ostwalt explains,

> Just as contemporary musicians use a secular medium to communicate a sacred message, we also see secular artists whose seemingly secular music communicates religiously meaningful lyrics. That represents the sacralization of the secular in which originally secular cultural forms take on sacred or religious functions through the subject matter or presentation of the art.
>
> (251)

One widely recognized and frequently critiqued example of a religiously meaningful secular song is Lil Nas X's song "Montero (Call Me by Your Name)." The song's title is an apparent nod to the 2017 film *Call Me by Your Name*, itself based upon the 2007 novel of the same name by André Aciman. In the novel and the film, a 17-year old spending the summer in Italy with his parents falls in love with a 24-year-old male student of his father's. Their romance is passionate but complicated. The phrase "call me by your name" is an invitation to express that passion. "Montero" is Lil Nas X's real first name. He wrote the following on his Instagram shortly before the song was released:

> dear 14 year old Montero, i wrote a song with our name in it. It's about a guy i met last summer. i know we promised to never come out publicly, i know we promised never to be 'that' type of gay person, i know we promised to die with the secret, but this will open doors for many other queer people simply to exist. you see this is very scary for me, people will be angry, they will say i'm pushing an agenda. but the truth is, i am. the agenda to make people stay the fuck out of other people's lives, and stop dictating who they should be. sending you love from the future.
>
> – lnx (twitter.com/LilNasX)

The song's lyrics express desire and are for the most part not explicitly religious, with the exception of the line "If Eve ain't in your garden/you know that you can/Call me when you want/call me when you need" and a reference to God "shinin' on me" during periods of wealth and success (Hill et al. 2021). The music video accompanying the song, however, uses clear Christian imagery to reconfigure the relationship between sin, sex, and self.

The video begins with a voiceover against the backdrop of a surreal cloudbank: "In life, we hide the parts of ourselves we don't want the world to see. We lock them away. We tell them no. We banish them. But here, we don't. Welcome to Montero" (Muino and Hill 2021). The camera then moves through the clouds, down to a landscape dotted with Greek-looking ruins (including a fallen statue with Nas's face) and a pink-toned fantasy landscape. We see Lil Nas X playing the guitar peacefully underneath a tree, but he is soon disturbed by a serpent, again with his own face, albeit with the addition of a third eye. Startled, Nas begins to run, but the flowers, a statue, and even the clouds take on the face of the serpent-Nas as the lyrics become suggestive: "You're cute enough to fuck with me tonight." As the two begin to kiss, the video focuses on a tree with a line from Plato's *Symposium* carved into the bark in Greek: "After the division the two parts of man, each desiring his other half" (Plato 191a). The argument in Plato's text is that human beings were originally joined together in pairs of various gender combinations, but, after becoming divided, must spend their lives seeking their other halves, their complementary selves.

This tension between the implied inadequacies of the Garden of Eden—and the fixation on **heteronormativity** among some Christians—and the Platonic construct of gender is compelling. The story of the Garden of Eden, found in the biblical narrative of Genesis 2–3, has been interpreted in many ways by Christians. One common interpretation identifies Eve, depicted as the first woman, as responsible for sin. When Eve accepts a forbidden apple from a serpent, and gives it to her husband Adam, the two are punished by God. Christians often depict this as the "fall" into sin, and argue that women are both more sinful than men and ought to submit to them in marriage. The authors of the notorious 15th-century witch-hunting guide, the *Malleus Maleficarum*, cite a range of Christian thinkers to justify their claims that women are more likely to be practitioners of witchcraft than men. Eve, they write, "seduced Adam" and passed sin to him; "therefore she is more bitter than death" (Kramer and Sprenger 1486: pt. 1, q. 6). Women are associated with both sexuality and sin in this text, and the supposed actions of witches are used to reinforce male (and Christian religious) authority.

More recently, as one example, conservative pastor and professor Denny Burk, writing on behalf of the Gospel Coalition, argues that because the biblical narrative depicts Adam as created before Eve, "Adam is given the position of authority" (Burk 2014). Furthermore, Burk interprets Eve's role as Adam's "helper" to mean that modern women are by God's design supposed to be married to men and subservient to them. In contrast, biblical scholar Susan Niditch, while acknowledging that while "Jewish and Christian traditions postdating the Hebrew Bible and a long history of Western scholarship have viewed woman's creation in Genesis 2 as secondary and derivative—evidence of her lower status" (Niditch 2012: 30), contends that this is a misreading of the Bible. Niditch says that, instead, Eve's curiosity about the apple reveals that she is the protagonist of the story, and that her curiosity is "quintessentially human" (31).

Some origin stories may fit our own experiences and others may not. The lyrics continue, "Call me out by your name/I'll be on my way like/Mmm mmm mmm." The scene shifts, however, to depict Nas dressed in a pink wig and pink fur stole being led by other versions of himself, each in a more spectacular blue wig and pieced-together denim uniform. They appear to be in the Colosseum, the ancient amphitheatre in Rome. He is put on trial by versions of himself, in front of an audience of thousands of versions of himself resembling metallic statues. While he pleads his case, singing "I want to fuck the ones I envy," the crowd throws things at him. He is eventually struck unconscious by a sex toy.

The most provocative and theologically important part of the video comes next. While Nas's character initially ascends toward heaven, he swiftly changes direction and engages in an erotic version of the **harrowing of hell**. The **Apostle's Creed** reads in part, "He suffered under Pontius Pilate, was crucified, died and was buried. He descended into hell." This image of Jesus descending into hell to preach to and gather the damned, demonstrating his power over evil, is a common topic of religious art, including in the work of Hieronymus Bosch, whose vision is characteristically bizarre. Bosch might appreciate Lil Nas X's video: only momentarily transformed into an angelic figure, Nas then becomes archetypically demonic as he slides on a stripper pole into hell.

In hell, Nas encounters Satan, who—unsurprisingly—also bears a version of Nas's own face. The lyrics continues as Nas descends: "Call me by your name/Tell me you love me in private." Wearing over-the-knee black stiletto latex boots and Calvin Klein underwear, Nas whispers into Satan's ear, "Fuck it, let's try it" as he climbs on his lap. Nas twerks and performs a lap dance; when Satan seems entranced, Nas reaches out and snaps Satan's neck. This seduction followed by swift violence is reminiscent of the actions of Judith and Jael, two women portrayed in the Apocrypha and the Bible, respectively. Judith, a Hebrew widow, ingratiates herself with Holofernes, an enemy general, and then cuts off his head and returns home with it. In Judges 4, Jael initially offers shelter to rival Canaanite general Sisera; when he is lulled to sleep she drives a tent stake through his head. Both women are regularly depicted in religious art. Here the video positions Nas as the unexpectedly triumphant hero who was previously overlooked and underestimated.

What does this mean? Coupled with Nas's letter to his younger self, the deliberate use of and interrogation of Christian imagery in the video suggests he is both sinner and savior. Some version of himself gives in to temptation: not the temptation to have sex with another man, but the temptation to damn himself for it. There are origin stories that would see this desire and coupling as good and even as part of divine design, the video suggests; it is the impulse to self-condemnation, not the impulse to love, that must be overcome. The desire to be called by the lover's own name conflicts not with God's will but with the deep-seated shame instilled by a hateful culture. Even the act of naming—so central to Adam's activity in Genesis 2—has biblical overtones. The video's opening voiceover, which establishes Montero as a place where banishment is no longer necessary, parallels Christ's call to those who have been suffering in hell. Those who have been damned can be redeemed. Nas-as-Jesus triumphs over evil; Nas-as-Satan fully embraces his queerness. It is provocative, and it is powerfully Christian.

This comports closely with Ostwalt's theory, which sees religious ideas engaging the broader cultural context. As he explains, "Secular and popular culture might contain more authentic belief than official religious theologies, because it is in the popular culture that one can encounter belief and values apart from and freed from paternalistic religious doctrine and dogma" (29).

Conclusion

Ostwalt identifies secularization as bidirectional, meaning that religious culture can affect secular culture and vice versa. Contemporary musical artists drawing on Christian images and symbols are a good illustration of his theory, as they ask questions of and sometimes reject aspects of the Christian tradition as they analyze it critically, using the various cultural and intellectual tools at their disposal in order to be true to their artistic vision—in other words, to create deeply religious music. Such music, because of its critical approach and willingness to engage a wider array of topics and a broader swath of the human condition, provides an opportunity to contribute substantively to contemporary Christian practice in ways that are at odds with the boundaries typically drawn around CCM, highlighting the complexity, mystery, and doubt inherent to religious life. Ostwalt's method of analysis offers a more accurate and revealing understanding of this phenomenon than unidirectional models, suggesting that his understanding of secularization is a better analytical tool. As Ostwalt argues,

> Whereas sacred music is defined by, bounded by, and limited by doctrine and dogma, secular music has no such limitations. Thus ... it is in secular music that we learn what we really believe, and it is through our response to secular music that we can fashion an ethic that is meaningful and relevant. Secular music, therefore, provides a more reliable measure of authentic belief, relevant ethics, and real commitment than sacred music, which can be defined by standards of belief that are no longer owned by those in the tradition.
>
> (255)

Summary

- For several hundred years, the decline of religion in Western society has been predicted. In the 1960s, sociologists of religion, following the lead of Peter Berger, developed a theory of secularization, arguing that Christianity is in decline in the United States and Europe, and that this process is irreversible. Sociologist of religion Conrad Ostwalt argues instead for a bidirectional relationship between the sacred and the secular. This suggests that religion may be changing in form rather than declining.
- To analyze Ostwalt's theory, the chapter examines contemporary Christian music (CCM) and its relationship with American evangelical Christianity, as well as other genres of popular music and their use of Christian images and symbols.
- A comparative analysis of CCM and other popular music suggests that CCM reflects the influence of secular forms of music, while secular music using Christian imagery reflects religious influence used outside of strictly religious contexts.
- Ostwalt's description of secularization accounts more successfully for the way that contemporary artists like Lil Nas X use Christian images and symbols than other forms of secularization theory, and his analysis

contributes to the ongoing problematizing of the larger claim that society is becoming less religious over time.

- Both Semler and Lil Nas X are engaging in religious reflection outside of the sphere of CCM and outside of explicitly religious settings like worship services, and both artists offer critiques of some Christian doctrine using Christian terms, images, and symbols. By doing so, they demonstrate that religious traditions can be used and interpreted outside of identifiably religious settings; music can be religious without being part of a religious body or bound by religious authority.

Discussion Questions and Activities

- How do you choose music to listen to in different situations? What genres of music do you find most meaningful? Why?
- Ostwalt suggests that artists who do not identify their music as Christian or religious, per se, might still be addressing issues of spiritual and religious importance. Do you agree? Can you think of examples?
- Why do some artists choose to use Christian or other religious concepts, language, and symbols in secular contexts? Why do some Christians object to this?
- Do Christians, or other religious people, gain or lose anything when artists use Christian concepts in their music outside of Christian contexts? What about nonreligious people?
- Do you think analyzing music and other forms of popular culture can reveal something about religious beliefs? Why or why not?
- What makes something (a song, book, poem, image) religious or nonreligious?

Glossary

Apostles' Creed A Western Christian (that is, Catholic and Protestant but not Orthodox) statement of faith whose origins trace back to the second century C.E. and whose wording was finalized several centuries later.

Bidirectional Moving in two directions; here, Ostwalt argues that sacred and secular forms of culture influence each other, and thus the interactions are bidirectional.

Evangelicalism A Christian religious movement that includes some or all of the following: an emphasis on personal religious experience, an insistence upon witness and mission, a loyalty to biblical authority, an understanding of salvation by grace through faith, a literalistic interpretation of the Bible, an emphasis on leading a life of personal holiness.

Family resemblances Qualities and characteristics shared between ideas or institutions, much in the same way that qualities and characteristics are shared between relatives. As in the case of a family, no one feature may be common to all members of the group—instead, there are over-lapping similarities. The idea was popularized by philosopher Ludwig Wittgenstein (2010).

Harrowing of Hell   A Christian teaching that Jesus was crucified and died, and then descended into hell to gather the souls of good people who died prior to Jesus's birth.

Heteronormativity   The social expectation that people are straight and cisgender (that is, their gender identity matches the sex they were assigned at birth), and the social rewards for behaving accordingly.

Origin story   A religious or cultural narrative explaining where a particular people, or people in general, come from.

Secularization   A diminishment of the importance of religion, especially in terms of social power or influence.

Stonewall   A 1969 riot at the Stonewall Inn, a gay bar in New York City, in which gay people refused to tolerate a police raid and fought back. This event is recognized as an important part of the gay rights movement.

Further Reading

Ostwalt, C. (2012) *Secular Steeples: Popular Culture and the Religious Imagination*, New York: Bloomsbury.
Ostwalt lays out a model of secularization, as described in this chapter, then uses it to examine an array of spaces, texts, and images in popular culture.
Partridge, C. (2013) *The Lyre of Orpheus: Popular Music, the Sacred, and the Profane*, New York: Oxford University Press.
Partridge offers insights into the sacred dimensions of popular music and its power to shape people's lives.
Radosh, D. (2010) *Rapture Ready! Adventures in the Parallel Universe of Christian Pop Culture*, New York: Soft Skull.
Radosh provides a glimpse into the contemporary evangelical subculture, spending time analyzing Christian music festivals, Christian theme parks, celibacy clubs, and much, much more.
Stark, R. (1999) "Secularization, R.I.P." *Sociology of Religion* 60, no. 3: 249–273.
In this important article, Rodney Stark analyzes and deconstructs early theories of secularization, arguing that they do not adequately account for the data on religious participation and belief, either now or historically.
Stephens, R. (2018) *The Devil's Music: How Christians Inspired, Condemned, and Embraced Rock 'n' Roll*, Cambridge, MA: Harvard University Press.
In this engaging book, Stephens provides a history of the relationship between Christianity and rock music, exploring its origins in Pentecostalism and the shifting attitudes toward rock among evangelical Christians.

Bibliography

Backus, F. (2022) "Rock Is America's Favorite Music—Just Not Among Young People," *CBS News*, April 3. Online. Available https://www.cbsnews.com/news/rock-music-hip-hop-young-people-opinion-poll/ (accessed 25 June 2022).

Baldridge, G. (2020) "The Dark Reality of the Christian Music Industry," State of Grace, Refinery 29, YouTube.com, June 20. Online video. Available https://www.youtube.com/watch?v=IEbyzZE5nzA (accessed 15 September 2021).

Baldridge, G.S. (2021) "Jesus from Texas," [Song, performed by Semler on *Preacher's Kid*]

Beaujon, A. (2006) *Body Piercing Saved My Life: Inside the Phenomenon of Christian Rock*, Cambridge, MA: Da Capo Press.

Berger, P.L. (2008) "Secularization Falsified," *First Things*, February, 23–27.

———— (1990) *The Sacred Canopy*, New York: Anchor.

Burk, D. (2014) "5 Evidences of Complementarian Gender Roles in Genesis 1–2," *The Gospel Coalition*, March 5. Online. Available https://www.thegospelcoalition.org/article/5-evidences-of-complementarian-gender-roles-in-genesis-1-2/ (accessed 25 June 2022).

Cash, E., S. Cash, F. Cash, M. Cash, and A. Bergthold. (2020) "Holy Water," [Song, performed by We the Kingdom on *Holy Water*, Capital Christian Music Group].

Crocker, M., J. Houston, and Salomon Ligthelm (2013) "Oceans (Where Feet May Fail)," [Song, performed by Hillsong United on *Zion*, Hillsong Music].

Daigle, L., P. Mabury, and J. Ingram (2019) "Rescue," [Song, performed by Lauren Daigle on *Look Up Child*, Centricity].

Goldstein, W.S. (2009) "Secularization Patterns in the Old Paradigm," *Sociology of Religion*, 70, no. 2: 157–178.

Gospel Music Association (2015) "GMA & CMTA Research Shows Popularity of Christian Music." Online. Available https://gospelmusic.org/news-gma-cmta-research-shows-popularity-of-christian-music (accessed 15 September 2021).

———— (2016) "47th Dove Awards, 2015–2016 Policy & Procedures Manual." Online. Available https://www.gospelmusic.org/wp-content/uploads/2016/02/2015-2016-Policies-and-Procedures-Manual.pdf (accessed 25 June 2022).

Hill, M., D. Baptiste, D. Biral, O. Fedi, and R. Lenzo (2021) "Montero (Call Me by Your Name)," [Song, performed by Lil Nas X on *Montero*, Columbia Records].

Hunt, E. (2021) "We Interview Semler About The Inspiration Behind Her Chart-Topping EP," *She's a Full on Monet*, February 11. Online. Available https://shesafullonmonet.com/grace-semler-baldridge-interview (accessed 15 September 2021).

Johnston, R.K. (1991) "American Evangelicalism: An Extended Family," In D.W. Dayton and R.K. Johnston (Eds.), *The Variety of American Evangelicalism*, Downers Grove, IL: Inter Varsity Press.

Kramer, H., and J. Sprenger (1486) *Malleus Maleficarum*. Online. Available https://pages.uoregon.edu/dluebke/Witches442/442MalleusMaleficarum.html (accessed 25 June 2022).

"Lauren Daigle On Defying Labels, Connecting With Fans, Grey's Anatomy, Adrenaline & More." (2019) 104.3 MYfm, YouTube.com, January 4. Online. Available https://www.youtube.com/watch?v=TUt4tKiEpKI (accessed 15 September 2021).

Martin, M. (2021) "Musician Semler Talks New Album 'Preacher's Kid,'" *NPR Music*, March 6. Online. Available https://www.wbgo.org/2021-03-06/musician-semler-talks-new-album-preachers-kid (accessed 15 September 2021).

Merritt, J. (2018) "Lauren Daigle and the Lost Art of Discernment," *The Atlantic*, December 8. Online. Available https://www.theatlantic.com/ideas/archive/2018/12/let-lauren-daigle-be-unsure-about-lgbt-relationships/577651/ (accessed 15 September 2021).

MRC Data (2022) *Year-End Report U.S. 2021.* Created in collaboration with Billboard. Online. Available https://mrcdatareports.com/wp-content/uploads/2022/01/MRC_YEAREND_2021_US_FNL.pdf (accessed 25 June 2022).

Muino, T., and M. Hill, dir. (2021) "Montero (Call Me by Your Name)," [Video, performed by Lil Nas X]. Online. Available https://www.youtube.com/watch?v=6swmTBVI83k (accessed 15 September 2021).

Niditch, S. (2012) "Genesis," In C. Newsom, S. Ringe, and J. Lapsley (Eds.), *Women's Bible Commentary*, 3rd ed., Louisville: Westminster John Knox Press.

Nielsen (2014) "2014 Nielsen Music U.S. Report." Online. Available https://www.nielsen.com/wp-content/uploads/sites/3/2019/04/nielsen-2014-year-end-music-report-us-1.pdf (accessed 25 June 2022).

Nolan, S. (2021) "Semler's 'Preacher's Kid' and the Limits of Inclusion," *The Gospel Coalition*, February 22. Online. Available https://www.thegospelcoalition.org/article/semlers-preachers-kid-limits-inclusion/ (accessed 12 September 2021).

Ohlheiser, A. (2014) "Jars of Clay's Christian Fans Lash Out after the Lead Singer Tweets for Same-sex Marriage," *The Atlantic*, April 25. Online. Available https://www.theatlantic.com/politics/archive/2014/04/jars-of-clays-christian-fans-lash-out-after-the-lead-singer-tweets-for-same-sex-marriage/361256/ (accessed 15 September 2021).

Ostwalt, C. (2012) *Secular Steeples: Popular Culture and the Religious Imagination*, 2nd edn., New York: Bloomsbury.

Plato. *Symposium*. Translated by Benjamin Jowett. Online. Available http://classics.mit.edu/Plato/symposium.html (accessed 15 September 2021).

Radosh, D. (2010) *Rapture Ready! Adventures in the Parallel Universe of Christian Pop Culture*, New York: Soft Skull.

Stark, R. (1999) "Secularization, R.I.P." *Sociology of Religion* 60, no. 3: 249–273.

Turner, M.P. (2010) *Hear No Evil: My Story of Innocence, Music, and the Holy Ghost*, Colorado Springs: Water Brook Press.

Williams, Z., C. Beathard, and J. Smith (2019) "There Was Jesus," [Song, performed by Zach Williams and Dolly Parton on *Rescue Story*, Provident Label Group].

Wittgenstein, L. (2010) *Philosophical Investigations*, Oxford: Wiley-Blackwell.

6 Ecology and Religion
Climate Change in Popular Culture

Dell deChant

Introduction

I grew up in Florida before it became the Florida everybody knows: No Disney World or Sea World, no Tampa Bay Buccaneers or Miami Heat, no massive urban sprawl with franchise restaurants on every corner, no manatee die-offs and sea-level rise. My life began at about the same time the world of traditional Florida was beginning to die, as this once largely rural, lightly settled, ecologically fragile state was beginning its transformation into one that is highly urbanized, densely populated, economically diversified, and severely damaged ecologically. When I was born, Florida had a population of about 3.5 million; today it is the third most populous state in the nation, with a population of over 21 million. The radical transformation of Florida has had a ruinous impact on the state's ecology and a lasting impact on my life and professional career.

Over 40 years ago I entered the academic world with a question I still wrestle with: What motivates people to actions of radical malice and radical good—to sacrifice everything (including their own lives at times) to perpetrate acts of both horrible violence and harm and acts of incredible compassion and love? Perhaps not surprisingly, my quest for an answer focused on religion, specifically religious systems appearing in times of social crisis and significant cultural change, and offering alternatives to the existing norms of their cultures—religions like Christianity and Buddhism, for example. As important as it is to study those religions of antiquity, my particular interest was in religious groups emerging in the contemporary world—a world that was clearly and dramatically experiencing social crisis and significant cultural change and generating religious responses that challenged current cultural norms and called for personal and social transformation.

The term scholars came to use to identify these groups is New Religious Movements, and the development of a subfield in Religious Studies dedicated to the study of these groups occurred at about the same time I was beginning my research. My early success as a scholar was owed, at least in part, to my good fortune of focusing my studies on a cluster of new religions that had been largely ignored or marginalized by other scholars.

DOI: 10.4324/9781003079729-7

This offered opportunity to present conference papers, publish articles, and contribute chapters to books.

Over time, my research on new religions brought me into contact with work that was being done in another young subfield of Religious Studies—Religion and Popular Culture. It was in this area that I published the most important of my three books—*The Sacred Santa: The Religious Dimensions of Consumer Culture*. That book presents a theory that our consumer-based economic system is predicated on a sacralization of the economy that offers sacred legitimation and powerful motivation to the perpetual consumption of material goods.

The Sacred Santa and the argument it developed was a turning point for me, one that brought my scholarship into direct engagement with my life as a Floridian. I had long been concerned with the ecological crisis, going back to my reading of Rachel Carson's *Silent Spring* as a young person and my witnessing of the destruction of Florida's environment throughout my life. I joined others at the first Earth Day in 1970, witnessed a massive oil spill in Tampa Bay when I was in my teens, saw woodlands and ponds destroyed for strip malls, and gopher tortoise colonies paved over for highways and subdivisions.

What is happening to the environment in Florida has been happening elsewhere—everywhere, really. It is just happening faster and more destructively here than most other places. Soon after the publication of *The Sacred Santa* it became evident that the argument developed in that book offered a unique approach to examining the ecological crisis. The substance of the argument, thus, allowed better insight into not only why individuals and culture as a whole are driven to consume material goods at a frantic and unsustainable pace (and often despite rational reasons not to), but also how to better understand how and why we seem incapable of responding to the ecological crisis and continue to engage in the very activities that are deepening and accelerating the crisis, which appears today to be nearing the point of apocalyptic catastrophe.

As well known to most, the ecological crisis has worsened dramatically in the decade since the first edition of this book contained my chapter on this topic. Today I am certain everyone reading this chapter is aware of the crisis. I suspect that some, perhaps many, have had first-hand experience with its direct consequences. A recent report notes that over 1/3 of all Americans have suffered a climate-related disaster in just the summer months of 2021 (Kaplan and Tran, 2021). Signs of ecological collapse regularly confront us in today's world, and popular culture is replete with accounts, from the endless fires in the American West, ever stronger hurricanes, floods in Germany and New York City, habitat loss for major predators (tigers, polar bears, panthers) hydraulic fracturing, GMOs and melting glaciers, invasive species and contaminated food supplies, disappearing bees, record-breaking heat, and the polar vortex that brought sub-zero temperatures to Texas. The list is long and lengthening.

Clearly, the ecological crisis is a significant feature of the contemporary world, and the study of religion and popular culture rightly includes ecology as a major subject area. Curiously, however, despite the widespread interest in ecological issues and questions for both scholars and the general public, there are relatively few academic texts that engage the religious dimensions of ecology in popular culture. This is not to say there are not important studies of religion and ecology or popular culture and ecology. There certainly are. In fact, these two subject areas represent important new areas of scholarly inquiry. What seems missing, however, are studies giving significant and explicit attention to religion in the context of the intersection of ecology and popular culture.

The purpose of this chapter is, thus, to offer an initial encounter with a largely underexplored subfield of ecology within the field of religion and popular culture. The encounter will be advanced with an initial section on theory and method that will survey the development of the subfield of Religion and Ecology, specify key terms used in studies of religion and ecology, and conclude with a summary of major theoretic concepts that typically guide studies of religion and ecology. The case study that follows will consider how these concepts might be reconfigured to better engage religion and ecology *in* popular culture, and better analyze and evaluate the religious dimensions of a well-known ecological issue (Climate Change) in popular culture.

Theory and Method

Historical Context

The field of Religion and Ecology is one of the newest areas of research in Religious Studies. It emerges in the context of both the growth of Religious Studies as a recognized scholarly field and the rise in public awareness of the ecological challenges facing the world. As a distinct subfield of Religious Studies, the origin of Religion and Ecology is typically traced to a series of conferences on "Religions of the World and Ecology," hosted by Harvard Divinity School's Center for the Study of World Religions from 1996 to 1998. As noted by one of the major organizers, Mary Evelyn Tucker, the conferences were intended to:

> Provide a broad survey that would help ground a new field of study in religion and ecology.... Recognizing that religions are key shapers of people's worldviews and formulators of their most cherished values, this research project uncovered a wealth of attitudes and practices toward nature sanctioned by religious traditions.
>
> (Tucker 2006: 407)

Most scholars working in this area recognize that the Harvard conferences, and subsequent publication of a ten-volume collection of papers, launched Religion and Ecology as a significant subfield within Religious Studies. There was also important work prior to the conferences, especially pioneering efforts of David Barnhill and Eugene Bianchi who established Religion and Ecology as a regular topic area at meetings of the American Academy of Religion (AAR) beginning in 1989 (Taylor 2008:1373). But long before the Harvard conferences and the appearance of Religion and Ecology at the AAR, a scholar of medieval culture and technology by the name of Lynn Townsend White, Jr. published the seminal article in the field, "The Historical Roots of Our Ecologic Crisis" (White 1967).

White's article was the first to engage issues (in this case, what he identified as a "crisis") in ecology in terms of religion. It was a bold and provocative study, which offered a rather severe critique of the role (and culpability) of religion in bringing about the degradation of the natural world. Following closely the publication of Rachel Carson's *Silent Spring* (1962), which arguably initiated the environmental movement in popular culture, White's article traced the origins of the West's cavalier attitude toward the natural environment and disregard of ecological systems to Christianity and (in White's reading, at least) the sacred sanction it gave to the exploitation of nature. White's "Roots" is still referenced by contemporary scholars, and it is fair to say that few texts have had as great an impact on a field of study as this short article has had on Religion and Ecology.

Today, Religion and Ecology is a vital, dynamic, and very diverse area of scholarly activity. The past two decades have seen the publication of numerous academic texts on Religion and Ecology, several substantial reference books, a number of collections, and two scholarly journals dedicated to the topic. Universities have developed specific concentrations in Religion and Ecology, and faculty at many schools of higher education have developed and continue to develop courses in this area.

Religion and Ecology Today

As a rapidly expanding and still emerging field, it is risky to specify distinct theories and methods unique to Religion and Ecology. Suffice it to say, general tools of scholarship used in the academic study of religion are also relevant in this area, with some being more important or more frequently encountered here than in other areas. Rather than presenting a wide collection of theories and methods, I will note those of particular importance for general purposes and basic familiarity. In this regard, several preliminary understandings are critical to our encounter with Religion and Ecology in Popular Culture.

First and foremost, as noted previously, despite the important and rapidly expanding work being done in both Religion and Ecology and Ecology and Popular Culture, the area of our particular interest has been largely overlooked—at least as a clearly delineated topic or subfield. This being the case, inquiries into Religion and Ecology in Popular Culture are best thought of as preliminary and rightly attentive to terms and concepts being used.

As Professor Clark explains in the "Introduction" to this book, the study of religion and popular culture necessarily begins with definitions, and he carefully presents a set of working definitions of key terms; specifically, religion, culture, and popular culture. You will find that this is not uncommon in academic texts in new and still developing areas of inquiry, such as religion and popular culture, religion and gender, religion and sports, religion and ecology, and others. If you happen to explore Religion and Ecology in other courses or on your own, you will find texts in this area usually give careful attention to definitions of key terms—especially religion.

In this regard, we are reminded of Daniel L. Pals's correct observation that: "As we proceed, it will be wise to keep in mind that the matter of defining religion is closely linked to the matter of explaining it" (Pals 2006: 13). In other words, there is a close link between definition of critical terms of a field and theories used to guide critical inquiries into subjects of that field. This is certainly the case in studies of Religion and Ecology.

Key Terms

So, as we consider Religion and Ecology in Popular Culture, our first concern is establishing a working vocabulary. For purposes of order and coherence, we will accept Professor Clark's descriptions of *religion*, *culture*, and *popular culture*, given in the "Introduction." Clark's description of *religion* will be nuanced a bit in the "Case Study" section with the addition of the concept of **the sacred**, and an explanation of the theoretic relationship between religion and the sacred.

From among the many other terms and concepts relevant to studies in this area, three are especially critical: **nature, the environment**, and **ecology**. For scholars of Religion and Ecology, these three terms have importance, and attention to their usage in the literature is necessary.

Most broadly, the term **nature** refers to the physical-material world, and all entities, features, properties, and processes occurring therein. In this broad sense, "nature" necessarily includes humankind. More typically, however, nature has referred to the physical-material world as it exists independent of human modifications or distinct from human control and manipulation.

Today, however, human life has so fundamentally altered the natural world that nature as an independent force no longer exists. In this regard, Bill McKibben's notion of "**the end of nature**" (McKibben 1989) has broad acceptance among scholars of religion and ecology. Further, in popular usage, nature has an antiquated, anachronistic resonance. What once might have been referred to as nature (or natural) today is referred to as "the environment" (or "environmental"). Thus, in this area, nature tends not to be used as frequently as it once might have been, although the first, broader meaning of nature (given above) remains valuable to understanding the planet and the life it sustains.

Increasingly, where nature once might have been used, **the environment** is the preferred technical term. Most broadly, the environment refers to the immediate context in which something exists or is located. It is often used as a synonym for nature now that the traditional sense of nature has been compromised and fallen out of popular usage. For example, in popular discourse, we more often hear of calls to "protect the environment," but not so much to "protect nature." The environment is not a synonym for nature, however; for what this usage reveals, subtly perhaps, is that nature, per se, does not exist independently of human contexts. The environment is always contextual, and human beings supply the context—affecting it, being affected by it, and defining it. Where "nature" may at times imply independence from humans, the "environment" seldom has such a connotation.

In a related sense, the derived term, Environmentalism, typically refers to outlooks, beliefs, and sources of action that respect and seek to protect the *natural* environment. Although "the environment" usually is taken to mean the natural environment, it can refer to any number of non-natural settings—e.g., the domestic environment, the economic environment, the political, the urban, the educational, and so on. Notably, however, when used without modification, it is usually understood to refer to the *natural* environment; and the term environmentalism is *always* understood this way.

In the context of the evolving meanings and nuances of terms previously presented, **ecology** has received broad acceptance as the covering term for academic enterprises concerned with the relationship of human beings to the world of nature (or the environment). Most generally, ecology refers to the study of the interrelationship of organisms and the world around them. Beyond this initial understanding, the term has come to mean the study of the interrelationship of all things in nature (as a whole) and the relationship between specific actions and distinct effects. Importantly, in the context of Religion and Ecology, according to a recent textbook, another way to understand ecology is as "a *morally instructive* system of interconnections, a claim about the interrelated character of nature that has instructive lessons to teach all people" (Bauman et al. 2011: 230; italics mine). Aside from these more academic meanings, in terms of popular culture, the meanings and implications of ecology are extremely wide ranging, politically and socially charged, publicly disputed, and economically problematic. It is of critical importance that all inquirers (from elementary school students in science classes to professional scholars) recognize this reality. Most do not.

Theoretic Elements to Consider and Reconsider

At this point we can consider three general theoretic elements of relevance to Religion and Ecology and how they might be reconsidered or reconfigured to engage this area in Popular Culture. First, Religion and Ecology is surprisingly normative and "activist"; second it tends to be unusually focused on traditional expressions of religion (what I have referred to elsewhere as "the usual suspects approach" (deChant 2008: 77–79 and 2014: 158, 162); and third it generally overlooks the relationship of this area to culture as a whole—in which environmental issues and ecological concerns have come to comprise a fiercely disputed terrain, and one contested by powerful secular forces such as business, politics, government, and the media. Each of these elements will be briefly considered here in the context of Religion and Ecology, and then reconsidered in light of Religion and Ecology *in* Popular Culture.

First, although it may be a bit surprising to some, Religion and Ecology is recognized by many as a field of inquiry in which scholars are allowed (even expected) to be activists. The passage from the textbook on Religion and Ecology cited previously is suggestive of this normative character of many studies of Religion and Ecology. Notice how the authors emphasize that ecology may be "morally instructive" and that the "interrelated character of nature has instructive lessons." Implied in these assertions is that there is an intrinsic value and even virtue in ecology. Moreover, more recently, they stress:

> Similar to critical theories that deal with race, gender, sex, sexuality, and class, scholars in the field of religion and ecology seek to make a practical difference in the world. This field exists not just to develop theories and ideas, but also to contribute to a more just and sustainable world.
>
> (Bauman et al. 2017: 8)

Underscoring the normative nature of this field, one of its major theorists, Roger Gottlieb, affirms that the study of religion and ecology emerged in the context of the massive ecological crisis facing the world today, and that one of the major questions that "form the heart of the study of religion and ecology" is "how must beliefs (and actions) change as we face the *environment*" (Gottlieb 2006: 6). Note again the normative character of this approach. The question is not whether beliefs and actions will change or even that they should, but rather *how must* they change.

While the normative approach may seem quite reasonable, and certainly worthy of serious consideration in today's world, some may find it problematic from a scholarly standpoint. Once ecology (however it may be conceived) is deemed morally instructive the neutrality and objectivity of the inquirer may be questioned. Further, if inquiry begins with the presupposition that we are confronted with a massive ecological crisis that requires change in (religious) beliefs and actions, the inquirer's objectivity may again be questioned, with the risk that the findings and conclusions of the inquirer are deemed to be compromised. Yet, such risks are common in this area of study. When considering religion and ecology in popular culture, we may find a more suitable method to be the neutral approach that is typical of Religious Studies.

The second consideration in our reflection on theoretic approaches to religion and ecology in popular culture is the recognition that all too often previous studies have focused their attention quite heavily on major world religions using the "usual suspects approach." While there are exceptions to the usual suspects approach, as will be noted below, for the most part the study of religion and ecology is restricted to explorations of beliefs, practices, and current attitudes of well-known and well-established religions. These studies also tend to be developed in the context of Lynn White's original critique of over 50 years ago (White 1967). That is, there is often a presumption that *mainstream* religion should be doing something about the "ecological crisis." Attention then is given to what mainstream religion is or is not doing—with accolades extended to activities deemed meritorious and encouragement to do more.

As we study religion and ecology in popular culture, I think we can do better than the usual suspects approach. We can consider what Bron Taylor terms "green religions" and "dark green religion," taking seriously the presence of important religious expressions in marginal movements such as neo-paganism, Native American spirituality, and New Age religions (Taylor 2006: 598–599); and even including the emergence of a non-supernaturalistic "civic earth religion" (Taylor 2006: 604–606). Even more successfully, as I will argue in the case study that follows, we can deploy the thought of Jacques Ellul (with some modifications) and discover the sacred function of seemingly secular cultural systems.

Case Study: Finding the Sacred in the Climate Change Debate

To introduce this specific case study (the Climate Change Debate), let me begin by noting the third and final theoretic feature of Religion and Ecology that we may reconsider—namely that studies in this area generally overlook the relationship of Religion and Ecology to culture as a whole. In doing so, they tend to minimize the reality that environmental issues and ecological concerns have come to comprise a much-disputed terrain, and one contested by powerful secular forces such as business, politics, government, and the media. The assertion that there is a massive ecological crisis, as routinely occurs in literature on Religion and Ecology, is far from a generally accepted fact in contemporary American culture. When reading the fine work by important scholars on the various issues and questions pertaining to religion and ecology, folks who are even marginally familiar with the wider world of culture are doubtless quite mindful that much (if not all) of what is being presented in these marvelous studies will be rejected out of hand by a large percentage of the American population and an overwhelming majority of the elected leaders of one of America's two great political parties. For them there is no more an ecological crisis today than there was one when Lynn White wrote his article in 1967. Moreover, for them, not only is there not a crisis, the very idea of one is a pernicious hoax concocted by a political elite.

Recent polling data indicates that there is growing acceptance of the relationship between human activity and climate change, with 57% of Americans *believing* there is a relationship as of 2020—up from the 47% that *believed* in the relationship in 2014 (Chinni, 2021). Still, there is little change in the number of Americans who affirm that there is no relationship: 32% in 2020 (Yale 2020), compared with 34% in 2010 (Blumner 2011).

More strikingly, in 2016 the United States elected a President who had once asserted that climate change was a hoax, invented by the Chinese (Jacobson, 2016). Although he has since backed off that assertion, the hoax assertion echoes the position of that 32% of the population who reject any relationship between climate change and human action and harmonizes with the view of Senator James Inhofe (Oklahoma), who also called global warming "the greatest hoax ever perpetrated on the American people" (Kolbert 2006: 160). Despite the assertions of a President and a major political party, in "legitimate scientific circles, it is virtually impossible to find evidence of disagreement over the fundamentals of global warming" (Kolbert 2006: 162).

It is here, on the furiously disputed terrain of contemporary public opinion about the environment, that Religion and Popular Culture may help us better understand and navigate the emerging field of religion and ecology. How this might happen will be presented in the context of an exploration of the heated climate change debate.

The volatility of the climate change debate in popular culture is hard to ignore and easy to observe. Those who are interested are invited to do some internet searches. What you will find is that there are a vast number of sources supporting the scientific consensus that climate change is a reality, and it is caused by human activity. In fact, there are many more today than there were ten years ago. However, there are also a significant number of sources disputing the scientific consensus and many that offer reasons for rejecting it. Besides the various websites and YouTube videos disputing and rejecting climate change, a brief survey of Amazon.com reveals numerous books that also dismiss the scientific consensus on climate change. Finally, not surprisingly, Facebook is perhaps the best source for internet support of climate change denial, with a recent report finding that Facebook sites "denying the reality of the climate crisis or the need for action were viewed at least 8 million times in the US in the first half of 2020" (Carrington 2020).

Whether looking for support or rejection of climate change and its causes, there is no difficulty in finding abundant sources. This abundance of sources supporting both positions presents us with what is aptly classified as an **availability cascade**, an ever-increasing phenomenon in popular culture (especially cyber culture) and a powerful force in shaping understandings and perceptions of large portions of the population. An availability cascade, which seems virtually inevitable in internet research and communication using social-networking systems, is "a self-reinforcing process of collective belief formation by which an expressed perception triggers a chain reaction that gives the perception of increasing plausibility through its rising availability in public discourse" (Kuran and Sunstein 1999: 683).

In terms of our analysis of the climate-change debate, this reveals that no matter which side of the issue you are on, there is an overwhelming amount of information (facts, data, evidence, authorities, books) to support your case. The issue is polarized, and the competing availability cascades assure us that the issue will remain polarized. Why change your mind when you can craft a torrent of supporting information for your view? Moreover, why consider a competing position when the position you have taken seems so obviously correct?

Doubtless many people do indeed form their views and convictions about climate change and numerous other issues due to availability cascades, and there does not seem to be any good reason to change one's mind or consider competing positions if one is captured in one of these cascades. Students of religion and culture, however, have a responsibility to get beyond the cascades of self-reinforcing facts and data—no matter how painful and unpleasant that may be. For us, the task at hand is to understand the matter before us; and to do that, we must set aside our personal beliefs and commitments.

What this means is that although one may have a rather profound personal interest in the environment and the relationship between human beings and the natural world, in order to understand and analyze this topic, one must necessarily set aside personal interest and commitment. This methodological approach is known as **bracketing**, and it is predicated on one of the guiding principles of Religious Studies—neutrality. If I were to allow my personal stand on the issue to guide my scholarship, I would quickly move in the direction of the side that I agree with, thus limiting my ability to understand the other side and to present that side fairly and honestly.

So, the first methodological step we are encouraged to take moves us away from the way Religion and Ecology is typically approached. In short, we *are not* taking a normative position on the issue; and unlike many scholars working in this area, *in terms of our research here*, we will not "consider nature to be sacred in some way" (Taylor 2006: 598). The status of the debate in popular culture does not allow us to do that. Note, nature may well be sacred (or not) for us, but the point is that *in terms of our research here* we have no commitment one way or another. What we do want to understand is the debate as it appears in popular culture, why it is so fractious, and how religion comes into play.

This brings us to the next methodological consideration; and, again, another departure from the traditional approach taken in Religion and Ecology. Rather than trying to compartmentalize and contextualize our study in terms of major religious traditions, we will take a broader approach.

While we certainly would learn something by using the usual suspects approach, what we would learn would not be all that meaningful or all that helpful for understanding the full fury and rigor of the climate-change debate. What we would find, by the way, is that most mainstream religions concur with scientific findings that climate change is occurring, is caused by humans, and humans must take action to mitigate its impact on future generations, with Pope Francis's *Laudato Si'* being a leading example (Bergoglio 2015).[1] While studying mainstream religious responses is notable and helpful, it skirts the larger issue, which is why this topic is so heated, and why the sides are so polarized.

So, instead of researching specific religious traditions, or resorting to an 'explanation by cascade' approach, we might apply a theory that expands the concept of the **sacred** and broadens the concept of **religion** so as to include cultural elements of a seemingly secular nature. The specific theory proposed here is derived from one introduced and first constructed by Jacques Ellul, namely that in the contemporary world, the sacred may be something more and something quite different from traditional notions of divinity (Ellul 1975). Further, and as a result, our relationship with the sacred is mediated through institutions other than traditional religions. For Ellul, and in brief, the Ultimate Power of a culture is the **sacred** of that culture; and **religion** is the human institution through which the sacred is mediated within a society (Ellul 1975: c. 3, 4, and 6).

Thus, for Ellul, technology is the sacred of contemporary culture, and politics is the dominant religious expression. In other words, technology is the Ultimate Power, and politics is the institution through which that Power is mediated in society. As I have argued elsewhere, Ellul's theory is extremely helpful; all it needs is a little fine-tuning (deChant 2002: 29–32). Specifically, the content of the two categories requires adjustment. Where Ellul argues for technology as the contemporary sacred, I argue for the economy; and where Ellul argues for politics as the religious institution that mediates the sacred, I suggest it is consumption—i.e., retail spending: shopping and buying products (deChant 2002: 36–40. For a thorough exposition of this theory and its deployment in an analysis of the religious dynamic of contemporary culture, see deChant 2002: 25–50).

Using this modification of Ellul's theory may help explain why the climate-change/global warming debate is so contentious. It is not about science, and the Keeling Curve, the greenhouse effect, or data generated by NOAA and NASA showing conclusively that the earth is warming and human activity generating CO_2 is the cause. Although both sides have their own respective availability cascades with torrents of facts and data, the substance of the debate does not ultimately concern facts and data.

The variation of Ellul's theory suggested above offers a new way to understand the debate in terms of the sacred and religion, in this case, the sacred of economic growth and expansion and the religion of consumption. What the hard science supporting climate change encounters in the world of popular culture are the deep-seated religious beliefs of postmodern America, a world constructed on glorious myths of **American Exceptionalism** and unfettered economic growth, fueled by cheap oil, and energized by personal religious rituals of consumption of material goods at ever-increasing rates. To reiterate and clarify, using this line of analysis, for contemporary American culture, the sacred (or Ultimate Power) is the economy, and our relationship with this sacred reality is fully experienced through the religion of consumption.

Ellul's theory, as modified here, gives us a better idea of why climate change, and various other ecological and social issues (like vaccines and election outcomes), cause such controversy. What is at stake is a sacred order of existence, and the religion that engages us with that sacred order. If the climate-changers are right, then it is this very order that is to blame for impending (and now appearing) global calamities. If global warming is actually occurring, and the dire consequences it promises are coming to pass, then the sacred world of American Exceptionalism, with its unending economic expansion and rituals of personal consumption, is coming to an end—and, ironically, bringing about its own demise.

For good reason, then, many leaders in government, commerce, and industry challenge and dismiss climate change and certainly its cause by human activity. It is not a scientific debate, although it may assume the rhetorical trapping of such a debate. The science appears pretty well settled. For some, it may appear political, and a case can be made for reading it this way.

Deploying the economy-as-sacred theory reveals that the denial of climate change is not based on science or even politics. Instead, it is a thoroughgoing rejection of climate change on religious grounds. The opposition rejects climate change arguments because they compromise the sacred reality (of the economic order) of American culture and undermine its religion (of consumption). Critics of climate change are as adamant as they are because they are on a religious mission to eliminate a heretical belief. When analyzed in this way, we may not be in a position to better resolve the climate change debate or any of the other disputed societal issues that surface in contemporary culture (like wearing masks during a pandemic), but we might understand just why they are so contentious and why they are more religious than they might otherwise seem to be.

Summary

- Ecology and ecological issues are popular topics in contemporary culture, and although scholars have given attention to distinct subject areas of (a) Religion and Ecology and (b) Ecology and Popular Culture, little attention has been given to Religion and Ecology *in* Popular Culture.
- Key concepts relevant to Religion and Ecology are: nature, environment, ecology, religion, and the sacred.
- To better address Religion and Ecology *in* Popular Culture certain theories and methods typically used by scholars of Religion and Ecology need to be reconsidered, specifically: (1) the normative/activist approach, (2) the focus on traditional expressions of religion, and (3) the tendency to overlook the relationship of Religion and Ecology to culture as a whole.
- Reconsideration and reconstruction of these three elements allows better understanding of Religion and Ecology in contemporary culture, and also why the issues in ecology are so contentious.

Discussion Questions and Activities

- In your own experience, does nature have a religious significance? If so, can you articulate its significance?
- In your estimation, why has so little work been done on religion and ecology in popular culture?
- Do you think that scholars of religion should take public stands on issues related to the "ecological crisis" (e.g., global warming, species extinctions, deforestation, and so on)?
- In your estimation, what is the best course of action for traditional religions to take in response to the "ecological crisis?"
- Have you ever experienced an "availability cascade" regarding a particular subject of study or research? How might you guard against being influenced by such a cascade?
- Research "Climate Change" on the internet and social media sites (like Facebook and YouTube). Find sites that support the scientific consensus on the reality of climate change and its anthropogenic (human-caused) origins and compare them with sites that dispute or reject the scientific consensus. **Bracket** your own stance on the issue and try to understand each position as viable and convincing.
- Read Senator James Inhofe's book, *The Greatest Hoax: How the Global Warming Conspiracy Threatens Your Future*, and compare it with Al Gore's *An Inconvenient Truth: The Planetary Emergency of Global Warming and What We Can Do About It*. How do they reveal competing concepts of the **sacred** and why would it be difficult for someone who agreed with Inhofe to accept Gore's "inconvenient truth"—and vice versa?

Glossary

American Exceptionalism   Mythic narrative affirming the glorious destiny of the United States, predicated on the belief that the United States is unique among all nations in the history of the world. Stress is given to various ideals (self-governance, freedom of association, economic opportunity, and others) as definitive of America's exceptionalism and the sources of its world-historic success.

Availability cascade   **Process** through which a claim becomes accepted by ever increasing numbers of persons due to the frequency of its occurrence in communication networks.

Bracketing   Conscious **suspension** of personal beliefs about a topic of professional inquiry for the purpose of maintaining greater objectivity.

Ecology   Study of the **interrelationship** of all things in nature (or the environment), and the full spectrum of relationships between specific entities, other entities, and the environment in which they exist. Also, an academic field that studies these interrelationships. In contemporary America, the meanings and implications of ecology are quite broad, complex, politically and socially charged, economically problematic, and much-disputed in popular culture.

"End of nature"   A **concept** developed by Bill McKibben in a book by this title, identifying the contemporary/postmodern era as a post-nature world; nature as something independent of human beings no longer exits—i.e., there is no physical-material world independent from human modifications or distinct from human control and manipulation.

The environment   The immediate context in which something exists or is located. Often used as a synonym for nature, now that the traditional sense of nature has been compromised and begun to decline in popular usage. For example, in popular discourse, we more often hear of calls to "protect the environment," but not so much to "protect nature." In this regard, a derived term, Environmentalism, typically refers to outlooks, beliefs, and sources of action that respect and seek to protect the *natural* environment.

Nature   Most broadly, the physical-material world, inclusive of all entities, features, properties, and processes occurring therein. Although humans are part of nature by definition, typically, nature has referred to the physical-material world as it exists apart from human modifications or distinct from human control and manipulation. In popular usage, nature has an antiquated, anachronistic resonance. What once might have been referred to as nature (or natural), today is referred to as "the environment" (or "environmental").

Religion   See Professor Clark's definition in the Introduction, but note the nuance given here, with religion being understood as the social institution that mediates a relationship between human beings and what they hold as sacred.

Sacred   Following the usage of Jacques Ellul and others, sacred is that which serves as the Ultimate Power or Principle of a culture. It is the ground of being and source of meaning and purpose. In this understanding, it functions as the supreme power/principle that is mediated by the social institution of religion.

Note

1   This work and the environmental commitment of Pope Francis represents a particularly intriguing convergence of history, religion, environmentalism, and popular culture – accentuated not coincidentally by the pope adopting the regnal name of one of the earliest and most celebrated religious environmentalists, St. Francis of Assisi (1181-1225).

Further Reading

Gottlieb, Roger S. (2006) *A Greener Faith: Religious Environmentalism and Our Planet's Future*, New York: Oxford University Press.
   Thorough study of religious environmentalism by one of the major scholars of Religion and Ecology. Attention is given to major themes, leaders, and initiatives.

Gottlieb contextualizes the religious dimension of environmentalism relative to topics such as secularization, politics, and consumerism.

Hay, Peter. (2002) *Main Current in Western Environmental Thought*, Bloomington: Indiana University Press.

Substantial survey of major intellectual and cultural forces behind and within the contemporary environmental movement. Attention is given to "Ecophilosophy," "Ecofeminism," "Green Political Thought," "Religion, Spirituality, and the Green Movement," and several other critical features of today's environmental movement.

Sturgeon, Noel. (2009) *Environmentalism in Popular Culture*. Tucson: University of Arizona Press.

Detailed examination of environmentalism in Popular Culture through the critical lens of cultural studies. Using "intersectional analysis," Sturgeon offers a critical study of the ways in which environmental issues and themes relate to large social concerns, especially problems in equality and social justice.

Taylor, Bron. (2010) *Dark Green Religion: Nature Spirituality and the Planetary Future*, Berkeley: University of California Press.

Most recent book by pioneer in the study of the religious dimensions of ecology. Taylor argues for an inner religious dynamic at work in a variety of environmental organizations, helping us understand how seemingly secular causes are better understood as functionally religious in orientation.

Bibliography

Bauman, Whitney A., Richard R. Bohannon II, and Kevin J. O'Brien (2011) *Grounding Religion: A Field Guide to the Study of Religion and Ecology*. New York: Routledge.

―――― (2017) *Grounding Religion: A Field Guide to the Study of Religion and Ecology*. 2nd edn. New York: Routledge.

Bergoglio, Jorge Mario (Pope Francis) (2015) *Laudato Si': On Care for Our Common Home*. Encyclical Letter. Vatican City: Libreria Editrice Vaticana.

Blumner, Robin (2011) "Enough of Us, Already, Let's Think Smaller." *St. Petersburg Times*, 30 January: 5P.

Carrington, Damian (2020) "Climate Denial Ads on Facebook Seen By Millions, Report Finds." *The Guardian*, 8 October. https://www.theguardian.com/environment/2020/oct/08/climate-denial-ads-on-facebook-seen-by-millions-report-finds

Carson, Rachel (1962) *Silent Spring*. Boston: Houghton Mifflin.

Chinni, Dante (2021) "Global Warming Perceptions by State: Most Americans Accept Human Fault." *NBC News*, 25 April. https://www.nbcnews.com/politics/meet-the-press/global-warming-perceptions-states-more-americans-accept-fault-n1265213

deChant, Dell (2008) *Religion and Culture in the West: A Primer*. Rev. Printing. Dubuque, Iowa: Kendall/Hunt.

―――― (2002) *The Sacred Santa: Religious Dimensions of Consumer Culture*. Cleveland: The Pilgrim Press.

―――― (2014) "Where's the Beef? Looking for Food in Religion and Ecology." Pages 155–172 in William D. Schanbacher (ed.), *The Global Food System*. Santa Barbara, CA: Prager.

Ellul, Jacques (1975) *The New Demons*. Trans. C. Edward Hopkin. New York: Seabury Press.

Friedman, Lisa (2018) "'I Don't Know That It's Man-Made,' Trump Says of Climate Change. It Is." *The New York Times*, 15 October. https://www.nytimes.com/2018/10/15/climate/trump-climate-change-fact-check.html

Gottlieb, Roger S. (2006) "Religion and Ecology—What Is the Connection and Why Does It Matter?" Pages 48–66 in Roger S. Gottlieb (ed.), *Oxford Handbook of Religion and Ecology*. New York: Oxford University Press.

Jacobson, Louis (2016) "[Hillary Clinton] Says Donald Trump Says Climate Change Is a Hoax Invented by the Chinese." *Politifact*. The Poynter Institute, 3 June. https://www.politifact.com/factchecks/2016/jun/03/hillary-clinton/yes-donald-trump-did-call-climate-change-chinese-h/

Kaplan, Sarah and Andrew Ba Tran (2021) "Nearly 1 in 3 Americans Experienced a Weather Disaster this Summer." *Washington Post*, 4 September. https://www.washingtonpost.com/climate-environment/2021/09/04/climate-disaster-hurricane-ida/

Kolbert, Elizabeth (2006) *Field Notes from A Catastrophe: Man, Nature, and Climate Change*. New York: Bloomsbury.

Kuran, Timur and Cass R. Sunstein (1999) "Availability Cascades and Risk Regulation." *Stanford Law Review* 51 (April): 683–768.

McKibben, Bill (1989) *The End of Nature*. New York: Random House.

Pals, Daniel L. (2006) *Eight Theories of Religion*. 2nd edn. New York: Oxford University Press.

Taylor, Bron (ed.) (2008) *Encyclopedia of Religion and Nature*. London: Continuum.

——— (ed.) (2006) "Religion and Environmentalism in America and Beyond." Pages 588–612 in Roger S. Gottlieb (ed.), *Oxford Handbook of Religion and Ecology*. New York: Oxford University Press.

Tucker, Mary Evelyn (2006) "Religion and Ecology: Survey of the Field." Pages 398–418 in Roger S. Gottlieb (ed.), *Oxford Handbook of Religion and Ecology*. New York: Oxford University Press.

White, Lynn Townsend, Jr. (1967) "The Historical Roots of Our Ecologic Crisis." *Science* 155: 3767 (10 March): 1203–1207.

Yale University (2020) *Climate Opinion Maps, 2020*. https://climatecommunication.yale.edu/visualizations-data/ycom-us/

7 Ritual Doing, Religious Doing

Understanding Harry Potter Fan Pilgrimages

J. Caroline Toy

Introduction

I first became aware of *Harry Potter* fan pilgrimage because of a human traffic jam. Fan pilgrimage as discussed here typically involves physical travel to filming locations, character or celebrity memorials, themed attractions, and more, by people who are very invested in a media text, group, or event. Traveling with family in the United Kingdom, we attempted to visit Christ Church College in Oxford to view its iconic architecture. Christ Church is also a well-known inspiration and filming location for the *Harry Potter* movies. When we arrived, during England's autumn school break in 2012, the line of families waiting to enter the college stretched out into the garden and changed our plans.

Years later, I found myself comparing two apparently different pilgrimage experiences. On a single overseas trip, I visited the Warner Bros. Studio Tour – The Making of *Harry Potter* on the outskirts of London, where I spent over half an hour circling the astonishing scale model of Hogwarts Castle used in filming, and walked the last 200 km of the Camino de Santiago, a renowned thousand-year-old Catholic pilgrimage route in Spain that now attracts Catholics, other Christians, spiritual seekers, and adventure travelers. I am not Catholic; I am a *Harry Potter* fan. The comparison stuck with me. In what ways, and why, are these experiences both pilgrimages?

As a result, I undertook an intellectual "pilgrimage": a quest to understand where religiosity lies in the landscapes and doings of fan pilgrimage. This exploration included a host of other questions: why do some scholars (and fans) acknowledge the religious resonances of pilgrimage in fandom while others ignore or deny them? What does sacred space mean without religious institutions or supernatural beliefs? Who gets to go on fan pilgrimage (and fit in) and who is excluded? What does "doing things" during fan pilgrimage (not just locations themselves) mean to fans who undertake it?

The last question motivates this chapter. There are many ways to "read" fan pilgrimage: by examining the destinations themselves, by considering the demographics of pilgrims, and/or by focusing on why certain stories or people inspire pilgrimage. However, what fan pilgrims *do*, and how they

DOI: 10.4324/9781003079729-8

talk about it, is a particularly rich entry point to thinking about how fan pilgrimage might be a kind of religious doing, even though it is not (usually) part of an organized religion. It also allows us to think closely about ritual as a kind of doing. Here we will use fans' accounts of doing rituals to think about **ritualization**, the strategic performance of ritual "scripts," and its effects in the spatial, social, and narrative landscapes of pilgrimage. I will argue that while this ritualization takes place in contexts that are about fiction, or are "fake" (constructed, dramatic, make-believe, and/or commercialized), fan pilgrimage rituals are a kind of religious doing that forces us to ask important questions about where we draw the boundaries of "religion."

Theory and Method

Definitions are a significant concern for this kind of study. What is ritual? What constitutes a pilgrimage? Why do we associate these types of practices with religion? What is a pilgrimage in the context of fan culture (and what is fan culture, anyway)? These are also terms whose definitions are matters of considerable dispute.

Ritual and Ritualization

Ritual, as a concept in European-influenced studies of religion, has largely referred to repeated actions, often ceremonial, that symbolize, enact, or idealize values or narratives. However, scholarly work on ritual has varied in its approach. Victor Turner, for example, an anthropologist with an interest in pilgrimage, followed earlier scholars in exploring rituals as social dramas of symbolic actions (1974). Scholar of religion Jonathan Z. Smith, on the other hand, examined ritual's relations to place and narratives (1982, 1987). In Smith's view, ritual *produces* sacredness (including sacred space, objects, and stories) through actions with special significance, rather than sacredness giving rise to ritual. Catherine Bell's work reasons that ritual is not best seen as a set of repeated actions with fairly fixed meanings (a "script"), but as ritualization, a "strategic way of acting" in which individual performances of ritual scripts in different situations change their meaning (1992: 7). That is, a ritual never quite looks the same, and never has quite the same meaning or effects; the performance is more significant than the script (Bell 1998).

Bell's interest in these performances over a more traditional definition of ritual is ideal for this ethnographic study of fan pilgrimage, as is Smith's understanding of the production of sacredness and space. This chapter draws on both, viewing ritual performance (or ritualization) as a strategic way of acting in response to narratives, values, and landmarks. Ritualization produces a sense of specialness or sacredness in and about its context. This definition prioritizes situational variability and *effects*—that is, ritualized ways of doing can make something special or make something happen.

These effects can include perceiving social belonging, developing identity, interpreting a narrative, shaping space, and participating in commerce, all given extraordinary significance.

Ritual Performance and Doing Religiously

To study fan pilgrimage, we must first articulate our understanding of the relationship between religion and ritual/ritualization, for two reasons. First, the validity of ritual as ritual (and pilgrimage as pilgrimage) is sometimes tied to it being "religious" or not, while there is no universal agreement about what "religion" (or for that matter, "secular") means. This has some-times resulted in certain types of "secular" acts being excluded from study as ritual. Second, if we prioritize ritualization and its special effects over ritual scripts, we can begin to see that the line between *religious* specialness and *non-religious* specialness is thin indeed (Taves 2009), and a productive thing to challenge. This is particularly true in the study of pilgrimage and is why we will use the term "sacredness" throughout. Common-sense and tra-ditional definitions of religion, which tend to focus on beliefs about the supernatural and the texts, rituals, and power structures that surround those beliefs, are not necessarily helpful.

Just as Bell argues that ritual performances are not simply enactments of beliefs, and Smith argues that rituals produce sacredness rather than being products of it, we will approach religiosity, or ways of being religious, as effects of special ways of doing. We will speak of religiosity in the sense of "**doing religiously**," a term with similar inflections that works better outside the context of a traditional, self-identified religious community or doctrine. Doing religiously is strategic doing, formal and informal, at the boundary of what "counts" as religion, that produces deeply meaningful experiences with lasting significance. Scholar of religion and popular culture David Chidester similarly describes "religious work" as "negotiating what it means to be human" regardless of the *content* of that work (2005: 18). However, religious work seems to subtly imply functions that take the place of religion, whereas doing religiously is a complex of actions and effects that may coexist with other religious or non-religious understandings of what it means to be human.

Pilgrimage

Pilgrimage is an ideal field for observing doing religiously. A global phenom-enon, pilgrimage is usually understood as structured geographic travel to a place associated with events, people, or narratives that have a high degree of significance. It is often highly ritualized, but this does not necessarily mean that all participants closely follow a set script together. Thus, for our pur-poses, **pilgrimage** is a genre of religious doing that *negotiates* geography, meaning, and social context in a space that invites competing understand-ings of what happens there. Pilgrims have a wide range of situational experiences to which they attribute extraordinary significance. Pilgrimage, then, can be a genre of religious doing (in its traditionally religious ritual repertoires and its effects) without any given pilgrim being a religious adherent, and it does not require a deity or supernatural belief system.

However, this is a point of scholarly dispute, with some scholars attempting to clearly separate (religious) pilgrimage and (secular) tourism. Peter Jan Margry, for example, argues that the term "secular pilgrimage" (pilgrimage without existential concerns about the supernatural) is inherently contradictory (2008). However, this is reductive, in part because any pilgrimage is about more than supernatural beliefs, interventions, or obligations. Another common but fallacious misconception is that pilgrimage ought to be distinct from commercialized experiences and merchandise. John Eade and Michael Sallnow more helpfully characterize pilgrimages (and specifically pilgrimage sites) as "realm[s] of competing discourses" that can accommodate different, perhaps contradictory narratives, practices, and personal beliefs (1991).

Especially productive for our purposes is the more recent view of pilgrimage as a complex interplay of social relations, space, power, beliefs, and practices. The special significances we associate with pilgrimage can happen—or not happen—in many different kinds of settings, activities, and intents. That is, pilgrimage "arises from contingent conjunctions of ... agents and practices at particular points in space and time" (Maddrell et al. 2016), including surrounded by tourists who occupy the same site just for fun (or with boredom), and in highly commercialized contexts. Viewing pilgrimage in this way allows us to see it as a field of negotiation: of individual with group, individual or group with narratives, individual or group with ritual practices, and so on.

Fan Pilgrimage

Fan pilgrimage, also called pop culture pilgrimage (or sometimes media tourism), is an ideal case for exploring these complexities. **Fan culture**—the practices of people who identify as fans—is commonly associated with celebrities, teams, events, and multi-media texts including books, movies, music, TV shows, comics, and so on. To most observers and many scholars it seems religious only in the pejorative sense of "cult" followers.[1] Indeed, the study of fan pilgrimage, by whatever name, has a tenuous relationship with the study of religiosity in pilgrimage. But at a minimum, it is of the same genre of practice as more traditional religious journeys: geographic travel to a place—constructed or otherwise—motivated by being a fan, typically involving ritualized practices, though such practices may not immediately strike an observer as religious. It is important to note that both academics and fans themselves document and produce scholarship on fan pilgrimage.

Scholarship on rituals and ritualization in fan pilgrimage (by those terms or others) is wide-ranging. Memorial messages and graffiti emerge in contexts as varied as Elvis Presley devotion, Princess Diana memorials, and filming locations from TV shows *Torchwood* and *Sherlock* (Alderman 2002; Doss 1999; Potts et al. 2018; Beattie 2014; Toy 2017). Staged photography—long acknowledged to be a form of ritual in tourism (MacCannell 1976)—filming location-hunting, and identifying fictional settings have been studied in relation to the city of Vancouver, *Blade Runner*, *Harry Potter*, mystery fiction, *Sherlock* again, and simply the phenomenon of fan photography itself (Brooker 2005, 2007; Larsen 2015; Reijnders 2011; Lee 2014; Öhman and Walden). Still other authors focus on activities intended to generate a sense of immersion, including official attractions dedicated to *Doctor Who* and *Harry Potter* (Garner 2016; Hills 2017; Waysdorf and Reijnders 2016). In these examples, fans may do some or all of the following: leave objects or messages, take photos of themselves or the location, and participate in themed activities like rides, dramas, dining, and shopping.

Methods

The case studies below examine ritualization and doing religiously at fan pilgrimage sites related to the *Harry Potter* films. The larger project from which they come, which also includes sites related to *Doctor Who*, *Torchwood*, and *Sherlock*, relies on ethnographic fieldwork such as participation in pilgrimage, observation at sites, and interviewing participants. These methods are common in anthropology, folklore, religious studies, and fan studies. *Harry Potter*-related sites discussed here include the Warner Bros. Studio Tour London; the Platform 9¾ photo op at King's Cross Station in London; and the Wizarding World of Harry Potter theme park in Orlando, Florida (WWHP).

While observations of ritual performances are valuable, the stories of what people do and what that doing means to them provide better insight into *ritualization* and its effects. The interviews discussed here are not intended to provide a summary or representative sample of what fans think about pilgrimage; rather, they explore some of the many ways that *doing* in fan pilgrimages—which, as Maddrell et al. (2016) theorize, is deeply dependent on people, feelings, geographies, and events—produces a variety of different, sometimes dissonant, experiences. The stories featured here will introduce three effects of ritualization in fan pilgrimage: production of sacred space, perception of social ties, and the relationship of identity and narrative.

Case Studies

Sacralizing Space: Jean and Louise's Story

As *Harry Potter* fans know, King's Cross Station in London is where Harry catches a train to wizard school. To board the train, however, he must first leave ordinary King's Cross for the hidden Platform 9¾ by running full-tilt at a brick wall that separates "muggle" departures from magical ones. Since early in the *Harry Potter* phenomenon, King's Cross has played host to a marker of Platform 9¾ in the main ticket hall: half a luggage trolley bolted to a brick wall and decorated with wizarding gear. Fans pose with the trolley as if they were pushing it through the wall to the magical platform. This is arguably the most imaginatively **liminal** location in *Potter* fan pilgrimage, as it marks the point at which Harry crosses from ordinary world to magical, and from being a muggle to becoming a wizard. Currently the trolley is located next to an official gift shop. Fans can visit and take their own pictures for free or purchase an official photo.

White French fans Jean (who was interviewed) and Louise (who participated in surveys but did not take part in an interview) traveled in the United Kingdom in 2016 as part of a special birthday trip to visit sites related to *Harry Potter* and *Doctor Who*. In London, they visited the Warner Bros. Studio Tour as well as King's Cross Station. While they had been to Platform 9¾ before, the coincidental timing of this visit—the day after actor Alan Rickman, who played Professor Snape, died—produced an extraordinary experience. When they arrived, they found crowds of fans leaving flowers, cards, and other objects in memory of Rickman (and Snape, who has one of the series' most dramatic death scenes). Jean related:

> it was a strange day. People simply gathered there, visiting the shop, and [leaving] flowers or candles. My girlfriend wanted to do something and we bought a postcard to leave a note. It was a sad day for fans I think.
>
> (Interview, January 15, 2019, edited for concision)

Though Jean (who is Catholic) did not consider Platform 9¾ or other destinations he visited like the Warner Bros. Studio Tour to be sacred space, nor did he describe himself as a pilgrim, what he describes is a common form of sacralizing public space through memorialization. It is seen in a religious context at shrines across faiths; at graves of or monuments to dead celebrities; and in a civic context at impromptu memorials for victims of mass violence. What Jean and Louise expected to be a fun photo op (which is how many visitors in this and other studies describe 9¾) actually became a sacralizing moment for the space as fans, without coordination, responded to events and each other by participating ritually. Louise, in her survey response, did not hesitate to call 9¾ "a sacred place, a place where fans go and gather during important events" like the one she witnessed.[2]

From these events, we might assume that places like 9¾ can *become* sacred spaces *if* ritual happens there. However, Louise's perspective is suggestive: the place *always* has the capacity for sacredness. Jonathan Z. Smith (1982), discussed in the previous section, characterizes sacred space as a "focusing lens" that gives special import to what happens in it, and is designated for that purpose. This is an apt way of understanding 9¾, since it is always being designated as such a place by activities that may not immediately seem like rituals, but are. The next account demonstrates how an apparently ordinary occurrence like staged photography contributes to both the sacralization of space and the importance of social engagement.

Ritually Performing Social Ties: Amelia's Story

Amelia is a White American fan who describes herself as "an anomaly when it comes to a lot of *Harry Potter* fans" because she first read and watched *Harry Potter* as an adult, despite having been roughly the target age when they first came out. Shortly thereafter, she visited Platform 9¾ (as well as other *Harry Potter* locations) with a study abroad trip in 2015. She identifies strongly with the qualities of Hufflepuff House, one of the four houses at the magical school Hogwarts, which she was sorted into by an official online quiz. Unlike Jean and Louise, Amelia visited Platform 9¾ on an ordinary day and took part in typical activities like standing in line, being photographed pushing the luggage trolley, and visiting the gift shop.

The photo op is both efficiently commercialized and ritualized. Visitors are offered their choice of scarves in Hogwarts house colors to wear. In the usual pose, the visitor pretends to run at the wall while one staff member stands just out of the camera's view to toss the end of the scarf in the air while pictures are taken, simulating speed. The whole process takes about a minute, a small fraction of the time spent waiting in line.

Amelia chose the Hufflepuff scarf. Though posed photography can be a ritual act in itself (MacCannell 1976), what Amelia perceived herself to be doing by wearing that scarf clearly demonstrates the strategic aspects of ritualization:

> People look down upon Hufflepuffs, we're not looked at as the cool ones … whereas I think it's great to be Hufflepuff. I like the traits that are associated with us, and so … I felt as though I had this connection, when I was able to put on the scarf and pretend as though I was … running into the wall to get through to Platform 9¾.
> … I felt this connection because, you know, you're at the station, and people are going about their business, about to board a train and there you are, about to embark on this journey of your own, and nobody bats an eye, which I thought was just so very cool and very unique.
> (Interview, December 4, 2018, edited for concision)

Amelia, as someone performing a ritual script (putting on the scarf, posing for the picture), is using that script strategically to do something that is both individualistic and deeply tied to her perception of Hufflepuff House as a magical "we" that transfers into the ordinary world. Taking part in this activity is an assertion of belonging to an imaginative group, some of whom are physically present and others of whom have been or will be, all under the public, non-magical eye. Amelia also commented that she preferred the in-situ 9¾ photo op in King's Cross to the "quote-unquote Platform 9¾" at the Warner Bros. Studio Tour, a much larger-scale reconstruction of the whole platform and train with several trolleys along the wall where visitors can take pictures. This seems to be a product of both proximity to the fictional point of embarkation into magic and being seen by hundreds of people, fellow fan pilgrims and ordinary travelers alike. We can see this even more clearly in the next story.

Performance, Belonging, and Narrative – Luna's Story

The Wizarding World of Harry Potter (WWHP) in Orlando, Florida spans two of the Universal theme parks, with Hogsmeade Village and Diagon Alley sections connected by a train (encouraging visitors to purchase a more expensive multi-park ticket). Both areas display enormous attention to detail in spaces, food, merchandise, and magical entertainment. They are designed to immerse the visitor in the magical story-world as if they are a part of it (Waysdorf and Reijnders 2016), as opposed to other Universal and Disney park areas where costumed characters maintain a focus on a distanced fictional plot. Being a part of the story-world is essential to this account.

Luna is an Asian-American fan who has a long history of involvement in *Potter*-related communities. Though she is not an academic, she has been recognized in both academic and fan circles for her studies of the *Harry Potter* texts.[3] She has two children, including a daughter who is also a dedicated *Harry Potter* fan. To mark her daughter's 11th birthday (the day magical children are admitted to wizarding school), the two of them traveled to the WWHP. One of the highlights of their visit was what Luna refers to as the "wand ceremony," a recreation of a child's visit to the famous Ollivander's wand shop to obtain their first wand.

The ceremony is a short interactive drama, where small groups enter a dim and mysterious wand shop and watch as one person—usually a child—selected by the attending "wand maker" actor, tries different wands, causing chaotic effects, until matching with the right one. (They can then purchase that specially-equipped wand as a souvenir—and use it to interact "magically" with certain locations in the park.) Luna spoke enthusiastically of much of the WWHP, but most notably about this experience:

> Getting my daughter chosen for the wand ceremony [was a highlight]. I had prepared her by telling her to dress up in costume, wear 11th birthday gear, stand in front, and "look excited" (unnecessary to tell her that). She did get chosen, the ceremony was extremely well done.... When my kid had her ceremony, she could barely breathe for excitement and I cried watching.
>
> (Survey response)

Later, in the interview, she elaborated, emphasizing how the public ritual of the wand ceremony focuses everyone's attention on the value of the unique individual:

> it's an immersive experience with an actor who remains in character the whole time as a wandmaker and lets you feel the magic of being *seen* and knowing that each individual person, and the magic within each person, is as important and worth just as much attention as anyone else. It doesn't matter if you are wealthy or a minority or an insignificant person who is used to being undervalued. There is one wand that is right for you, the same as anyone else. And the theater around this attraction is designed to let you feel that, whether you're the one chosen or you are watching someone else go through it. [...] The experience of being seen and having something core to one's self be brought to light is always emotional, and this attraction ceremonializes it and enacts it in front of witnesses. That is genius, and very beautiful. The shared witnessing elevates it.
>
> (Interview, January 7, 2019)

This is a story in which the strategic dynamics of ritualization are particularly clear. What is Luna *doing* with the ritual as she experienced and narrated it? She reflects that it asserts her daughter's equal and unique worth in the real world, paralleling the wand's significance in the magical world (you have to have a wand that recognizes and works for you to grow up magical, and to be without a wand is to be marginalized). Scholars of religion, particularly those who study Christian theology, may call attention to Luna's use of "witnessing" and being seen, which recalls Martin Buber's (1970) concept of "I and Thou," describing interaction with someone else who is not alienated, or even entirely separable, from one's own self. We should not overemphasize this; Luna does not identify herself as religious. However, we should not neglect the strategic importance Luna grants to being witnessed, and bearing witness, while participating in a ritual that, like Platform 9¾, reflects an entry point into the magical world. Jean, Louise, and Amelia used ritualized actions at Platform 9¾ for different purposes—Jean and Louise to join in a moment of collective memorialization and Amelia to assert her place as a fan—and Luna's story of the wand ceremony goes still further: asserting worth as a human.

Analysis

This leads us to an important question: does the presence of ritual in a pilgrimage framework, even with these effects we recognize as religious, justify considering fan pilgrimage in the frame of doing religiously? After all, fandoms are not self-identifying religious groups, and most fans do not identify spiritually or religiously with their fan affiliations (indeed, these four do not). Fan pilgrimages are also subjected to one common (though misguided) critique of "secular" pilgrimage, tourism, and other fannish practices: their close association with mass media and commercialization supposedly invalidates the possibility that they might be religious. This critique rests on a misconception that religiosity is separate from "profane" life, one that is not borne out by pilgrimages across the globe. Organized tours, souvenirs, and other forms of commercialism are common in many pilgrimages that are clearly religious. We *regularly* consider commercialized experiences to be valid manifestations of religious doing.

Rather, in this case as in many intersections of popular culture and religion, doing religiously is powerfully entangled with commercial participation. Chidester (2005: 18), exploring the meaningful ways people use materials acknowledged to be fake and specifically commercial, identifies doing religiously as religious work, "engaged in negotiating what it means to be human." In the case studies above, we see fans' pilgrimage rituals deployed in the way Chidester describes. In Jean and Louise's case, the work emerges spatially; in Amelia's, through how she perceives herself as belonging to an imaginative community; and in Luna's, in relation to a fictional narrative. Luna's example is also interesting because it is the most literally scripted; in her story, the *effects* of fictional drama and real-world performance intersect closely. All this work is genuinely meaningful and religious, among the "fake" stuff of theme parks and photo ops.

In fact, this allows us to introduce an interesting complication to the idea that fan pilgrimage is religious doing "despite" its fakeness and commercialism. Understanding fan pilgrimage as a phenomenon of doing religiously that is based on, and communicates through, fiction raises the question of what it means to deploy fictional narrative in this way. The narratological concept of "fictionality" (Nielsen, Phelan, and Walsh 2015) describes a mode of communication in which both speakers/performers and listeners/observers know that something literally untrue is being said or depicted, but the falseness itself is used to communicate something true. This theory was formulated to help understand parody, but is applicable here. Recall Jean, Louise, Amelia, and Luna's stories; a consistent undercurrent is the importance of seeing, being seen, and enacting things about themselves in a fictional milieu. Their uses of rituals grounded in fictional characters, plots, identities, and abilities *gain* significance *because* they are fake. Ritualization in fan pilgrimage highlights both fakeness—including disjunctures between real and fictional worlds—and meaningfulness. This is a significant component of how its religious doing operates.

Luna's story is a particularly informative example: a fictional scene (based on a very specific event in *Harry Potter and the Sorcerer's Stone*) rendered as a commercialized ritual has real effects in asserting identity and human value that parallel the fictional ones, with no claim that *Harry Potter* (or magical abilities) are literally real.[4] On the contrary, participating in this brief reiteration of made-up things, in a specially designated place and before a comprehending audience, has extraordinary communicative, emotional, and even existential significance. That is, discourses and experiences that are fully understood to be false on one level are also understood to convey truth that eludes serious description. Similar dynamics operate in Jean, Louise, and Amelia's stories.

Conclusions

We have seen that ritual and ritualization in fan pilgrimage are a kind of religious doing, sharing with other forms of religious doing significant effects on participants' emotions, sense of belonging, and negotiating what it means to be human. Interlocutors' stories show that ritualized fan pilgrimage experiences are driven by, and contingent upon, intersections of space, narrative, and people. These stories emphasize that *ritualization*, the strategic deployment of ritual scripts in different situations, is a powerful, compelling overlay on spaces that may accommodate many purposes, from ordinary train stations to expensive theme parks. Furthermore, they demonstrate that fan pilgrimage is religious doing not *in spite of* its self-conscious fakery, but *because* its fictional foundations lend it power for participants.

It bears emphasizing that this does not make fan culture a religion, nor fan pilgrimage an experience that participants necessarily see as religious. Indeed, none of the interlocutors discussed in this chapter identified religiously with *Harry Potter* fandom or described their pilgrimages as religious. Jean described himself as Catholic Christian, Amelia described herself as Jewish, and Louise and Luna did not identify with any religion. The term "sacred" resonated with Louise as a descriptor for Platform 9¾; Luna did not find that she felt spiritual or like she was in a sacred place, but acknowledged others may; and Amelia and Jean did not attribute sacredness or spirituality to their experiences at all. Most other interlocutors in the larger project felt similarly, although some were quicker to embrace the idea of sacredness, and a few who were strongly connected to faith communities discussed a complex relationship between faith, fan pilgrimage, and identity. The point of this analysis is not to attribute a religious identity to any interlocutor or argue that any aspect of fan culture necessarily constitutes religion.

Rather, these stories ask us to question our assumptions about what is and is not doing religiously, for the sake of better understanding ritual and religiosity as they intersect with popular culture in a secularizing world. Indeed, what constitutes religiosity in such a world to begin with? Some (for example, Bickerdike 2016) have contended that pop-culture-based religious work is a replacement for religion: traditional faiths wane, but humans still crave meaningful stories, connections, and rituals. However, this is shortsighted; as Charles Taylor (2007) argues, secularization is not the disappearance of religion, but a reconfiguration of religiosity among a range of other cultural phenomena and choices. I concur with Taylor and Matt Hills (2013) that contrary to this "loss hypothesis" theory of replacing religion, the complexities of doing religiously in fan pilgrimage suggest a need for more application of ways we understand fan culture to how we study contemporary religiosity.

Summary

- Fan pilgrimages—journeys by fans to special fandom-related spaces—frequently include practices like ritual that we can classify as "doing religiously," though they take place in an ostensibly non-religious milieu and fan pilgrims usually do not identify fan practices as religious.
- Using methods like interviewing and close observation of fans' rituals, we can better understand how rituals acquire meaning and give significance to narratives for both individuals and groups.
- Ritualization—strategic performance of scripted ritual activities—in fan pilgrimage is a means by which participants make meaning from encounters with fictional worlds and each other, and negotiate their identities, belonging, and values.
- The "religious work" of fan pilgrimage is not produced *in spite of* its concern with fiction, fakery, and commercialism. Rather, the fictional context and sometimes-commodified practices *lend power* and lasting significance to rituals and experiences, as described here by fan pilgrims.

Discussion Questions/Activities

- This chapter has examined activities—certain rituals in *Harry Potter* fan pilgrimage—that are not usually considered religious, in order to understand ritual and religiosity in new ways. What are other activities we could examine this way?
- What other examples of travel involve rituals and/or ritualizations? Are these necessarily pilgrimages? Why or why not?
- It is common to assume that pilgrimage—unlike the examples here—involves some kind of belief in the superhuman: devotion to a deity, teacher, or saint, desire to experience a miracle like healing, and so on. Why do you think so many people assume pilgrimage has, or must have, these superhuman aspects?
- In this chapter we explored ideas like doing religiously, ritualization, and pilgrimage outside the boundaries of self-identifying religions. Look up a more "traditional" pilgrimage and learn about it. (Consider the Islamic *hajj* to Mecca, Jewish pilgrimage to the Western Wall, Christians visiting Santiago de Compostela, Buddhists traveling to Bodh Gaya, or Neo-Pagans at Glastonbury.) In what ways does your chosen pilgrimage seem to operate outside its religious tradition? How does it intersect with other people, practices, and interests?

Glossary

Doing religiously   Performing activities that produce sacredness, special-ness, belief, moral centering, sense of the superhuman, existential anchorage, or another effect of super-normal significance, or performing activities with the intent to produce such effects. Put another way: ways of being religious manifested in actions, as opposed to religious life defined primarily by beliefs or affiliation with an established religion.

Fan People "who display a degree of enthusiasm about a person, media text, genre, or activity" *(Fanlore)*. A person can be a fan without being part of a fandom (a loose community of fans).

Fan culture The practices of fans. Common features include consuming, discussing, or critiquing media; social media engagement; collecting merchandise; attending concerts, games, openings, or conventions; creating transformative works (e.g., fan fiction); exchanging memes; and more. A person can be a fan without actively participating in these practices.

Fan pilgrimage Pilgrimage to filming locations, character or celebrity memorials, fannish events, or themed attractions, among others.

Liminality Often defined as a state of being "betwixt and between," liminality is the experience of being outside of or in transition between typical categories or statuses, whether because none apply or several overlap. See Turner (1974).

Pilgrimage A genre of doing religiously that involves a journey to a significant place, negotiating geography, meaning, and social contexts. Often considered a type of tourism. A pilgrim need not necessarily identify as religious.

Ritualization Strategic ways of acting in a specific situation, responding to narratives, values, traditions, liturgies, and/or landmarks that produces a sense of specialness or sacredness in and about its context. "Ritual" refers to practices or the scripts (common, established actions for such purposes) through which ritualization occurs.

Notes

1 Matt Hills (2002) has written extensively on the reclamation of "cult" allegiances in fan culture. However, outside of fan studies, attributing cultishness to fandom generally conveys a perception that fans are irrational, overzealous, and out of touch with the real world.
2 Platform 9¾ has been the site of happier mass fan gatherings, such as Epilogue Day, September 1, 2017, when Harry and friends are said to deliver their children to the platform.
3 In the interest of protecting Luna's identity, her published works and others' works in which she has been recognized must remain unnamed.
4 English editions outside the United States: *Harry Potter and the Philosopher's Stone.*

Further Reading

Bell, Catherine (1992) *Ritual Theory, Ritual Practice.* Oxford: Oxford University Press.
Essential reading for understanding contemporary takes on ritual and performance. Bell deconstructs the category of "ritual," focusing on strategic, situational

"ritualization" and its power dynamics. Also see Bell's chapter "Performance" in *Critical Terms for Religious Studies*.

Chidester, David (2005) *Authentic Fakes*. Berkeley: University of California Press.
Chidester explores the use of popular culture commodities, symbols, and brands to do "religious work." He challenges common preconceptions that religiosity is serious, distinct from profane concerns like consumption, and concerned with truth. Rather, genuine religiosity can emerge through play, fakery, and commodities.

Doss, Erica (1999) *Elvis Culture: Fans, Faith, and Image*. Lawrence: University of Kansas Press.
Doss explores the material culture (art, music, kitsch, places, etc.) of Elvis Presley fans. The book includes an examination of pilgrimage to Graceland. This analysis has useful applications for study of other fan cultures' rituals, pilgrimage, and material culture.

Hills, Matt (2002) *Fan Cultures*. London: Routledge.
Hills's theorization of fans' attachments, activities, and psychology is essential reading in the study of fan culture. Hills's exploration of the relationships between "cult" and fan culture, and fan culture and geographies, inform this chapter.

Maddrell, Avril, Alan Terry, and Tim Gale, eds.(2016) *Sacred Mobilities: Journeys of Belief and Belonging*. Farnham: Ashgate Publishing.
This collection of recent essays on "sacred mobilities" (encompassing a greater variety of journeys than "pilgrimage") includes a wide range of historical and new pilgrimages in religious and secular contexts. The volume breaks down distinctions between religious and secular, focusing on sacredness across all the journeys described.

Potts, Liza, Melissa Beattie, Emily Dallaire, Katie Grimes, and Kelly Turner (2018) *Participatory Memory: Fandom Experiences Across Time and Space*. http://participatorymemory.org/book/index
This interactive digital book was produced through participant-observation fieldwork. It explores fans' activities at many sites, several related to *Harry Potter*. While it does not take a religious studies perspective, it examines ritual activities in detail with visual and audio illustrations. (Faculty may find it useful as a model of experiential learning.)

Bibliography

Alderman, Derek H. (2002) "Writing on the Graceland Wall: On the Importance of Authorship in Pilgrimage Landscapes." *Tourism Recreation Research* 27 (2): 27–33.

Beattie, Melissa (2014) "A Most Peculiar Memorial: Cultural Heritage and Fiction." In *Who Needs Experts? Counter-Mapping Cultural Heritage*, edited by John Schofield, 215–224. Farnham, Surrey, UK: Ashgate.

Bell, Catherine (1992) *Ritual Theory, Ritual Practice*. New York: Oxford University Press.

——— (1998) "Performance." In *Critical Terms for Religious Studies*, edited by Mark C. Taylor, 205–224. Chicago: University of Chicago Press.

Bickerdike, Jennifer Otter (2016) *The Secular Religion of Fandom*. London: SAGE Publications.

Brooker, Will (2005) "The Blade Runner Experience: Pilgrimage and Liminal Space." In *The Blade Runner Experience: The Legacy of a Science Fiction Classic*, edited by Will Brooker, 11–30. Columbia University Press.

——— (2007) "Everywhere and Nowhere Vancouver, Fan Pilgrimage and the Urban Imaginary." *International Journal of Cultural Studies* 10 (4): 423–444.

Buber, Martin (1970) *I and Thou*. Translated by Walter Kaufmann. New York: Simon & Schuster.

Chidester, David (2005) *Authentic Fakes: Religion and American Popular Culture*. Berkeley: University of California Press.

Doss, Erika (1999) *Elvis Culture: Fans, Faith, and Image*. Lawrence, KS: University Press of Kansas.

Eade, John, and Michael J. Sallnow (1991) "Introduction." In *Contesting the Sacred: The Anthropology of Christian Pilgrimage*, edited by John Eade and Michael J. Sallnow, 1–29. London and New York: Routledge.

"Fan." n.d. Fanlore. Accessed November 15, 2019. https://fanlore.org/wiki/Fan

Garner, Ross P. (2016) "Symbolic and Cued Immersion: Paratextual Framing Strategies on the Doctor Who Experience Walking Tour." *Popular Communication* 14 (2): 86–98.

Hills, Matt (2002) *Fan Cultures*. Sussex Studies in Culture and Communication. New York: Routledge.

——— (2013) "Sacralising Fandom? From the 'Loss Hypothesis' to Fans' Media Rituals." *Kinephanos* 4 (1): 7–16.

——— (2017) "The Enchantment of Visiting Imaginary Worlds and 'Being There': Brand Fandom and the Tertiary World of Media Tourism." In *Revisiting Imaginary Worlds: A Subcreation Studies Anthology*, edited by Mark J.P. Wolf, 246–265. New York and London: Routledge.

Larsen, Katherine (2015) "(Re)Claiming Harry Potter Fan Pilgrimage Sites." In *Playing Harry Potter: Essays and Interviews on Fandom and Performance*, edited by Lisa S. Brenner, 38–54. Jefferson, NC: McFarland and Company.

Lee, Christina (2014) "'Welcome to London': Spectral Spaces in Sherlock Holmes's Metropolis." *Cultural Studies Review* 20 (2): 172–195.

MacCannell, Dean (1976) *The Tourist: A New Theory of the Leisure Class*. New York: Schocken Books.

Maddrell, Avril, Alan Terry, and Tim Gale, eds. (2016) *Sacred Mobilities: Journeys of Belief and Belonging*. London and New York: Routledge.

Margry, Peter Jan (2008) "Secular Pilgrimage: A Contradiction in Terms?" In *Shrines and Pilgrimage in the Modern World: New Itineraries Into the Sacred*, edited by Peter Jan Margry, 13–46. Amsterdam: Amsterdam University Press.

Nielsen, Henrik Skov, James Phelan, and Richard Walsh (2015) "Ten Theses about Fictionality." *Narrative* 23 (1): 61–73.

Öhman, Tiia, and Satu Walden (n.d.) "Fangirl Quest: Film Tourism & Other Fantastic Adventures." Accessed May 7, 2018. http://fangirlquest.com

Potts, Liza, Melissa Beattie, Emily Dallaire, Katie Grimes, and Kelly Turner (2018) *Participatory Memory: Fandom Experiences Across Time and Space*. http://participatorymemory.org/book/index

Reijnders, Stijn (2011) *Places of the Imagination: Media, Tourism, Culture*. Franham, Surrey, UK: Ashgate.

Smith, Jonathan Z. (1982) "The Bare Facts of Ritual." In *Imagining Religion: From Babylon to Jonestown*, 53–65. Chicago: University of Chicago Press.

——— (1987) *To Take Place: Toward Theory in Ritual*. Chicago: University of Chicago Press.

Taves, Ann (2009) *Religious Experience Reconsidered: A Building Block Approach to the Study of Religion and Other Special Things*. Princeton: Princeton University Press.

Taylor, Charles (2007) *A Secular Age*. Cambridge: Harvard University Press.

Toy, J. Caroline (2017) "Constructing the Fannish Place: Ritual and Sacred Space in a *Sherlock* Fan Pilgrimage." *Journal of Fandom Studies* 5 (3): 251–266.

Turner, Victor (1974) *Dramas, Fields, and Metaphors: Symbolic Action in Human Society*. Ithaca: Cornell University Press.

Waysdorf, Abby, and Stijn Reijnders (2016) "Immersion, Authenticity and the Theme Park as Social Space: Experiencing the Wizarding World of Harry Potter." *International Journal of Cultural Studies* 21 (2): 173–188.

8 Sacred Writings

The Biblical Canon and the Marvel Cinematic Universe

Elizabeth Rae Coody

Introduction

My mother loves to recall the time she tried to convince me as a small child to give away some well-loved books. I was usually generous, but this time I refused because "Books are our friends." I could not give away friends! Gathering many more friends led me to the study of the Bible, which I found cropping up all over literature, particularly in the West. What books the Bible actually contains, though, is a more complicated question than I might have expected from lessons in Christian Sunday School. The word "Bible" in English traces back to the plural Greek *biblia*, which is the plural of "book." Although what we normally call "the Bible" is the Christian Bible (and this text includes books holy to Judaism as well) it was already the word for a collection of books before it was used this way. These crowds of friends are organized through a complex social network that involves who makes the cut, what power comes from being "in" or "out" of a canon, and what even fringe acquaintances might tell us about religious power.

Canon studies is a part of biblical studies that discusses broadly what is "in" or "out" of the Bible or a Bible. Taken most simply, a **canon** is a defined list, a collection of texts with some kind of borders. The canon I'm examining in this chapter is the Christian canon. What is on this or any other canon list or inside those borders or how porous these borders are reflects authority and power; what falls outside of the canon can be anything from simply less authoritative works of piety to heretical dangers. Canonization is the process by which followers of Jesus chose which books to include— either implicitly (through repetitive use) or explicitly (by prescriptive decision-making). The borderland is the negotiation between the extremes of what is "in" or "out." The definition of this border for Christianity is one over which people have been willing to die. These stories matter to how people live and die, but nonreligious stories matter too. Similar decisions about what counts as "in" or not are used in popular culture as well, and the current conversation often takes on similar dangerous language. The "Fandom Menace" is a play on the film *Star Wars, Episode I: The Phantom Menace* (1999), and a way to refer to a particular group of **extremely online** comics and film fans that coalesced around a hatred of and personal attacks

DOI: 10.4324/9781003079729-9

around the Rian Johnson directed *Star Wars, Episode VIII: The Last Jedi* (2017). This group of internet trolls is characterized by a disdain mainly for Disney properties, which includes both Star Wars and Marvel works that would include people of color and women in major roles, as creators, or in industry leadership (MacFarland 2022). This demarcation of "in" as particularly white supremacist is not a new phenomenon, of course; the worrying "Great Replacement Theory" that is popularized here (the false and violence-charged claim that white people are being socially replaced by minorities) has roots from before the United States Civil War.[1] But, the relatively new centrality of geek culture around video games, comics, and superhero stories in abusing and harassing vulnerable and minoritized populations is worth trying to understand.[2]

In popular culture, what counts as "in" particular storylines changes over time and through cultures. What is "in" or "out" of the cultural canon has been the focus of decolonization or post-colonial studies, which considers specific changes in cultures that result from colonial movements. Comparing popular culture to literature that has shaped the historical character of people over time and religious literatures sometimes causes distress in certain religious people. These are often the same people who are troubled by the notion that religion has been shaped by culture, a notion that Jeffrey Mahan discusses in the important collection *Religion and Popular Culture in America* (2017). He clarifies that this notion requires a particular definition of religion, one that specifies that religion "has a substance or essence that is not reducible to other forms of culture." But, he points out that whatever they point to, it is the human practices of religion and the reinterpretation of stories in particular that changes to "respond to our current situation" (Mahan 2017: 121). This distress over the idea that religious practices are cultural activities is also tied closely to superheroes in the United States. That is, if religion is just one of the things that people do as part of their culture, the idea goes that they might confuse or replace religion with culture. For example, in the February 1943 issue of *Catholic World*, Rev. Thomas E. Doyle wrote an article titled "What's Wrong with Comics?" that laments: "Like it or not, there are plenty of American children who know more about the man-wonder Superman than they do about Christ or any of the great characters of the Bible" (Hajdu 2008: 82). This anxiety morphed into a social movement in the United States that led to widespread burning of comics and even a Supreme Court trial that alleged they were corrupting the youth of America (Hajdu 2008). Religious leaders argued that young people might confuse their moral instructions in churches with the bad moral influences from comics.

Whether it causes distress or not, superhero stories have a power over people's lives that is quite "religious" in many ways. However, even when treated seriously, I submit here that there is still more easy access to these conversations than to conversations about what counts as biblical canon. My argument in this chapter is twofold: that the study of the active and lively movement of canons of popular cultural products can teach readers something about the behaviors of canon in the biblical text in ways that might make these movements more accessible, and that the long history of study of the canon is bound up with popular culture. This is one way that popular culture has pedagogical value (that is, teaches people) in a way that is often more difficult to do with the more distant biblical texts. When students have ready access to preexisting and intricate canons in popular culture, they can apply complex scholarly textual methods to them to interrogate the method and to gain insights into the popular culture they already know.

Theory and Method

The biblical canon is deceptively complicated; most students who sign up for academic courses that address the Bible seem to assume that "the Bible is the Bible." That is, most think that the book that they bring to class probably has the same things in it that their classmates do, regardless of differences in their translation, theology, or culture. This is often one of the first points a class on the Bible in an academic setting needs to address. A Bible that the average person purchases might not contain "just" the same ideas in different languages (already a complex notion to hold) but might not even contain the same books! Sometimes this is a disturbing idea for students, both religious and non-religious.

These ideas are not equally disturbing for users of the Bible, though: "Jews have tended to be far more relaxed than Christians about the diversity within the canon" since real and effective authority is from other written collections of Jewish oral traditions (that is the Oral Law or the Mishnah, a work of interpretation of the Bible) (Barton 2003; cf. Cohen 2012). Catholicism tends not to be as concerned with inconsistencies either, since magisterium or the way the Pope and Catholic Bishops interpret the Bible is a primary source of authority. As John Barton has it, "It is Protestant Christians for whom the shoe pinches most," since Scripture is the highest court and must be its own interpreter (22). While Judaism and Catholic Christianity both have built-in interpretation of the Bible that can help practitioners understand how to use the Bible in their lives, Protestant Christianity does not have these kinds of authorities. Instead, everyday Protestants and their leaders are equal in terms of their rights and responsibilities for interpreting the Bible. This is a freedom, but it also means that Protestants do not have a built-in layer of interpretation to help them with a complicated book.

If students have grown up in a religious setting that tends to view the Bible as an unshakable authority without a set interpreter as many Protestant Christians do, multiple versions of the Bible can be theologically disturbing. They might ask: "How can the Bible be infallible (or never wrong) if I have not considered that it has different versions?" For students who have not grown up in these same religious settings, this can still be disturbing for cultural reasons. They might ask, "How can my friends and colleagues be following a book that comes in so many different forms?" To both, it is worth exploring the borders that have created the canon.

Students want this answer to be simple, but of course, even the definitions of these terms are tremendously difficult to pin down. Even practiced scholars who specialize in this field will often use the terms canon and scripture inconsistently. Lee Martin McDonald is a long-time scholar of canon, but he admits that it took another scholar named Eugene Ulrich to bring the problem of terminology "to his attention" and that he hopes to correct it going forward (McDonald 2007: 18 fn 26). To Ulrich, a common definition must be concretely established before a conversation can begin, but it is by no means simple (Ulrich 2002). To help with this inconsistency, McDonald proposes that when we say "the Canon of Scripture" we mean either (1) rule of faith articulated by the scriptures or (2) list of books accepted as scripture (McDonald 2002).

Criteria for a Canon as a List of Books

Even if we grant that a list of books is what makes a canon for most Christians, we must recognize that this list of books is still not set in stone by any means. A quick glance at the differences between the lists of the books in a Catholic and Protestant Bible will demonstrate that point. Perhaps the most expedient way to understand how a canon is established is by understanding why different books are added and subtracted from the list. Again, these reasons are not set in stone, but having an informed guess at the kind of criteria the community used to establish the list of books accepted as scripture gives us a good place to start a conversation. To get us going, I will explain how the books that students find in their Bibles met the different church's criteria for membership in the Christian canon using the canon criteria presented by McDonald (2002: 413–439) as a guide. These criteria include antiquity, apostolicity, orthodoxy, use, and adaptability.

First, an item in the canon must have the quality of "antiquity" or to be old enough to make it to a list. Even a basic timeframe for this criterion is difficult to agree on, but these historical debates are outside the scope of this chapter. Arguably, the oldest texts in the Hebrew Bible are poems, perhaps from Deborah in Judges 5 from around the tenth or eleventh century BCE (Riches 2021, 9). But, it's the compilation and "canonization" or organizing into an authoritative list that is the crux of the argument. That is, it does matter when something was written, but it matters more to the study of canon how it is received. Suffice it to say here that the Hebrew Bible developed in concert with early rabbinic Judaism around the first century CE, and probably took on the final form in Hebrew later than most students estimate for this book with an ancient reputation. Once students reason that the writings about Jesus's life could not exist before his birth, they have an early date for the gospels. Although some early Church figures such as Irenaeus (writing ca. 170–180) claimed that the four gospels were all that was necessary, we know that by the end of the first century, collections of

Paul's letters were already circulating (McDonald 2007: 289–290). What made something canon was not standardized or considered orthodox until at least 200 years later. As McDonald summarizes, "In the second century, many (but not all) churches used the Letters of Paul in their worship and teaching, and some of them were even acknowledged as Scriptures by the middle to late second century and were used in admonitions to Christians" (2007: 320). Essentially, the idea that things have to be "old" is difficult to establish as a firm number. Not a promising start to establishing what makes the list!

Second, an item must have "apostolicity" or be able to be traced to the authority given to it by an Apostle or disciple follower of Jesus. This idea gets murky when questions of actual authorship arise in the field of Biblical Studies. It is commonly accepted in Biblical Studies—as well as other academic disciplines—that ancient texts claiming to be written by a specific person (usually a famous one) aren't necessarily written by that person. In fact, the idea of having an established author for a text is a fairly recent idea. But even if all texts that claim to be written by traditional, famous authors are accepted, what should Christians understand about the apostolicity of figures like Moses, who is key to understanding the scriptures Jesus used, but was not himself alive during the time of Jesus and so could not be Jesus's disciple? If someone understands Moses to be an author of a text, does that text meet the criterion of apostolicity or not? Or does the question of criteria change in reference to the Old Testament?

The third idea—that a book must have "orthodoxy"—is easier to establish by family resemblance, but that doesn't mean it's easy to set. Orthodoxy here means authorized or generally accepted theology or ideas. The philosopher Ludwig Wittgenstein popularized the idea of understanding concepts by "family resemblance": that concepts that are connected do not share one essential feature, but are better understood as connected by overlapping similarities. That is, every book of the Bible does not share the same exact theological stance on every topic; some do not necessarily address common ideas at all. But, an interpreter can find a set of ideas in common if they look for them. For example, even though the book of Esther does not contain any explicit references to God, the subject of the story includes devoted Jews praying and conducting other activities that are common to other books.

Fourth, the idea of "use" starts to take the authority out of the hands of priests or authoritative religious figures and begins to give power to anyone who uses the text. This one can get uncomfortable fast! While the idea of a democratized scripture list can be freeing and interesting, it means that minority and unpopular opinions might begin to take up weight in deciding what the canon list is.

Finally, "adaptability" recognizes that the items included in a canon are going to be changed to fit their times and contexts. This criterion admits that the items that fit best on the list are the ones that are best at applying to new situations. All this allows (or probably is what allows) a community to receive a list of texts as its canon.

These are great ways to understand the books that exist in the canon, but some fit better than others. Even if we say that there is no hierarchy—that books are simply "in" or "out" and of equal weight—these boundaries are not set firmly either across time or location. Bibles simply do not have all the same books in them, but most people continue to work in the world as if they do. So, what does having a canon allow a community to do with texts that they might not do otherwise? What do you do with an "accepted" list of books when you have them?

What a Canon Does

Theorist of religious studies Jonathan Z. Smith went a long way toward creating a comparative study of canon in his 1977 essay "Sacred Persistence: Toward a Redescription of Canon" (1982). In this chapter, I want to concentrate on a few of his ideas. First, that a canon is a type of list. More specifically, that list must be understood to be a closed and unchanging one if it's understood as a "canon" and not simply a "catalog." Then, once it is closed, the community around that list must overcome the textual limitations that they have imposed on themselves. Once the list is closed, people have only to work with the texts in the list, and therefore, they create new ways of interacting with those texts to be creative in ways that neither add nor detract from the canon list.

A key occurrence when a canon is created is what Smith calls the "*necessary* occurrence of the hermeneute" or a person to interpret the canon (1982: 48). That is, once the canon is established as a list of texts that are set, you have to have people "whose task it is continually to extend the domain of the closed canon over everything that exists *without* altering the canon in the process." If you want to make sure that your canon can truly work as a key to the universe, then you need interpreters to make sure that they both keep up with the movement of the world around the canon and can keep an eye on making sure that the canon stays where it is. In Christian tradition, this is often done by a preacher who knows their congregation well. Preaching or "homiletics" is the "attempt to make the 'text' speak to a quite particular situation," something that requires them to know both their people and their Bible quite well (51) What a canon requires of people is "ingenuity"—you must be clever and inventive if you hope to make all meanings from a closed list of books.

This idea of having a "closed" canon is deceptive as well. When we talk about a list being "closed" in this context, scholars are suggesting that this is a list that can neither have items added or removed. Theorist and author Umberto Eco explores the idea of what lists can do throughout his work and particularly in *The Infinity of Lists* (2009). As the title suggests, Eco argues that lists or catalogs suggest infinity by their forms, "a potential infinity" (15). Yet, when lists are finite, they must have bounds or limits. As I note above, these bounds for the biblical canon are difficult to establish.

But, once they are bound, Eco would claim that the items within take on a hierarchy. The "form" establishes an order (12).

Scholars like Ernst Käsemann have even argued that there should be a way to recognize a "canon within a canon" where there is an established selection and focus on this core of texts in order to ease concerns about diversity within the text (1964). Certainly, anyone in a tradition that uses the biblical text for devotional purposes will be able to recognize that certain parts of the Bible are more important than others, whether they would like this to be the case or not. Christians, even solely cultural Christians who otherwise do not have a regular devotion or study of the Bible, can repeat the main ideas of John 3:16 or say who Noah is; however, they will probably struggle explaining the main ideas of Jude, even though it is a very brief book. Why should this be? These concepts are difficult to explain fully and are often fraught with emotional charge. One way to do this explaining or to explore the concepts that are at work in the Bible is to connect it to different forms of popular culture.

An Older Popular Culture Connection

Since academic studies of popular culture are relatively new in scholarship compared to other parts of the field, scholars sometimes enjoy being the first person to put two ideas together. But my chapter isn't the first example of the study of the biblical canon and popular culture. Happily, it has a history! Ronald A. Knox wrote an article for the June 1920 issue of the journal *Blackfrairs* called "Studies in the Literature of Sherlock Holmes." In this article, he walks through several claims about Sherlock Holmes in order to establish "true" or "genuine" Holmes from what he says might be fakes created by the character Dr. Watson "for his own purposes" (156). Knox treats the whole thing seriously and uses the same methods he would otherwise use in Biblical studies. There were several others who used the methods of "Higher Criticism" (as the primary methods of Biblical studies were known then) on Holmes stories. Critic and author Dorothy Sayers with her usual tongue-in-cheek flair says of the "game" that it has:

> the aim of showing that, by those methods, one could disintegrate a modern classic as speciously as a certain school of critics have endeavoured to disintegrate the Bible. Since then, the thing has become a hobby among a select set of jesters here and in America. The rule of the game is that it must be played as solemnly as a county cricket match at Lord's: the slightest touch of extravagance or burlesque ruins the atmosphere.
>
> (1946: 7)

Knox defends his right to study Holmes in this way since "anything is worthy of study, if that study be thorough and systematic" and that Sherlock Holmes's detective methods (carefully selected) are useful. While I think

Sayers is exaggerating when she makes the claim that criticism is "disintegrating" the Bible, she goes on to say that it is not Knox's game that bothers her, but rather "how easy it is for an unscrupulous pseudo-scholarship to extract fantastic and misleading conclusions from a literary text by a series of omissions, emendations and distortions of context." She's concerned by authors who are not playing.

Play is a great strength of what people can do with popular culture. Characters and ideas are built to be enjoyed, engaged, and even tampered with in a way that biblical characters and ideas are usually not. Dan Clanton argues that this sort of "imaginative malleability" is what makes a medium like comic books in particular appropriate to compare with biblical interpretation. In a comparison of his own, Clanton suggests that:

> if we compare the character of Moses in the pseudepigraphical *Testament of Moses*, we will find a different character, different stories and different emphases that reflect the different communities that produced, edited and transmitted these texts. Similarly, if we compare Bob Kane's original 1939 Batman with other, later Batmen—such as those drawn and written by Neal Adams, Frank Miller, Jeph Loeb and Paul Dini, to name a few—we will see some stark differences not only in characterization but also in tone, themes, and morals.
>
> (2012: xvi–xvii)

Notice that the point of connection starts with two characters: a hero and a superhero. He goes on to explain how this comparison between Moses and Batman can be theorized for biblical interpretation:

> Put differently, not only the interpretive potentialities inherent in the format of comic books, but also the creative communal continuities— by which I mean the web-like systems of meaning(s) that are constructed between (a) a character's history, (b) the story arc of a specific narrative, and (c) the knowledge and reactions of the communities of "fanboys"—parallel the process by and through which the biblical text interprets itself and has been interpreted in various communities, discourses, genres, and time periods.
>
> (2012: xvi–xvii)

It is with creative continuity, narrative flexibility, and attention to irony that comics lend their most valuable talents to biblical interpreters. Comic books are a wonderful medium to work with for people interested in books and religious ideas (cf. Lewis and Kraemer 2010), but for this chapter, I want to look at how ideas and concepts from comics have been translated into film and beyond. While not all comics include superheroes, comics are the modern birthplace of the superhero genre. As Chris Gavaler argues, although "heroes" are centuries old, the "tradition of direct influence" of the superhero genre after 1938 "evolved from Siegel and Shuster's first thirteen-page Superman episode in *Action Comics* #1" (2018: 2). The characters and stories from Marvel Comics moved into movies at the end of the 2000s and have held a strong share of the market there since. What is in or out of the Marvel canon, though, has a complexity that we can play with that rivals even the biblical text.

Case Study

The Marvel Cinematic Universe (or MCU) is a **shared universe** that was begun in earnest after the success of the film *Iron Man* (2008). Having thousands of different creators work together to create a major film series in one universe is an undertaking that requires an "imaginative malleability" that both holds authority and allows a releasing of control on the corporate, narrative, thematic, and even existential levels. Understanding this balance in the MCU gives some insight into the way canon works here in terms of a different sort of authority, but surprisingly similar discussions of orthodoxy and adaptability.

While there were older films with a similar serial format and characters established in other media (the James Bond films for example) the MCU film series has been by far the most profitable and widest-reaching such effort in history. The current international box office for the growing 39 films in the series has climbed to nearly $27 billion since 2008, and these numbers will certainly grow even before this book comes to print. That is more than double the number from its closest U.S. counterpart the *Star Wars* film series, which has earned around $10 billion since 1977 with 15 films (Nash Information Services). Both series are currently owned by the Disney Corporation, but I hesitate to say that they have them fully under control either in the films or in the public mind. Even viewed from a strictly legal point of view, these characters are not all equally held by the same corporation. The borders of the MCU canon have been in chaos for years starting on the corporate level.

Marvel Comics was a name created in 1961 for a comic book company, formerly Timely (1939–1951) and then Atlas Comics (1951–1961). Marvel Studios was established as a film company in 2002 as part of the larger Marvel Entertainment corporation and makes the films of the MCU. This might make it sound like there is a simple source of authority for the MCU; however, this does not mean this corporation is the sole authority or owner of the elements of the canon. Before establishing its own studio, Marvel had sold rights to comic book characters to established film studios. For example, New Line Cinema owned Iron Man rights until 2006. All of Marvel has been owned by the Disney Corporation since 2009, soon after the run-away success of the first *Iron Man* film and the birth of the MCU. Marvel superhero characters the X-Men spent decades owned by the 20th Century Fox studio, which meant that Marvel could not use their long-establish "mutant" myths on screen until 20th Century Fox was acquired by Disney in 2020.[3] This means that "mutants" and X-men can now be part of the MCU, but even now it does not own the rights to all its characters. Rights to Spider-Man and several related characters were procured by the Sony film studio in 2002 and since then studios have had to make deals to use the characters (Barker 2020). All this rights-swapping and billion-dollar deals have a real effect on the average movie goer, even if they never pay attention! That is, the characters that get movies made about them or not, the legions of creators who get jobs (and do not get jobs) are wrapped up in a complex web of copyright, licensing, and even corporate relationships. Control of what goes on in these stories is therefore not just the purview of artists and writers, but under the supervision of teams of attorneys—or so we might understand. To create a film in the official canon of the MCU takes a particular set of closely guarded permissions and access to a set corporate authority.

This corporate authority is invested in the success of the stories it tells. From a story point of view in the MCU, there have been three "Phases" of a large overarching story completed in 2019. The first phase started with *Iron Man* in which billionaire playboy and genius scientist/weapons manufacturer Tony Stark was kidnapped in Afghanistan by a vague terrorist organization. With help from an Afghan doctor, he builds a mechanical war suit that he uses to escape. Home after his ordeal, he eventually decides to perfect the suit and become a superhero calling himself Iron Man. The project boasted a charming and rambunctious star in Robert Downey, Jr. and people loved it. This love created something like an "orthodoxy" or a generally accepted set of ideas that still basically guide what the MCU can do.

The MCU orthodoxy has a particular tone and a basic character of its shared reality. While there is of course political and technological fantasy involved in the film, it was grounded in a familiar American action movie reality. It treated the danger characters were in somewhat seriously, but it was not "gritty" or "dark" in its portrayal of this reality. This put it in contrast with the DC Batman films in Christopher Nolan's critically acclaimed *Dark Knight* trilogy at the time (2005–2012). There was a market for this sort of older children-to-adult but lighter superhero that was more successful than could have been reasonably hoped: the film grossed $585 million (the eighth highest of 2008), earned critical praise, and was nominated for two Academy Awards. The risky move of making a superhero film had paid off. But, this success was not guaranteed. When just one month later the studio put out *The Incredible Hulk* (2008) as a story taking place in Tony Stark's universe, success was modest. The film grossed less than half what *Iron Man* did and still ranks as the lowest grossing of any MCU film. There are a lot of excellent ways to think about how and why this happened, but suffice it to say here that people generally agreed that this movie wasn't as good as *Iron Man*! However, a cameo from Robert Downey, Jr. at the end of the film establishes beyond a doubt that these two films are taking place in a shared universe. The MCU was officially running.

This orthodoxy does change, but the changes happen "conservatively"— meaning that the changes are slow and carefully adhere to the established traditions. Millions and soon billions of dollars were on the line with each new decision; it was important to keep the products grounded in what worked. The studio followed up Stark's adventure with *Iron Man 2* (2010), then *Thor* (2011) took the series in another direction. Here, Marvel begins to establish on film their very own "gods"—here from Norse mythology. They also chose Shakespeare veteran Kenneth Branagh to direct, signaling how seriously they wanted these characters taken. Despite the fact that the film has gods and monsters fighting larger than life battles, they also establish how the MCU's magic and science work in this world. The film takes time to make sure audiences know that this world takes what might ordinarily be seen as magic in traditional fables as science. Here two scientists have a discussion about the wild events they are seeing, and their assistant Darcy Lewis chimes in:

DR. ERIK SELVIG: I'm talking about science, not magic.
DR. JANE FOSTER: Well, "magic's just science we don't understand yet." Arthur C. Clarke.
SELVIG: Who wrote science-fiction.
FOSTER: A precursor to science fact!
SELVIG: In some cases, yeah.
FOSTER: Well, if there's an Einstein-Rosen bridge, then there's something on the other side. And advanced beings could have crossed it!
SELVIG: Oh, Jane.
DARCY LEWIS: A primitive culture like the Vikings might have worshiped them as deities.
FOSTER: Yes! Yes, exactly. Thank you.

Things that look like magic to movie-goers might be going on (lightening-wielding gods, extraordinary hammers, spell-casting Loki, etc.), but the filmmakers want them to rest easy that it was advanced science fiction in this universe. These multi-million dollar stories have to be incredibly careful with ideas. Even so, they occasionally make "continuity errors" that interrupt the timeline or need a "ret-con" or "retroactive continuity" explanation to fix. These are common in comics, where several different creators often work on the same character or team, and it took prodigious memories to keep ideas organized before the advent of digital archives. In the 1960s Marvel editors famously occasionally offer a "No-prize" (that is, no actual reward but the honor) for fans who offer explanations for silly errors.

However, film fans and the Marvel Studios corporate creators seem less tolerant of these sorts of mistakes; the creators perceive themselves as protecting the livelihoods of thousands of people. A disaster could be ruinous, so they must be protective of the traditions or conventions of their work as they establish them. This orthodoxy and tradition has expanded now into nearly 40 films, more than 10 Marvel Television series for broadcasting, streaming, and cable, and now a quickly expanding set of Marvel Studios series for their Disney+ Streaming service. Marvel Studios has taken some risks over the years since, hiring creative or non-action directors or taking chances on less well-known characters, but these risks are done conservatively.

However, as seen above, in order for a canon to work in the world, it needs to be able to speak to the world as it changes or be adaptable. Where can the MCU really break out of its shell? How can it be creative and stay relevant even as the studio clings closely to what it has done before? There are some moves happening "in" the canon. Kevin Feige has been the president of Marvel Studios and the primary producer of the MCU since 2007; thus, he is the representative of the corporate authority discussed above. He and his team continue to hire proven directors to helm these films, but often choose those with an unconventional or strong style to help differentiate them. James Gunn's new direction from Earth-based stories out into space for the MCU starting with the first *Guardians of the Galaxy* (2014) was a soft step in this direction. This ensemble of characters was less familiar to general audiences and included more "alien" creatures further afield from the usual humanoid stars—notably a talking raccoon-creature named Rocket and an anthropomorphic tree who only ever says the line "I am Groot." New Zealand director Taika Waiti put his own quirky humor and a brash often-neon color palette on his Thor entries of the series in *Thor: Ragnarok* (2017) and *Thor: Love and Thunder* (2022). Director Cholé Zhao of the MCU ensemble film *Eternals* (2021) was better known for critically-acclaimed and independent films like her 2020 Best Picture Academy award-winning *Nomadland*. Director Sami Raimi's MCU entry *Doctor Strange and the Multiverse of Madness* (2022) was notable for having more of the director's own signatures: a chase from a demonic Scarlet Witch that looked straight out of his *Evil Dead* (1981); a zombie make-up for Doctor Strange and the demonic "deadites" from *Army of Darkness* (1992); and even a small role for his friend and regular player, actor Bruce Campbell. Still, Feige is the concentrated source of authority for the MCU here. Should he or the production staff object to a director's vision, that film would not be produced.

However creative, these are all "in" the canon and must move slowly. While they are increasingly different, they all have a certain MCU flavor characterized by staying relatively safe and stable: a big CGI-driven fight in the third act, a teasing post-credit scene that ties the film into an upcoming film or film-spanning villain, or lightening up serious character ideas from comics. For example, Tony Stark does not have a problem with alcohol in the films, though his struggle with alcoholism played out several times in the comics (e.g. Michelinie et al. 1979). The films share common tropes even when applauded for a newer look or drawing from mythologies that have not yet been tapped in the MCU, such as *Shang-Chi and the Legend of the Ten Rings* (2021).

One possible solution to this lack of flexibility and a way toward adaptability in the story comes with the expansion of the shared universe into a shared multiverse; that is, the live action series have followed the comics precedent of claiming that there are multiple timelines or universes that exist simultaneously where characters can act or react in any imaginable way. This was discussed in the time-travel plot of *Avengers: Endgame* (2019) then played out on screen in the Disney+ series *Loki* (2021), and then explicitly in the film *Spider-Man: No Way Home* (2021). This allows creators maximum range in the context of a shared universe; that is, they can do whatever is allowed by the production team and just claim it to be in another universe than the usual one, traditionally numbered "616." Therefore, in another universe, *Doctor Strange and the Multiverse of Madness* (2022) can introduce a number of characters that filmgoers were excited to see and then have the Scarlet Witch slaughter them on screen. These characters will inevitably return as part of other universes. In this way, a film or television show can be allowed to share only tacit resemblances with the larger MCU and still share the same multiverse.

A multiverse seems to offer the maximum freedom or adaptability allowed by a shared universe under a single studio's authority. As they must remain true to a core conservatism and need years to produce, these films cannot speak quickly to the world as it changes or easily to niche communities. The solution is a resistance movement called loosely Marvel "**fanfiction**"—fiction written by fans of Marvel outside of Marvel canon. These are not under the authority of Marvel Studios; they are completely outside of editorial control.

In fanfiction, anyone can take characters or ideas from the MCU and do whatever they want with them. These stories are not written for monetary profit, but mostly to build communities of fans. Often, what people want to do is make a canonical relationship blossom into something more than friendship—explicitly sexual or not. The MCU has some romantic couples (Stark and his eventual wife Pepper Potts, for example), but these relationships and their development is often frustrated or subsumed in the building of the action-oriented stories. They are almost all explicitly heterosexual. Sex or any sort of erotic or even romantic interlude is relatively rare in the MCU, especially in the films. The studios are aware of the attractiveness of their characters, though. Famously, the camera often takes a moment to linger on their shirtless male stars, a number of whom are named "Chris" (Evans, Pratt, Hemsworth) in what is commonly called a "thirst" trope. That is, their audiences desire these men, and the studios strive to provide what their audiences want to consume.

When people watch films or take in popular culture that can be called "consumption"; they are simply taking in or consuming what they are given. In contrast, taking something produced for one reason and then using it in your own way—for yourself or as a "do-it-yourself" activity—is called "prosumption." Alvin Toffler, who coined the term for business and technology developments, saw this as the combination of producing and consuming (1980). The activity of taking something established in a canon and doing what you want with it is an act of prosumption. Prosuming the MCU often involves reimagining these stories centered on different characters–usually other than the largely white, wealthy, cisgendered, heterosexual male central characters. Often fans imagine off-screen LGBTQ+ relationships between established beloved characters that would cause controversy if on-screen.

These characters participate in different kinds of relationships and in different kinds of interlocked stories that may be part of a **fanon** or a canon that is completely made by fans outside of the usual canon. Sometimes these stories are personal and might involve **headcanon** or a logic of character or story that exists only in an individual's mind. In Marvel fandom, sharing a headcanon explanation for a continuity error might win a No-Prize. But fanon can also expand into its own canon; networked lists of stories and tropes can be incredibly complex and developed in a network like Archive of our Own (AO3). While Marvel Studios and Marvel comics own the rights and authority to their characters, there is not much control being exercised over prosumption. That is ultimately to Marvel's advantage. Allowing active fans to produce their own works using their characters gives them a way to "extend the domain of the closed canon over everything that exists *without* altering the canon in the process" (Smith 1982: 48). In this way, Marvel both maintains their authority and gives up their control in order to create the maximum adaptability while still protecting the orthodoxy of the characters on screen.

Conclusion

No one entity owns the rights to the Bible itself, even though Bible-publishing is a $425 million annual business in the United States. Some publishers own copyrights to their translations, but the text is freely available. There is no central authority of the Bible. Marvel Studios is the central authority for and corporate owner of the MCU. MCU characters are jealously controlled by a powerful and sometimes litigious corporation. Yet in both cases, the nature of canons that thrives on both orthodoxy and adaptability requires that there is a certain amount of give and take around what is and is not allowed. It is an advantage for Marvel to allow fanfiction and other acts of prosumption (like cosplay, as Wolff discusses in this volume). Doing this, even if the characters act or appear in non-canonical ways, allows the Marvel canon to truly adapt. So, what is the equivalent resistance to conservative canon or control for the Bible? How can we recognize the prosumption of the Bible? By studying the reactions and uses that fans put the MCU canon to, I say we can better see the same impulses in Bible.

When comparing the Bible and the MCU, it is important not to overplay the similarities. Both have a mind-boggling number of characters, settings, ideas, and possible nuances. Both require some knowledge of background to make sense of later works. Both have a multitude of possible ways of presenting and remixing the stories that are in their bounded canons. While Marvel thrives on invention and Bible interpreters try to hue close to their text, they both draw toward a rather conversative sense of what is correct or allowed to be done with their material. There is risk in drawing too far from a set of family resemblances that is in both cases difficult to draw a precise border around. However, if we are to learn from the way popular culture remixes the elements of sacred traditions, the pull toward prosumption and adaptability can show us the possibilities of a canon that is used more freely in the world. Watching what creators do with the Bible, even when it's far from orthodox, can help us understand the Bible and the world.

Summary

- The study of "canon" goes beyond the Bible into literature and other groups of stories in many forms, but the roots of the study are inextricably linked to biblical study.
- The biblical canon relies on borders that need criteria, but these boundaries are difficult to explain and maintain even though many religious people find them self-evident.
- The Marvel Cinematic Universe (MCU) is a shared universe in a series of motion pictures that has a valuable and successful canon.
- While MCU borders do have legal borders, these are constantly being negotiated and resisted, especially by fans in acts of prosumption.
- When fans prosume the MCU canon, they do not harm it—rather, this use of the canon allows the canon to adapt beyond what it would otherwise be able to do.
- Similarly, the prosumption of the Bible allows interpreters to adapt the Bible to their changing world in acts that are similarly beyond control for better or worse.

Discussion Questions and Activities

- How might "antiquity" apply to the MCU? These characters were established in the 1960s; is that the time scale? What about "use"? What elements are useful to the MCU and what have you seen stop coming up because it wasn't useful? What might count as apostolicity in the MCU? I thought about maybe those who followed creator Stan Lee, but perhaps you could measure this by degree of relationship to Iron Man or Nick Fury. What other possibilities are there?
- Relate the study of "canon" in this chapter to the use of canon in another popular culture property. How does *Star Wars* use the idea of canon differently in the fandom versus in the corporation? How do licensing and copyright policies change or try to change canon?
- It is important not to draw false equivalence between notions of "canon" in Christianity, Judaism, and other religious traditions. Many religious traditions have sacred writings, but they may not treat them the same. Even within traditions, writings are treated very differently. Discuss how writings in two different popular culture canons have

varying degrees or types of importance or influence on other forms. You might compare the writings of Sir Arthur Conan Doyle to fans of the BBC series *Sherlock* to the writings of Julia Quin to the fans of the Netflix series *Bridgerton*.

- How important is it that comics characters stay consistent from comic to comic? What about when drawn or written by different creators over time (e.g. the character of Black Panther has gone through several important changes over the years, including going from largely white creators to now many Black creators). What about when characters or comics ideas crossover into TV and film (e.g. the source of Ms. Marvel's powers changing from the 2014 comic series to the 2022 Disney+ streaming series)?

- Update the current earnings and box office for film franchises named here. Where does this money come from and where does it seem to be going? Who controls the types of stories that are told in the "official canon" of these franchises?

- Read up on the nonprofit "Organization for Transformative Works" (OTW) and their site the "Archive of Our Own" (archiveofourown. org). What is the purpose of this organization? What are some popular fandoms being "prosumed" on the site when you search it?

Glossary

Authorized Works   A border case for canon, where a new author takes up a series or character defined by a (usually) dead author. An example: *The Monogram Murders* (2014) by Sophie Hannah is a sequel to Agatha Christie's Hercule Poirot novels, and was authorized by Agatha Christie, Ltd.

Canon   Defined collection. While this is the only requirement for a "canon" of any kind the idea often takes on a sense of this definition that includes boundaries around what is acceptable, endorsed by certain authorities, or follows in a coherent set. In the Bible, the list of accepted books of scripture. In media franchises, a defined list of accepted stories.

Extremely Online   An event or person that is closely engaged with Internet-centric culture. While it can refer to phenomena that do not have much influence outside of digital spaces, these borders are porous and many ideas cross over quickly. The digital world is part of the real world.

Fanfiction   Fictional stories that use and manipulate characters, settings, ideas, and concepts from existing media, especially in combination other media or alternative universes (AU) or forms.

Fanon/Headcanon   The stories that do not exist in authorized, licensed media, but are held to be true or told by fans, either individually (usually though not always "headcanon") or collectively. These may come from subtext in existing media or be entirely formed by fans. Ideas of fanon may be as simple as a character's never-mentioned favorite food or make up vast relationship networks formed outside of the canon.

Prosumption   The act of creating for one's own use; in this context, it is the activity of fans who use characters and ideas from already existing media to make their own costumes (cosplay), stories (fanfiction), games (especially fan-created roleplaying games or characters), rituals (for example, Jedi for *Star Wars* or Vulcan for *Star Trek* wedding rituals), or other unlicensed materials, originally a term from marketing combination of "production" and "consumption" related to DIY (do-it-yourself) cultural theory.

Shared Universe   A fictional world built by different creators contributing different works that take place in a common place but may stand alone. Comics historian Don Markenstien set out rules for "universe" used in this way (1970).

Scripture   A writing or set of writings that hold some authority in a religious tradition, usually establishing, relating or deriving from a set of norms or values.

Notes

1 The racist idea that white people are obligated to seize control from every other race undergirds much American history (cf. Gin Lum 2022). The Great Replacement Theory terminology itself comes from French nationalism in the early 1900s. In the contemporary United States, it is regularly touted by white supremacist, anti-immigration, and voter suppression groups and has been the understood or explicit motivation behind hate crimes through the last several decades.

2 One important point of inflection for a modern connection between hate speech and geek culture was in the primarily 2014–2015 "Gamergate" misogynistic harassment campaign where politically and socially "alt-right" trolls used online means to force women into hiding both online and in real life for their physical protection. It is commonly taken to be a model for this type of harassment since.

3 The studio tried to work around this by creating the "Inhuman" character in comics and on-screen. These characters were just different enough from mutants to avoid legal action, but with acquisition of 20th Century Fox they can now be "ret-coned" into being mutants. See the Disney+ series *Ms. Marvel* (2022), where the inhuman explanation of her powers from the comics has been changed to a mutant or X-men-related ability (Wilson and Alphona 2014).

Further Reading

Coogan, Peter (2006). *Superhero: The Secret Origin of a Genre*. Austin, Texas: Monkey Brain Books.
  Establishes useful scholarly foundations for the literary study of superheroes and includes a detailed history of the roots of the modern superhero. It is especially useful when combined with Gravaler 2018, which takes the ideas further.

Lewis, A. David, and Christine Hoff Kraemer eds. (2010). *Graven Images: Religion in Comic Books and Graphic Novels*. New York & London: Continuum.
  A collection of essays by scholars and comics creators that observes the crossover between religion and independent and mainstream comics. Essential for understanding how comics have a unique voice in religious conversations.

Hajdu, David (2008). *The Ten-Cent Plague: The Great Comic-Book Scare and How It Changed America*. New York: Farrar Straus and Giroux.
A well-researched and exciting book about the incredible success and then public outcry against the comics industry in the 20th century in the United States. Explores how this period has changed the character of American comics and the industry for generations.

McDonald, Lee Martin (2007). *The Biblical Canon: Its Origin, Transmission, and Authority*. Peabody, MA: Hendrickson.
A clear and expansive introduction to the Christian biblical canon that treats the origin, choices of books, and what constitutes the Bible with care. McDonald spend a long career on these topics, and his historical reconstruction of events that have led to the Bible is important to understand.

Smith, Jonathan Z. (1982). "Sacred Persistence: Toward a Redescription of Canon," *Imagining Religion: From Babylon to Jonestown*. Chicago: University of Chicago Press.
A relatively short by important essay that shows both the style of a classic scholar in the study of religion and how this type of scholarship can deftly treat the foundations of biblical studies. Smith deploys a dizzying number of references from all over the academic and intellectual world but centers himself as a historian of religion.

Knowles, Christopher, with illustrations by Joseph Michael Linsner (2007). *Our Gods Wear Spandex: The Secret History of Comic Book Heroes*. San Francisco: Weiser Books.
This book takes the position that superheroes have taken over in the modern world the roles that gods and demigods played to ancient people. An interesting consideration for anyone interested in understanding religion and popular culture.

Gamzou, Assaf and Ken, Koltun-Fromm ed. (2018). *Comics and Sacred Texts: Reimagining Religion and Graphic Narratives*. Jackson, Mississippi: University of Mississippi Press.
An important piece of comics and religious studies theory. This diverse collection of essays uses a variety of fields to explore how comics expand the meaning of the holy in different religious contexts.

Bibliography

Barker, Stephen (2020). "MCU, Sony, Fox: The History of the Marvel Character Movie Rights." *Screen Rant*, October, 22. https://screenrant.com/mcu-sony-fox-marvel-character-movie-rights

Barton, John (2003). "Unity and Diversity in the Biblical Canon." In *Die Einheit de Schrift und Vielvalt des Kanons/The Unity of Scripture and the Diversity of the Canon*, edited by John Barton and Michael Wolter, 11–26. Berlin/New York: Walter de Gruyter Press.

Clanton, Dan, ed. (2012). *The End Will Be Graphic: Apocalyptic in Comic Books and Graphic Novels*. Bible in the Modern World 43. Sheffield: Sheffield Phoenix Press.

Cohen, Norman J. (2012). *The Way into Torah*. Nashville: Jewish Lights Publishing.

Eco, Umberto (2009). *The Infinity of Lists*. Translated by Alastair McEwen. New York: Rizzoli.

Gavaler, Chris (2018). *Superhero Comics*. New York: Bloomsbury Academic.

Gin Lum, Kathryn (2022). *Heathen: Race and Religion in American History*. Cambridge, MA: Harvard University.

Hajdu, David (2008). *The Ten-Cent Plague: The Great Comic-Book Scare and How It Changed America*. New York: Farrar Straus and Giroux.

Käsemann, Ernst. (1964). "The Canon of the New Testament Church and the Unity of the Church." In *Essays on New Testament Themes*, Translated by W. J. Montague, 95–107. London: SCM.

Lewis, A. David, and Christine Hoff Kraemer (Eds.) (2010). *Graven Images: Religion in Comic Books and Graphic Novels*. New York & London: Continuum.

MacFarland, Melanie (2022). "Let's All Stop Ignoring the Fandom Menace. It's Real, and it's Winning." *Salon*, June 30. https://www.salon.com/2022/06/30/marvel-star-fandom-menace-gamergate/

Mahan, Jeffrey H. (2017). "Popular Culture in Religion." In *Religion and Popular Culture in America*, edited by Bruce David Forbes and Jeffrey H. Mahan, 121–125. Oakland, CA: University of California Press.

Markstein, Don (1970). "The Merchant of Venice Meets the Shiek of Arabi." *CAPA-alpha* #71, September. https://www.toonopedia.com/universe.htm

McDonald, Lee Martin (2007). *The Biblical Canon: Its Origin, Transmission, and Authority*. Peabody, MA: Hendrickson.

McDonald, Lee Martin (2002). "Identifying Scripture and Canon in the Early Church: The Criteria Question." In *The Canon Debate*, edited by Lee Martin McDonald, 413–439. Peabody, MA: Hendrickson.

Michelinie, David, Bob Layton, John Romita, Jr., and Carmine Infantino (1979). "Demon in a Bottle." *The Invincible Iron Man*. Issues #120–128. New York: Marvel.

Nash Information Services (2022). "Movie Franchises." *The Numbers*. https://www.the-numbers.com/movies/franchises

Riches, John. (2021). *The Bible: A Very Short Introduction*. Oxford: Oxford University Press.

Sayers, Dorothy (1946). Foreword to *Unpopular Opinions*. London: Victor Gollancz, Ltd. Camelot Press.

Smith, Jonathan Z. (1982). "Sacred Persistence: Toward a Redescription of Canon." In *Imagining Religion: From Babylon to Jonestown*. Chicago: University of Chicago Press.

Toffler, Alvin (1980). *The Third Wave*. New York: Morrow.

Ulrich, Eugene (2002). "The Notion and Definition of Canon." In *The Canon Debate: On the Origins and Formation of the Bible*, edited by Lee Martin McDonald and James A. Sanders, 21–35. Peabody, MA: Hendrickson.

Watts, James W. (2006). "The Three Dimensions of Scriptures." *Postscripts*, no. 2: 135–159.

Wilson, G. Willow and Adrian Alphona (2014). *Ms. Marvel, Volume 1: No Normal*. New York: Marvel.

Part II

Genres in Popular Culture

9   Cinema and Religion
The Horror Genre

Douglas E. Cowan

Introduction

It's not too much to say that one line, one single bit of movie dialogue, changed the direction of my intellectual life.

It's Hallowe'en, 2005, and a bout of flu has landed me on the couch. To that point in my career as a sociologist of religion, I was content researching and writing about NRMs (new religious movements), and religion on the Internet, and I imagined continuing that. Little did I know what that fateful afternoon had in store. Too lazy, really, to get the remote from the far side of the room, I settled in to watch a *Hellraiser* marathon run by a local television station. I recognized Doug Bradley's iconic character, Pinhead, from the box art at the video store, but I'd never watched the films. I was far more into science fiction than horror, more rocket ships than torture racks, more *Star Wars* than *Saw*. From Pinhead's cassock-like leather outfit, however, to his constant references to souls in torment, and an explicit, ongoing concern with the battle between good and evil, the *Hellraiser* **mythos** piqued my interest.

In the first installment, *Hellraiser* (1987), which is based on Clive Barker's novella *The Hellbound Heart* (1986), an intricate puzzle box opens a portal between our world and a dimension inhabited by creatures known as Cenobites—former humans now horribly mutilated, trapped in eternity by their own desires, and living in **ersatz** community defined only by their shared suffering. Many *Hellraiser* fans may not be aware of it, but 'cenobite' is an explicitly religious term and means a professed religious person—a monk or a nun—who lives as part of a community, rather than as a hermit. Indeed, an early draft of the *Hellraiser* screenplay included a scene showing their rude monastic cells. There is religion here, that is, the reality of an unseen order that impinges on our own, just not the kind that feels either familiar or comforting.

The marathon continued, exploring and expanding the *Hellraiser* mythology. *Hellbound: Hellraiser II* (1988) shows us a glimpse of what Hell itself *might* look like. Rather than hellfire, brimstone, and hordes of cackling demons, it is a bleak, gray labyrinth through which we wander alone, chased forever by the memories, fears, and desires that brought us there in the first place (see also Barker 2015). In *Hellraiser III: Hell on Earth* (1992),

DOI: 10.4324/9781003079729-11

Pinhead explicitly challenges the dominant religion in North America, performing a blasphemous mockery of the Eucharist from behind the altar of a Catholic church. When an outraged priest protests his sacrilege, shouting, "You'll burn in hell for this, demon!" the Cenobite responds amiably, "Burn? Oh, such a limited imagination." Theologically implicit lines such as these are common throughout the first several entries into the franchise. In *Hellraiser*, when the terrified Kirsty wants to know what the Cenobites are, Pinhead tells her, "We are explorers in the further regions of experience. Angels to some, demons to others." To another character in *Hellraiser III*, he explains, "There is no good, Monroe, there is no evil. There is only flesh." And to Joey, the female lead in that film, he pledges, "Down the dark decades of your pain, this will seem like a memory of heaven." Heaven and hell, angels and demons, souls cast in the balance between good and evil, the hope of eternal salvation weighed against the prospect of endless suffering—these are all explicitly religious concepts that, although they have become a generalized part of our cultural lexicon, make no real sense apart from the theological traditions in which they come embedded.

One brief bit of dialogue in *Hellraiser: Bloodline* (1996), the fourth entry in the series and by far the most ambitious, provoked a singular tilt in my scholarly life. Although legions of *Hellraiser* fans abhor this installment, I admit that it remains my favorite because of the possibilities it opens for exploring the religious imagination. Filling in the puzzle box's origin story, the **liminal** Cenobite realm, and the future of the doorway between our world and theirs, the narrative moves uneasily between eighteenth-century France, the late modern period, and some indeterminate time in a science fiction future. Rocket ships meet torture racks in a sci-fi/horror **hybrid**. In the twentieth-century timeline, Pinhead tries to coerce a New York architect into building a permanent portal between the dimensions, one through which Cenobite legions could pass in force and at will. When the architect meets his 'employer' for the first time, however, the young man exclaims in terror, "Oh, my God," to which, in his inimitable fashion, Pinhead responds: *"Do I look like someone who cares what God thinks?"*

And I thought, 'No, you don't. Not really.' *Why* don't you care what God thinks? What has happened to the God in which so many hundreds of millions have placed their trust? Has he been banished by science, as an earlier sequence in the *Hellraiser: Bloodline* suggests? Does the presence of the Cenobites—angels to some, demons to others—render him irrelevant? Or, while those hundreds of millions still profess belief, does Pinhead in some way reflect a paradox of the late modern world: we may still believe in God, but we don't seem to care what he thinks. And what does *that* tell us about the often-ambivalent relationship we have with our gods and our devils, our angels and our demons?

In that moment I wasn't sure what Pinhead meant, nor what I thought his statement could mean in terms of religious belief, religious studies, or even the relationship between religion and fear—but I've spent the last 15 years trying to figure it out (Cowan 2008, 2010, 2018, 2019, 2022).

Theory and Method

More than anything, as I have written elsewhere, I've come to realize that, rather than "competitors in the arena of the human imagination," religion and horror "are cultural siblings, modes of storytelling and worldbuilding that share an intimate and paradoxical concern for the same questions that lie at the fluctuating, often terrifying core of what it means to be human" (Cowan 2022: 6). Indeed, as Bram Stoker Award winner Dennis Etchison writes, "horror stories are popular existentialism," which is to say, horror, especially supernatural horror, shows us aspects of the religious imagination at work in popular culture and, not infrequently, in real time (in Winter 1985: 62).

Put broadly, we advance knowledge in distinct but interrelated ways: we fill gaps and we correct mistakes. Both are on display when we consider the problem of religion and cinema horror. For some, horror films do not seem to have much to do with religion, or at least with religion as we commonly recognize it. One seems out of place with the other. Reviewing Rupert Wainwright's 1999 film *Stigmata*, for example, Ron Burke writes, "You do not expect to find religion and spirituality in a horror film" (1999). While he seems to have missed completely such milestone movies as *Rosemary's Baby* (1968), *The Exorcist* (1973), and *The Omen* (1976), critics such as Burke are often limited by a definition of religion so narrow that they may not even recognize religion's onscreen variations when confronted by them. Indeed, more than any others, the three films above brought Satan into mainstream cinema (see Cowan 2008: 167–199), and *The Exorcist* has been named by the National Film Preservation Board of the U.S. Library of Congress to the National Film Registry. Put differently, "cinema horror is replete with religion and always has been."

Other scholars, however, reject the possibility that cinema horror has anything useful to say about religion, faith, spirituality, and humankind's ambivalent relationship with its gods. This more vexing problem speaks directly to our common inability to imagine or appreciate metaphysical realities other than those to which we are committed. Writing in the *Journal of Religion and Film*, for example, Bryan Stone opines that since "it offends, disgusts, frightens, and features the profane, often in gruesome and ghastly proportions … other than pornography, horror is the film genre least amenable to religious sensibilities" (2001). Like many who dismiss any meaningful connection between religion and horror, he concludes that

> the mere fact that horror films rely heavily on symbols and stories as mere conventions to scare the hell out of us does not make a case for religious vitality in our culture; in fact, their persistence eviscerated of any deeper connection to our lived question may be a good example of the decline of the religious in our culture.
>
> (Stone 2001)

In this case, rather than a gap to be filled, Stone's is a mistake that needs to be corrected. For one thing, he assumes that religion—which often implies the notion of "real religion" or "my religion"—is not regularly offensive, disgusting, frightening, or gruesome. History demonstrates clearly, however, that it has been all of these—and a good deal more. For another, by invoking the notion of "religious sensibilities," Stone falls prey what I call the **good, moral, and decent fallacy,** "the popular misconception that religion is always (or should always be) a force for good in society, and that negative social effects somehow indicate false or inauthentic religious practices" (Cowan 2008: 15–16). Neither sociological nor historical evidence supports this claim. Indeed, as historian of religion Jonathan Z. Smith writes, "Religion is not nice; it has been responsible for more death and suffering than any other human activity" (1982: 110). Human sacrifice to the gods in a variety of cultures, religiously motivated genocide in the Hebrew scriptures, wars of religion between competing sects in mediaeval Europe, the hideous history of witch hunts and heresy trials in a variety of traditions—all of these point to the historical reality that we are never quite so vicious as when we unleash our savagery in the name of our gods and in the service of what we consider true belief.

At this point, some critics contend that those who commit what seem to us as horrific acts did not really understand religion. They did not "get it right," as it were, and their interpretation of the human/divine relationship was not sophisticated enough to see beyond such mundane human realities as greed, anger, temptation, and cruelty. The problem, though, is that once again this defines religion in terms that are far too narrow. For the Aztecs, human sacrifice to the god Huitzilopochtli *was* traditional religion. For the Roman Catholic hierarchy in fifteenth-century Spain, the requirement to root out heresy was not based on a misunderstanding of Christian theology but on their commitment to what they believed was the *only correct understanding* of it. In some Muslim majority countries even today—Pakistan, Nigeria, and Yemen, for example—blasphemy remains a crime punishable by death, a sentence vehemently contested by hundreds of millions of their co-religionists in other countries (see Fiss and Kestenbaum 2017; Saeed 2015). To suggest that the other side "just didn't get it" is altogether too easy, too parochial, too slick. It limits our ability to see the myriad ways in which religion is reflected and refracted—shown to us and changed for us—throughout history and, now, in such popular culture products as cinema horror.

In order to avoid such pitfalls as the good, moral, and decent fallacy, researching cinema horror requires what phenomenologists call *epoché*, the willingness to bracket one's assumptions in the quest for **eidetic vision,** a glimpse of what is really there. This does not mean that we eliminate our biases. That is impossible. But, in the interest of understanding something more deeply, we can do our best to set them aside. For example, if my faith commitment compels me to believe that all other religions than my own are false at best and satanic at worst—a position held by millions of Christians around the world (see Cowan 2003a, 2003b)—and I am not willing to bracket those assumptions, this may very well prevent me from interpreting my data in a way that is at least fair, if not necessarily objective. What some may regard as a deeply held belief—for example, that the ability to function in the world depends on **propitiating** this or that god—I may simply dismiss as demonic activity, or even possession. But in doing so I impose my own theological views in a way that obscures and distorts the lived reality of another religious believer. This is particularly important if we want to gain something from cinema horror. Simply because a religious tradition does not look like ours does not mean that it is not meaningful for someone else.

When I began researching what became *Sacred Terror*, literally a couple of weeks after that Hallowe'en *Hellraiser* marathon, two simple questions drove my work: what do we fear and why is religion so often implicated in our fearing?; that is, if we accept the premise that religion and spirituality are and always have been integral to the horror genre, and if we reject the notion that cinema horror has nothing to teach us about these things, then what can we learn about what we fear, why we fear, and how we manage our fear? And how do those relate to our ages-old quest for meaning and purpose?

The method is simple: we have to watch a lot of movies, and with a critical eye. We cannot watch a few films and expect to say anything significant about the genre. As science fiction legend (and sometimes horror writer) Ray Bradbury advises, "See every film ever made. Fill up on the medium" (in Witkin 1994: 31). The methodological moral here is that we cannot make any kind of useful generalizations from one or two installments of *Hellraiser*, or by cherry-picking a few examples from the recent spate of so-called **torture porn** films, or by considering only the latest crop of "tween" vampire films without knowing the history of the undead on screen. We also have to watch them critically. While they may be entertaining, we seek to understand more than their value as entertainment. As we watch, as we immerse ourselves in our subject, we begin to see patterns, meaningful relationships between onscreen action and off-screen reality. It is then that we realize, for example, that although they both feature species of the undead, vampire films are fundamentally different from mummy movies. Vampire films are often heavily sexualized, while mummy movies are presented as tragic love stories. Beyond the concern with survival after death, not all zombie movies are even marginally related to religion, while others are religious from beginning to end. Whatever patterns emerge from studies such as these, there will always be anomalies and outliers, but we can only know this through a deep and thorough familiarity with the genre.

This brings us to a second important methodological point. In *Le surrealism au cinema*, Greek critic and filmmaker Ado Kyrou told his readers to "learn to look at 'bad' films, they are sometimes sublime" (1963: 276). Sad or not, the reality is that very few films are very good. Even "blockbusters" are often marred by clumsy direction, artless writing delivered by actors unequal to the task, and special effects that highlight the film's shortcomings rather than add to its achievement. This is true for horror films at least as much as for any other genre. That said, cinema horror is one of the most durable genres in cinema history and no major period in North American or European cinema has been without its scary movies. Cinema horror maintains a devoted, often sophisticated fan base. While most modern horror movies do not see theatrical release but go straight to streaming, many franchises produce multiple installments, each of which was eagerly awaited and debated by enthusiasts. Moreover, it appears that no other genre attracts the amateur filmmaker like horror. From backyard zombie movies to class-project vampire films, we remain as enamored of scary movies now as we have been of scary stories for centuries. There is much to see, then, but what can it tell us?

For more than 20 years now, anthropologists, sociologists, and cultural studies scholars have used a concept known as **sociophobics** to help understand the nature of fear in society. Some things we fear because they have served our survival as a species, others because we are taught to fear them. This is sociophobics which means that much of what we fear, why we fear those things, and how we manage those fears are socially constructed behaviors (see Scruton 1986). We all share similar physiological responses to fear—increased heart rate, a dump of adrenaline into our bloodstream, often sweating and shaking—but what causes these reactions is at least in part a product of socialization. Bollywood is one of the largest film industries in the world that makes movies in every conceivable genre. Zombie films, however, simply don't play well in India. Since cremation is the most common method of corpse disposal in India, there is no body to reanimate and, thus, no cultural history of the walking dead. In Haiti, on the other hand, although zombiism plays only a minor role in **Vodun**, it has a long history and strong cultural resonance among the Haitian people. In short, it makes sense as a fear in one place, but not in another.

Religion and cinema horror reveal a number of different, though often interrelated sociophobics. These include, though are not limited to: fear of sacred places; fear of death and of dying badly; fear of supernatural evil; fear of religious fanaticism; fear of the flesh and of religion's inadequacy. Let us consider each of these briefly, then one in more detail.

We fear sacred places. In *To Take Place*, Jonathan Z. Smith points out that "when one enters a temple, one enters marked-off space," that is, space specifically set apart for interaction between the seen and the unseen orders (1987: 104). They can be places in which we meet our own god or gods. As we saw in *Hellraiser III*, though, this invokes the potential for God's absence, for the inability of the sacred place to provide an accustomed sanctuary. They can be places set aside for other gods—the site of worship for one group but the locus of terror for another—or places abandoned by one faith and taken over by a competing tradition. There are places where many cultures believe that the worlds of the living and the dead most intimately connect: graveyards, cemeteries, cremation grounds, tombs, and mausolea. From *The Mummy* (1932; 1999) to *Poltergeist* (1982, 2015) and from

White Zombie (1932) to *Raiders of the Lost Ark* (1981), when we disturb the sacred resting places of the dead, we often invite horrific retribution (see Cowan 2008: 93–122).

Our fear of death, however, frequently has less to do with the brute fact of dying than with the potential for dying badly and, perhaps more importantly, not remaining dead. Ghost stories, vampire lore, mummy movies, zombie films, and the kind of reanimation horror epitomized in Mary Shelley's *Frankenstein* have been staples of cinema horror since the turn of the twentieth century. Although there is no reason to assume that the spirits of those who loved us in life should wish to harm us once they have passed over, cultures throughout the world have exhibited/included elaborate rituals regulating the relationship between the living and the dead. Whether we carelessly fail to honor these rituals or deliberately ignore the requirements of the relationship, the ghostly soul in torment has animated films as diverse as John Carpenter's *The Fog* (ignore the Rupert Wainwright remake) and Takashi Shimizu's *Ju-On* (which he remade for Western audiences as *The Grudge*), and as wide-ranging in theological implications as Tim Burton's *Beetlejuice* and *Corpse Bride*, and Steve Beck's *Ghost Ship* and *13 Ghosts* (see Cowan 2008: 123–166).

Fear of ghosts, however, is only one species of our fear of supernatural evil, especially when this evil is internalized (as in a possession film) or externalized (as in the threat of metaphysical mayhem visited upon our world). Fearsome demonic entities and shadowy satanic groups have figured in films ranging from such Hammer films as *To the Devil ... A Daughter*, *The Devil Rides Out*, and Val Lewton's 1943 classis, *The Seventh Victim*, three now-iconic films that brought Satan to the mainstream cinema in the late 1960s and early 1970s. *Rosemary's Baby*, *The Exorcist*, and *The Omen* blended fear of the satanic cult, the dark side of Roman Catholicism, and, in what one critic calls "*The Exorcist* for Protestants" (Jones 2002: 189), fundamentalist Christian fascination with the end-times and the identity of the Antichrist with A-list stars and major studio production values. Anyone familiar with Christian predictions of the Antichrist, which show up in dozens of novels beginning at the turn of the twentieth century, will find Richard Donner's *The Omen* somewhat plodding and predictable. Because it appeared at the height of renewed interest in Christian prophecies of the end-times, however, it was a huge financial success for Twentieth Century-Fox. Indeed, the money realized by *The Omen* allowed the studio to finish a little space opera George Lucas was making called *Star Wars* (Zacky 2001; see also Cowan 2008: 167–200).

For decades, onscreen fear of the devil has been accompanied by fear of those who worship him and who seek to prosecute his designs in the world. In *Rosemary's Baby*, since the entire story is told from one young woman's point of view, are the meddling neighbors, Minnie and Roman Castavet, merely annoying or are they truly part of a satanic cult dedicated to the devil's progeny? Are the Palladists in *The Seventh Victim* really just a Greenwich Village social club, or is something more sinister afoot? One of the most important aspects of this particular sociophobic is the onscreen conflation of witchcraft and Satanism. Although modern Pagans have worked diligently for decades to distinguish their religious practices from those of **theistic Satanists**, films ranging from *Horror Hotel* to *The Craft* have either implicitly or explicitly reinforced a cultural fear of witches and devils that is several centuries old. Cults and covens onscreen highlight offscreen fears of religious fanaticism, the willingness of people to carry out unspeakable acts in the name of their god (see Cowan 2008: 236).

Finally, there is what I call the "**metataxis** of horror," our fear that everything we know—or think we know—about the sacred order could be turned upside down in a matter of moments. If in his famous 1841 poem "Pippa Passes" Robert Browning writes, "God's in his Heaven / All's right with the world," horrific metataxis in cinema horror asks us to consider, "What if God's not there? What if heaven has turned to hell?"

Case Studies in Horrific Metataxis

In his classic work *The Sacred Canopy*, sociologist Peter Berger writes that "all socially constructed worlds are inherently precarious," religious worlds, arguably, most of all (1967: 29). Because they are concerned with the relationship between the seen and the unseen, the empirical and the metaphysical, religious worlds are open to challenge on a variety of fronts and require ongoing reinforcement among believers. Berger also points out that "the sacred has another opposed category, that of chaos. The sacred emerges out of chaos and continues to confront the latter as its terrible contrary" (1967: 26; see also Beal 2002; Cowan 2018). That is, whatever we consider sacred is constantly threatened by the potential for chaos, although "chaos" is often a matter of perspective. When the Israelites tore down the sacred poles of the Canaanite peoples, when Christians demolished or appropriated religious sites across Europe and the Americas, when the Taliban shelled Buddhist statues in Afghanistan, what seems to one group as chaos was to the other the righteous establishment of cosmic order. By proposing a change in the sacred order, cinema horror not only challenges our assumptions about that order but also questions our commitment to it. Although they appear in many different forms, cinema horrors challenge the dominance of the sacred order in three basic ways: inversion, invasion, and irrelevance.

First, horrific metataxis *inverts* popular categories of religious interpretation and expectation. Churches become centers of evil rather than sanctuaries, clergy work for the forces of darkness rather than the common good, and supernatural beings we believe are on our side turn out to be anything but. According to a 2000 survey, for example, 77% of Americans believe that "angels, that is, some kind of heavenly beings who visit Earth in fact exist," a belief that "cuts across almost all ranges of education, income, and lifestyle" (Shermer 2000: 244). Five years later, another study found that more than 80% of Americans believe either "absolutely" or "probably" in the existence of angels (Baylor Religion Survey 2006). This almost certainly accounts for the enduring popularity of films such as *It's A Wonderful Life* and television series such as *Highway to Heaven* and *Touched by an Angel*. In all of these, angels are inevitably helpful, compassionate, beautiful, and devoted to the betterment of the human condition.

But, as I write in *Sacred Terror*, what if they're wrong? "What if angels are unlike anything we might think or imagine?" (Cowan 2008: 69). If the message of these pop-cultural representations above is 'Be not afraid,' what if the angelic proclamation in cinema horror is 'Be afraid. Be very afraid'?"

In Gregory Widen's 1995 film *The Prophecy*, the archangel Gabriel has staged a second war in heaven. Bitterly resentful of the divine love lavished upon humans, whom he considers little more than "talking monkeys," Gabriel leads a rebellion designed to return the legions of angelic beings to what he considers their rightful place in the heavens. This film focuses on the concept of horrific inversion in two separate ways. First, the war in heaven threatens the entire sacred order. What becomes of angels and demons—a fairly simple, stable cosmic order—when those closest to God choose to follow the path trod first by those who rebelled against him? More interesting, though, especially in the context of popular belief in angels and their inherent goodness, is the second focus: what the Bible actually says about angelic beings. In the film, one of the principal characters is a young homicide detective, Thomas Daggett, who is trying to solve a series of puzzling murders and finds himself on the front lines of Gabriel's insurrection. A lapsed Catholic who almost entered the priesthood as a young man, Daggett is presented as an authority on angels and serves as our chorus throughout the film, explaining how the current popular conception of these beings is distinctly at odds with their representation in the sacred texts. As Daggett says,

> You ever read the Bible, Katherine? You ever notice how, in the Bible, when God needed to punish someone, make an example, or whenever God needed a killing, he sent an angel? Did you ever wonder what a creature like that must be like? Your whole existence spent praising your God, always with one wing dipped in blood? Would you ever really want to see an angel?

The point here is that this is not a fanciful reading of scripture, nor an unreasonable interpretation of the biblical stories in which angels appear. An angel with a flaming sword guards the entrance to Eden after humankind's expulsion in Genesis 3, while in Numbers 22, another angel threatens the prophet Balaam. The Hebrew people may have benefited from the angel of death's grisly night's work in Exodus 12, but how horrifying must that have been for everyone else? To the Egyptians at the time, the angel of Yahweh must have seemed like some terrible invading force. Indeed, consider how frightening it must have been for an angel of the Lord to appear to a young woman named Mary (see Luke 1:26–38). Why is it that when angels appear, their first words often address our fears, not our hopes?

Indeed, *invasion* is the second level of horrific metataxis. Rather than insurrection and inversion, we fear that the sacred order of things may be displaced through attack and occupation. Offscreen, this is demonstrated clearly when dominant religions try to limit or prevent the activities of new-comer faiths. Onscreen, we see this in films such as 1970s *The Dunwich Horror*, which is based on H. P. Lovecraft's famous 1929 short story of the same name; *Hellboy* (2004), Guillermo del Toro's effects-driven homage to Lovecraft; and most obviously in Stuart Gordon's 2001 *Dagon*, which is adapted from Lovecraft's 1936 story, "The Shadow over Innsmouth."

Set in the squalid town of Imboca on the Pacific coast of Spain, *Dagon* shows us survivors of a shipwreck finding themselves in a town overtaken by inhabitants deformed in one way or another. Some have tentacles where arms should be while another has piscine teeth and speaks in guttural grunts. The survivors seek shelter in what appears to be a Catholic church, but discover that it has been re-consecrated as "The Esoteric Order of Dagon." In this film, our chorus is Ezequiel, an elderly man who has lived in the village since childhood, but who has somehow escaped the horrific transformation. Many years ago, Imboca was a prosperous fishing village, but one day the fish disappeared and the town began to suffer. Being pious Catholics, they prayed for the return of their livelihood, but still the fish did not come.

One day a fishing captain named Cambarro tells the people that he knows a god that can bring back the fish, that can bring prosperity home to Imboca. On the rocky shore, Cambarro throws a small golden pyramid carved with the Dagon symbol into the sea. "I hear first time new prayer," mutters Ezequiel sadly. "I wish I never hear. I wish I never see. Soon, Imboca rich … people go against God. No worship Cristo. All worship Dagon, or die." As he speaks, we are shown flashbacks of the villagers smashing the furniture and religious statuary in the Catholic church and murdering the parish priest. The crucifix is replaced by the symbol of Dagon, and Cambarro leads the villagers in prayer to their new god. "All worship Dagon or die," says Ezequiel quietly.

Compounding this particular fear is the possibility that the cosmic order will not return to what we consider "normal."; that is, there will be no happy ending, no resolution, no ultimate step back from the abyss. In many films, at least in the case of North American cinema horror, the world does return to normal. Good triumphs as evil is defeated—or at least deflected or deferred.

In *The Dunwich Horror*, Wilbur Whateley's attempts to bring back the Old Ones—elder gods who ruled aeons before the arrival of the religions with which we are now familiar—are defeated in a battle of magical wits by the scholar of all things esoteric, Professor Armitage. The sacred order has been threatened, but the Old Ones are beaten back once again. Similarly, in *Hellboy*, Rasputin's efforts to open the portal for the elder gods are thwarted by agents of the Bureau of Paranormal Research. However refracted through the events of the film, this return to normalcy is a hallmark of

North American horror. If nothing else, it opens the way for the invasion of seemingly innumerable sequels.

Ado Kryou's advice about bad movies notwithstanding, some sequels are simply better left unmade. Friedkin's *The Exorcist* is a cinema horror classic, but the two sequels that followed it—even given the star power of Richard Burton in *Exorcist II* and George C. Scott in *Exorcist III*—were dismal by comparison. Fifteen years after *Exorcist III*, however, and more than three decades after Friedkin's original film, directors Renny Harlin (*Exorcist: The Beginning*) and Paul Schrader (*Dominion: Prequel to The Exorcist*) made prequels to fill in the backstory on Father Lankster Merrin, the exorcist played originally by Max von Sydow. Jeremy Slater's two-season television series, *The Exorcist* (2016–2018), takes place in the original storyworld, though following an adult Regan MacNeil facing the possession of her own daughter. In the two versions of Merrin's backstory, however, we encounter elements of the third sociophobic, insignificance, that is, the fear that God may not be there when we need him, or that his presence simply doesn't matter.

For Merrin, the encounter with unthinkable evil begins in 1944 in a small town in Nazi-occupied Holland. Partisans have killed a German SS soldier and his commander seeks the guilty party. Father Merrin, the parish priest, pleads with him, assuring him that no one in the village could have done this thing. Gathering everyone in the square before the village church, the officer demands that Father Merrin choose ten townspeople for summary execution. Horrified, he cannot and the officer shoots a young woman in the head. "That was for making me wait," he says in Schrader's version. If Merrin does not comply, the entire population will be massacred. The priest begs the officer to shoot him instead. In Harlin's version, the German holds his pistol to a young boy's head, demanding again that the priest choose. Merrin's lips move in prayer and the soldier sneers.

> "Are you praying?" he asks. "To God?"
> "Shoot me," Merrin says once more.
> "God is not here today, priest," he replies, and shoots the child.

A small scene, given different weight in each version of the film, but it embodies one of the singular fears of religious people: what if God is either not there or powerless to act? This is the fear that lies at the heart of **theodicy**, the justification of God in the face of suffering. Here in the small village square is the classic problem of evil that has plagued believers for millennia and provided anti-theists with their most powerful argument against the existence of God. If God is all good and all-powerful, how can such atrocities occur? Arguments ranging from God's tears in the face of human free will to God's willing self-limitation have sought an answer to this question, but cinema horror raises the dilemma for us again and again. Where is God? From *Hellraiser III* to *Dagon*, *Dominion*, and numerous other films, prayers prove ineffective against monstrous evil. Rather than simply movie set pieces for the establishment of a particular horror narrative, these are sociophobic artifacts that reveal significant aspects of our relationship with the divine.

Conclusion

In the late modern West, the problem for many people is not secularization but ambivalence, not a decline in the importance of religion, but a deep-seated uncertainty about the power of the unseen order to affect our lives, either positively or negatively. Rather than dismiss cinema horror as unworthy of discussion—after all, it is arguably the most durable of all cinema genres—these films function as significant cultural artifacts of this ambivalence, especially where they challenge accepted (and often naïve) understandings of the Christian Church. From *Hellraiser*'s Pinhead to *The Exorcist*'s Pazuzu to the myriad demons, devils, and sundry dark forces that challenge the sacred order, what many of these films say, in no uncertain terms, is "Your god is too weak"—a prospect that is more frightening to believers than the possibility that God does not exist. By studying how these films terrify an audience, these ideas of inversion, invasion, and irrelevance can reveal the gaps in our knowledge of each other and ourselves.

Summary

- Embrace surprise in your research. Don't be afraid to check out the side-quests and dark alleys of your intellectual interests. It is never enough to watch only one film in a franchise, or one version of a film. Be open to what comparison can tell you.
- Many critics have overlooked the presence of religion in cinema horror or have dismissed its importance as a cultural indicator of religious belief. Both problems require correction. Popular culture remains one of the most powerful means of shaping our perceptions.
- These corrections require that we bracket our assumptions about the relationship between religion and cinema horror in order to see more clearly what these important cultural products reveal.
- Cinema horror reveals a number of specific sociophobics—culturally constructed and conditioned fears—all of which point to the need for more in-depth consideration of transnational horror.
- Cinema horror can teach us significant things about the way we view religion. Despite continued suggestions that we live in an increasingly secularized world, these films continue to tell us that we maintain a strong, though ambiguous relationship with the unseen order.

Discussion Questions and Activities

- In small groups or in a short writing, talk about your emotional and intellectual reactions to different horror films that you have seen. Why do you think you react the way you do? Is there a particular type of horror film that frightens you more than others? Why do you suppose that is?

- The author of this chapter claims above: "From backyard zombie movies to class-project vampire films, we remain as enamored of scary movies now as we have been of scary stories for centuries." Do you agree or disagree with this claim? How might you defend your answer in class?
- Watch a series of franchise films and plot the emerging worlds these films create and recreate. How do they reflect and refract offscreen examples of religion? How does the mythology evolve and develop?
- How do horror films re-imagine accepted cultural references? Watch a series such as *Wishmaster*, for example, and discuss how these re-present the image and idea of the genie. Research the *djinn* and ask which popular representation is more faithful to the legendary sources. If there are changes, why do you think that is so?
- Using the concept of sociophobics described in this chapter, analyze some of your favorite horror films or the current top horror films. What are the kinds of fears represented and why do you think they are presented in the ways they are?

Glossary

Eidetic vision From the phenomenology of Edmund Husserl, this means to see what is in front of one, rather than what one expects to see. Presumes **epoché**.

Epoché From the phenomenology of Edmund Husserl, this means to bracket one's assumptions in an attempt to understand phenomena on their own terms.

Ersatz False or imitation.

Good, moral, and decent fallacy The mistaken belief that goodness, morality, and decency can serve as definitional attributes for "religion." They can't. Full stop.

Hybrid Horror cinema is often less genre-specific than a hybrid form that transcends any particular style, with many films (e.g., Ridley Scott's masterful *Alien*) sitting perched on the boundary between, say, horror and science fiction.

Liminal Based on the work of anthropologist Victor Turner, has come to mean an in-between space, somewhere that is not one place or another, but somehow both and neither.

Metataxis A change in the accepted order of life, a disruption in the way we view the world and accept it as viewed.

Propitiate To satisfy the demands of something or someone.

Sociophobics The social construction of fear. The sociological position that what we fear, the ways we express fear, and how we resolve our fear are all culturally conditioned.

Theistic Satanists   Those who worship Satan as a religious practice, not to be confused with satanic dabblers, who use Satanic worship as a means of social rebellion.

Theodicy   Literally, the justification of God, that is the arguments made to justify the existence of God in the face of suffering and evil.

Torture Porn   A subgenre of horror films that emphasizes torture, mutilation, and sadism, often with sexual overtones, that began to appear in the early 2000s. Many critics consider these films a resurgence of the splatter, slasher, and Italian *giallo* films of the 1970s and 1980s.

Vodun   The Afro-Caribbean religion popularly sometimes known as Voodoo, Voudou, Voudoun, or Vaudou.

Further Reading

Beal, T. (2002) *Religion and Its Monsters*. New York: Routledge.
One of the first academic analyses of the ways in which the monstrous informs our understanding of religion. A scholar of biblical literature, Beal looks at the dark side of religion revealed in sacred texts ranging from the Hebrew scriptures to the Ramayana.

Carroll, N. (1990) *The Philosophy of Horror, or Paradoxes of the Heart*. New York: Routledge.
An excellent discussion of the horror genre in its literary, artistic, and cinematic forms. Carroll's work is particularly useful for his "third way" approach to horror, walking a path between metaphysical acceptance and psychological dismissal.

Cowan, D.E. (2008) *Sacred Terror: Religion and Horror on the Silver Screen*. Waco, TX: Baylor University Press.
One of the few in-depth discussions of religion and horror cinema, which includes the popular horror-science fiction hybrid. Cowan uses the principle of sociophobics—the concept that what and how we fear is socially constructed—to consider why so much of cinema horror relies on religion.

—— (2018) *America's Dark Theologian: The Religious Imagination of Stephen King*. New York: New York University Press.
The first in-depth investigation of how Stephen King treats the religious imagination in his horror fiction, the book explores the religious imagery, themes, characters, and, most importantly, questions that haunt King's novels and short stories.

—— (2022) *The Forbidden Body: Sex, Horror, and the Religious Imagination*, New York: New York University Press.
Taking a broad approach not limited to horror cinema or popular fiction, but embracing also literary horror, weird fiction, graphic storytelling, visual arts, and participative culture, this book explores how fears of bodies that are tainted, impure, or sexually deviant are made visible and reinforced through popular horror tropes.

Jancovich, M. (1996) *Rational Fears: American Horror in the 1950s*. Manchester: Manchester University Press.
Although generally dismissive of the relationship between religion and horror, Jancovich's book is useful for the ways in which it demonstrates the relationship between offscreen life and onscreen representation, in this case the various sociophobics associated with the Cold War period.

Scruton, D.L. (ed.) (1986) *Sociophobics: The Anthropology of Fear*. Boulder, CO: Westview.
The classic text on the exploration of fear and fearing as culturally conditioned experiences.

Bibliography

Barker, C. (1986) *The Hellbound Heart*. New York: Harper.
———— (2015) *The Scarlet Gospels*. New York: St. Martin's Press.
Baylor Religion Survey (2006) *American Piety in the 21st Century*. Waco, TX: Baylor Institute for Studies of Religion.
Beal, T. (2002) *Religion and Its Monsters*. New York: Routledge.
Berger, P.L. (1967) *The Sacred Canopy: Elements of a Sociological Theory of Religion*. New York: Anchor Books.
Burke, R. (1999) "Review of *Stigmata*." *Journal of Religion and Film*, 3/2, Online. Available www.unomaha.edu/~jrf/stigmata.htm (accessed February 21, 2021).
Cowan, D.E. (2003a) *Bearing False Witness? An Introduction to the Christian Countercult*. Westport, CT: Praeger.
———— (2003b) *The Remnant Spirit: Conservative Reform in Mainline Protestantism*. Westport, CT: Praeger.
———— (2008) *Sacred Terror: Religion and Horror on the Silver Screen*. Waco, TX: Baylor University Press.
———— (2010) *Sacred Space: The Quest for Transcendence in Science Fiction Film and Television*. Waco, TX: Baylor University Press.
———— (2018) *America's Dark Theologian: The Religious Imagination of Stephen King*. New York: New York University Press.
———— (2019) *Magic, Monsters, and Make-Believe Heroes: How Myth and Religion Shape Fantasy Culture*. Berkeley and Los Angeles: University of California Press.
———— (2022) *The Forbidden Body: Sex, Horror, and the Religious Imagination*. New York: New York University Press.
Fiss, J., and Kestenbaum, J. G. (2017) *Respecting Rights? Measuring the World's Blasphemy Laws*. Washington, DC: U. S. Commission on International Religious Freedom, Online. Available www.uscirf.gov/publications/respecting-rights-measuring-worlds-blasphemy-laws (accessed August 15, 2022).
Jones, D. (2002) *Horror: A Thematic History in Fiction and Film*. London: Arnold.
Kyrou, A. (1963) *Le surréalisme au cinéma*. Paris: Le terrain vague.
Lovecraft, H. P. ([1929] 2001) "The Dunwich Horror." In *The Thing on the Doorstep and Other Weird Stories*, ed. S.T. Joshi, 206–245. New York: Penguin Books.
———— ([1936] 1999) "The Shadow over Innsmouth." In *The Call of Cthulhu and Other Weird Stories*, ed. S.T. Joshi, 268–335. New York: Penguin Books.
Saeed, A. (2015) "Limitations on Religious Freedom in Islam: Rethinking through the *Maqasid*?" In *Routledge Handbook of Law and Religion*, ed. Silvio Ferrari, 369–380. New York: Routledge.
Scruton, D.L. (ed.) (1986) *Sociophobics: The Anthropology of Fear*. Boulder, CO: Westview.
Shermer, M. (2000) *How We Believe: Science, Skepticism, and the Search for God*, 2nd Edition. New York: Owl Books.
Smith, J.Z. (1982) *Imagining Religion: From Jonestown to Babylon*. Chicago: University of Chicago Press.

——— (1987) *To Take Place: Toward Theory in Ritual.* Chicago: University of Chicago Press.

Stone, B. (2001) "The Sanctification of Fear: Images of the Religious in Horror Films." *Journal of Religion and Film* 5/2, Online. Available www.unomaha.edu/~jrf/sanctifi.htm (accessed February 21, 2021).

Winter, D.E. (1985) *Faces of Fear: Encounters with the Creators of Modern Horror.* New York: Berkeley Books.

Witkin, M. (1994) "A Defense of Using Pop Media in the Middle-school Classroom." *The English Journal* 81/1, 30–33.

Zacky, B. (dir.) (2001) *The Omen Legacy*, DVD. Hollywood, CA: Prometheus Entertainment.

10 Food and What's Cooking in Pop Culture
Lord of the Lembas

Jonathan Sands Wise

Introduction

I stumbled upon the *Lord of the Rings* (hereafter *LOTR*) in high school by some chance or providence, and was immediately engrossed. J.R.R. Tolkien, an Oxford professor and good friend of C.S. Lewis, wrote the trilogy (along with other connected stories, like *The Hobbit*) through the middle of the 20th century, and I am far from the only person to find in these stories a powerful myth that is both immensely enjoyable and deeply powerful in ways that can be hard to explain. In fact, *LOTR* has been chosen as the top book of the 20th century (or of the millennium!) in several polls by magazines and Amazon.com. When Peter Jackson set out to turn the *LOTR* into a trilogy of movies, first released in 2001, 2002, and 2003, there was little doubt that they would be popular, but through a combination of the material and brilliant direction, they became cultural phenomena, not only earning nearly $3 billion at the box office, but also winning an unprecedented number of Academy Awards for a fantasy film series.

But what is it about these odd fantasy stories about hobbits (short, human-like creatures with simple tastes), dwarves, elves, orcs, and wizards that is so interesting? I cannot speak for everyone else, but I always had a sense that these stories were somehow deeper and more meaningful than many other tales. Certainly Tolkien accomplishes this in part by creating a well-established fantasy world, one that feels like it has all of the complexity and unexplained depth of the real world that we inhabit. I believe that he also imbues these stories with the world view that he knew best as a medieval scholar at Oxford: the world of *LOTR* builds on the moral and metaphysical world of the high middle ages in Europe and most of the Mediterranean, a view that is equal parts Greek philosophy, Judeo-Christian-Arabic religious interpretations of that philosophy, and Germanic myths and politics. I have had the great pleasure of teaching classes and writing articles exploring the ways that this medieval worldview underlies Tolkien's work for much of my career, and I believe that one clear connection lies in his understanding of food, ethics, and culture, though this is not unique to Tolkien. As someone who loves to study food *almost* as much as

DOI: 10.4324/9781003079729-12

I love to eat, this study allows me to combine two passions by exploring how Tolkien's use of food and scenes of eating allow us to get a deeper understanding of his characters.

Symbols and Suppers: The Use of Food as a Symbol

Hobbits, the delightful creatures at the heart of *LOTR*, love to laugh and eat and drink, just like me. In the first movie, *The Fellowship of the Ring*, we find four hobbits—Frodo, Sam, Merry, and Pippin—fleeing from mortal danger with Aragorn, the future king. They have a mysterious Ring of Power which must be destroyed to permanently defeat Sauron, the evil and powerful being that first created the one Ring. Sauron has sent the Black Riders, former men and kings who accepted lesser rings from Sauron and have become powerful evil creatures that can only do Sauron's will, to capture the Ring. In this moment of danger, as they flee through the wilderness, Aragorn is bewildered to find the four hobbits getting out food supplies in mid-morning to eat breakfast, since they already ate breakfast earlier. Pippin explains, "We've had *one*, yes. What about second breakfast?" As Aragorn disgustedly turns away and disappears over the hill, Merry says, "Don't think he knows about second breakfast, Pip." Alarmed, Pippin follows him up the hill: "What about elevensies? Luncheon? Afternoon tea? Dinner? Supper? He knows about them, doesn't he?" Merry shakes his head resignedly, "I wouldn't count on it."

Indeed, all four hobbits will have to learn to eat different food, and often to go without food, during their quest, but they do not love food the less for that. Throughout the films, the hobbits' simple, generous, appreciative, and joyful approach to food (and drink) defines their characters and allows us as viewers to understand the movies at a deeper level. This is not unique to *LOTR*; across pop culture, scenes centered around food and drink enrich stories by connecting to broader and older narratives of eating and drinking, while giving us unique and valuable insights into the moral character of those who eat and drink. The centrality of the symbolism of food and drink in pop culture should not surprise us, because in many ways, food is equally central to all of human life (cf. Ferry 2003: 2, 7; Bower 2004: 3). What we eat, when we eat, how we eat, and with whom we eat, go far to define who and what we are as creatures. Food is at the intersection of culture and nature: we *must* eat because we are animals, but we *want* to eat because it fulfills desires, defines identities, and brings us joy. It is our cooking and our sharing, our waiting for others to eat and our asking a blessing on our food, our celebrations and banquets, and who is or is not invited—in short, the cultural and religious practices that surround our eating—that set us apart from other animals and even from each other (Kass 1994: ch. 4). Eating is a defining act of humanity; it defines us culturally, personally, religiously, and ethically, as well-mannered or wild, as patient or fiery, and even as good or evil.

According to a Christian reading of a widely shared and well-known foundational story of the Western world, it is when one man and one woman eat a fruit that was forbidden to them that sin and evil first enter into the world and human hearts (Genesis 3). Later in the biblical story, in his covenant with his chosen people, Israel, God commands them to keep three annual feasts, including the Feast of Unleavened Bread, or Passover, with which they are to remember that he passed over, or spared them, in Egypt (Exodus 34:18–24), and God also commands Israel to observe carefully the eating of specific foods in specific ways (e.g., Leviticus 11). It is at the observance of the highly ritualized and symbolically ordered Feast of the Passover that Jesus later institutes a so-called "new" covenant, one that is still commemorated today with the ritual of the Eucharistic Feast (Matthew 26:20–30). In this Eucharist, or Communion, Jesus's followers eat broken bread (Christ's body) and drink wine (Christ's blood) and in partaking of their lord, they seek not to consume him, but—as Augustine of Hippo, a Christian theologian of the fourth and fifth centuries, claimed—to be consumed by him (Augustine 1960: 171). Finally, in both the Christian and ancient Jewish traditions, the final revealing of God—the apocalypse— is envisioned variously as a peaceful age of eating one's own bread and wine where even the dietary habits of wolves and lions are changed (Isaiah 65:17–25), or as the Banquet of Heaven, a wedding feast to which even (especially!) the beggars are invited (Matthew 22:1–14). For many religions, and conspicuously so for Jews and Christians, every great moment of religious time, from the fall to redemption to the unveiling of the new age, is instituted, ritualized, and accomplished with eating.

It is both as a natural indication of our ethical state and as a symbol of our deepest religious beliefs that we turn now to the place of food in pop culture. In what follows, I will suggest some specific ways that movies can use eating and food as religious symbols that imbue these scenes with important meaning, and can show us what sort of characters we are dealing with.

Theory and Method

Two Pinches of Symbolism and a Dash of Gluttony: A Medieval Recipe for Reading

There is no one shared method for reading texts or cultural artifacts regarding food, but reclaiming a medieval tradition of reading and combining it with a medieval theory of eating provides us with one clear option. In what they called an allegorical reading of the text, medieval theologians and philosophers posited that besides the **literal meaning**, every biblical text (and at least most literature) was believed to have a **spiritual meaning** (Beichner 1967). While the literal meaning was meant to inform or entertain, depending on the genre, the spiritual meaning was meant to instruct by placing each text within a larger Christian universe and teaching the reader whom they should imitate (or not).

So, for example, while God commanding Abraham to sacrifice Isaac on Mount Moriah (Genesis 22:1–19) literally means that God did so command

Abraham, for Augustine the entire story has a further spiritual meaning as well: this is a prefiguring of God the Father sacrificing his own son on what (according to tradition) is the same mountain, and hence is a **symbol** of the sacrifice of Jesus on the Cross (Augustine 1984: 394–395). This adds new depths of meaning to both stories, and makes the ram in the bushes into a symbol of Christ, sacrificed so that we do not have to be. As Christians later read the story, they use this odd story of near filicide to understand what happens on the cross at the place Abraham calls "The Lord Will Provide" (Genesis 22:14). We can extend the spiritual reading further by noting that along with referencing past or future realities, stories also have a spiritual meaning for us *now*, what is commonly called a **moral** reading. That is, just as Abraham was held to the impossibly high moral standard of absolute obedience, so we too are to be perfect in our everyday lives, and yet by God's mercy there is a provision made for us when we fail. The central insight here is clear: stories gain meaning by reading them in light of other stories, past or future, and also have a basic moral meaning in that they tell us how we should live our own lives.

Stories do not, and cannot, include every detail of their characters' lives. Imagine a movie that recorded every single activity that someone undertook during a day in real time, or a novel that tried to describe every thought that someone had. This would, doubtless, be incredibly boring! When everyday activities are included by writers and artists, then, we should wonder why. For example, if we see someone going to the bathroom in a movie, something besides the ordinary better happen while they are in there, something that tells us more about this person or their situation, or it just isn't effective (or interesting) storytelling. So when we see someone eating in a story or even in a painting or other work of art, we should ask, "Why is the artist showing us such mundane details?" The medieval theory that every text has spiritual senses points us to an interesting way to understand the inclusion of the mundane in modern day storytelling: in the enactment of such everyday practices, the artist can make interesting and meaningful reference to other stories that imbue their work with deeper and more nuanced meaning than would otherwise be possible (eating as a symbol). In addition, the artist can more effectively teach us something about the character of the person who is eating (eating as a moral practice).

Eating as a Symbol and Moral Practice: A Classical Example

A quick example will help us fill out this theory and make it clearer, so let us turn to a pop culture artifact of an earlier age in which food is clearly being used both symbolically and as a moral marker: Augustine's *Confessions*. Augustine was one of the most famous men of his day in early Christian Rome. A brilliant rhetorician and orator who converted in midlife to Christianity and soon became a Bishop in Africa, Augustine's autobiography, the *Confessions*, was one of the most popular and famous works of both his own time and of the later Middle Ages. In it, Augustine reminisces at length about a seemingly harmless adolescent prank he committed with his friends at the age of 16. He then spends page after page lamenting how horribly sinful and lost he was at this time. The story itself is quite simple and brief:

> In a garden nearby to our vineyard there was a pear tree, loaded with fruit that was desirable neither in appearance nor in taste. Late one night—to which hour, according to our pestilential custom, we had kept up our street games—a group of very bad youngsters set out to shake down and rob this tree. We took great loads of fruit from it, not for our own eating, but rather to throw it to the pigs; even if we did eat a little of it, we did this to do what pleased us for the reason that it was forbidden.
>
> (Augustine 1960: 70)

This is a seemingly harmless prank, especially since Augustine has hinted in the same chapter that he was committing much greater thefts, getting drunk every night, and possibly even having affairs with married women! So why does Augustine make such a big deal about this particular bit of food-related fun?

Augustine has many reasons for including this vignette, but one clear reason is for the symbolic value of this particular crime and the deeper notes of meaning it infuses into the story. Any biblically literate person reading a story about someone eating forbidden fruit in a garden might immediately think of the Christian reading of Adam and Eve in the Garden of Eden, chowing down on the fruit of knowledge and learning way more than they ever wanted to know about the "evil" part of the Tree of Knowledge of Good and Evil. Augustine's act of eating from the pear tree is hence an imitation of this original act of sin and pride, which makes his act symbolic of any other human sin. This "first" sin, according to the theology of original sin that Augustine helped make the orthodoxy of the Western Church, is not only a single sinful act, but is the one act in which all of humanity corporately fell together; all of us participated in this one sin of our aboriginal father and mother. In mimicking this original sin, therefore, Augustine is symbolically committing The Sin, not just any sinful act, and the tortured discussion of motivations that follows is meant to apply to all sin.

While committing a crime reminiscent of the original sin shows us pretty clearly where Augustine is at morally, not every reference would be so clear, so we can use other aspects of this story to understand more about Augustine's character. Medieval moral theology provides us with an interesting way to interpret when people are eating correctly in its discussion of the Capital Vice of **Gluttony**. As medieval ethicists such as Thomas Aquinas developed the tradition of the seven capital vices, they tried to provide concrete advice on how to avoid the vices. Thomas, for example, argues that there are five ways to go wrong with regards to eating, and Rebecca

Konyndyk De Young, a contemporary scholar, helpfully captures these under the mnemonic FRESH, standing for Fastidiously, Ravenously, Excessively, Sumptuously, and Hastily (Konyndyk DeYoung 2009: 141ff). To eat too daintily or fastidiously is to be too picky; in other words, one way of being gluttonous may be to eat *too little*. Ravenous eaters are the opposite, bolting down their food in an orgy of swallowing, both hands full of food waiting its turn to enter their all-consuming maws. The excessive eater is the one we normally think of when we picture gluttony, the over-weight person who simply eats far too much, while the sumptuous eater is our other picture of gluttony, the person who covers his or her plate with nothing but rich, fatty, and/or sweet foods. Finally, the hasty eater is the person who eats *too soon*, and so generally eats alone, before everyone else sits down to the meal (Konyndyk DeYoung 2009: 141ff).

In eating of the pear tree, Augustine devours, or even carelessly throws away after only one bite, raw fruit with a bunch of so-called friends. Likewise, rather than eating at an appropriate time, they raid the garden at night, and then throw out the pears that fail to live up to their fastidious desires. Augustine does not eat for the good of his body, nor for the good of his community, since he joins others in sin and steals from a neighbor. Neither does he eat for the glory of God, since he rejects God's law and willfully sins against God in the theft. Augustine steals and eats the pears only because he thinks that it will be fun for him to do so. His eating is an entirely self-centered and deeply disordered act. While not every author would have the background understanding of a medieval theory of gluttony that Tolkien, a medieval scholar and devout Catholic, undoubtedly had, the basic insight here is broadly applicable: how and what people eat, given the relevant cultural context, shapes our understanding of their personality and character.

To summarize, food is often used in movies, books, stories, and art generally for two often connected purposes: first, as a symbol that imbues the artifact with more meaning by deliberately referring to some other story, act, or artifact; and second, as an indication of the character of the person or people eating. Food and other common objects are especially powerful symbols for these purposes precisely because of their universality: everyone must eat, and so how and what you eat defines the sort of person (or hobbit) that you are.

Case Study

Apples and Rings: Symbols and Stories

Of course, the *Lord of the Rings* trilogy begins with a party. In a scene that neatly parallels Augustine's story of the great pear robbery, *The Fellowship of the Ring* shows Merry and Pippin steal and set off some fireworks at Bilbo's birthday party. As the movie opens, we learn that Bilbo, an old hobbit, is about to throw a huge birthday party for himself, and that

Gandalf, a wizard and even older friend, is going to attend and set off fireworks. After Gandalf selects from his wagon some relatively innocent fireworks, Merry and Pippin sneak up and steal the largest firework they can find, which turns out to be a large and rather dangerous dragon. Merry hands the firework to Pippin, who sneaks it off, and as Merry backs around the corner trying to look innocent, we see him take a large and conspicuous bite out of a bright, shiny apple: another Adam who has given in to temptation.

This scene uses the apple and the reference to the Garden of Eden lightly, as it is often used in contemporary culture. There is no hint here that Merry is sunk in the depths of irreparable sin, desperately in need of grace and mercy, as Augustine's parallel usage is meant to show. Indeed, Merry is a good hobbit, and he is far more of a mischievous imp than a depraved sinner in the *LOTR* films. Clearly, the meaning of symbols can alter over time, and taking a bite of an apple is now largely a symbol for unimportant, even "innocent" sins, if such an oxymoron makes any sense, perhaps because our culture takes sin of all sorts less seriously than many of the ancients did. The movies do, however, retain much of Tolkien's own Catholic view of the seriousness of sin in the symbolism of the Ring of Power, which acts as a substitute for Adam and Eve's fruit in these stories, symbolizing the destructive pursuit of corrupting power. Just like the forbidden fruit, the Ring is inherently attractive and tempting because it appeals to the pride, desire for power, and selfishness of all those who come into contact with it, whether they ultimately surrender to this temptation or not. Even more, the Ring has the same effects as the "original" fruit, giving knowledge and enhanced vision of a sort, but only at a great and terrible price for the bearer, for all its added knowledge is ultimately skewed such that the bearer sees only the evil of the world, never its full reality.

The movies demonstrate this parallel between the Ring and the Fruit in multiple scenes, especially in others' reactions to the Ring. Gandalf, Galadriel (a powerful and good elf), and Aragorn show their wisdom in refusing even to touch the Ring, though all feel its powerful pull and struggle against the temptation to seize this great power. Boromir, apparently a good and noble man from the old and powerful city of Minas Tirith, is too proud, and so proves unable to resist, trying to seize the Ring by force when Frodo will not give it to him. All believe that they would take the Ring to do good, but the wise know that they would not be able to use the Ring for such purposes: instead, it would use them. Most powerfully of all, when old Bilbo sees the Ring again, he becomes a veritable demon for a moment, his image twisted and distorted as if reflected in an evil fun house mirror. In each case, the person involved becomes aware soon afterward that they were acting almost under an external compulsion, but only *because* of their own interior weakness.

In the world that Tolkien has created, there are forces beyond those in our own world, forces that we might deem magical or mysterious. Whenever Frodo is near the Black Riders, he feels a desperate desire to put the Ring on his finger, even after learning that doing so makes him *more* visible to the servants of Sauron though it makes him invisible to others. When Frodo puts on the Ring, it warps his perception (and the viewer's) with a tunnel effect, mirroring the shape of the Ring itself; distances become distorted, Frodo becomes pale and disoriented, his eyes staring but unfocused, and he hears nothing clearly but only as through a tunnel and with a vague ringing. The world becomes a rushing wind that blows colors past him, and while he can see evil entities more clearly, the rest of the world fades into darkness and shadow. The ring conceals Frodo to the living entities around him, but also reveals to him the presence of the evil and the undead. Unfortunately, it also reveals him to the evil realities (the Black Riders and Sauron). Wearing the ring makes it appear that evil is the only reality, just as sin does for human beings.

The same pattern is evident in the temptation of the forbidden fruit in Genesis, both its temptation and its distorting power and revelation. For Adam and Eve, according to a common Christian interpretation, the temptation is to a powerful knowledge that would make them more like God, but the knowledge actually gained from the forbidden fruit is a distorted knowledge. While Adam and Eve learn certain truths about reality (e.g., they are naked), it is not so much *what* they learn as *how* they now perceive this reality that is altered. They already knew that they were naked in their innocence, but in their guilt, this becomes a matter of apparent shame (Genesis 3:10 and 21). The Ring, in a parallel fashion, changes the perception of its bearer. The third film in the trilogy, *Return of the King*, powerfully demonstrates a similarly sobering change in perception through a repeated line at the beginning and end of the film that neatly references the universal experience of eating: "we even forgot the taste of bread."

As the third film opens, director Peter Jackson gives us a quick summary of what the Ring is and how it was found by a hobbit-like creature called Gollum long ago. Gollum's friend actually found it, but Gollum is quickly corrupted by its seduction and kills his friend to steal the Ring. Under its baleful influence, Gollum ceases to see anything but his own desires: the Ring is "precious" *to him*, and he will kill anyone to possess it. But no one possesses the Ring any more than one can truly possess sin—we do not possess our sin, it possesses us. As opposed to food, which we consume and make part of ourselves, the Ring consumes its bearer and makes it part of itself, a pitiful ring-wraith, like the Black Riders.

Warped and distorted by the Ring, Gollum becomes more and more like a hollow caricature of a hobbit, nothing more than skin stretched over bones; or as Bilbo puts it when describing how the ring has made him feel after many years of hiding it, he feels "stretched, like butter spread over too much bread." Rather than eating cooked food, a symbol of civilization, Gollum begins to catch fish with his bare hands and to eat them raw; the camera spares us nothing here, dwelling almost lovingly on Gollum's few blackened teeth as they tear into the still-living fish's back, juice squirting out from between his chewing teeth. Even his name, as Ralph Wood points out in *The Gospel According to Tolkien,* is derived from his voracious appetite: Gollum is a nickname given to him because of the repetitive swallowing noise he makes (Wood 2003: 56). Like the Ring that has come to possess him, Gollum is now nothing but a voracious appetite. He desires no good, not even his own; his desires now revolve endlessly around the gold Ring that he endlessly revolves his fingers around, stroking it and speaking to it, calling it "My Precious." Gollum's voiceover as the film begins is addressed to his Precious, and it is a powerful device for characterizing the extent of Gollum's corruption and loss: "And we forgot the taste of bread, the sound of trees, the softness of the wind. We even forgot our own name."

The power of the Ring is strong. Even Frodo, who is praised for his humility and courage in resisting the Ring for so long, is eventually warped by it. He becomes jealous of the Ring, unwilling to allow Sam, his most faithful and dear friend, to touch or even to speak of touching it. As they make their way up Mount Doom to destroy the ring in *The Return of the King,* we get the full sense of Frodo's loss of self when he eerily echoes Gollum's earlier voiceover. As Sam tries to cheer Frodo with thoughts of strawberries and cream, Frodo confesses in a weak and fading voice, "I have forgotten the taste of bread." Frodo is becoming like Gollum, unable to participate in the civilized community of love that bread represents, unable even to remember why such a community is attractive. We will look more at the symbolism of bread shortly, but to see why it is a symbol of civilization, consider that first the wheat must be raised by settled farmers, then ground and turned into flour. The yeast, too, the leavening agent, must be preserved in a starter that must be occasionally fed with more flour and water, making it difficult or impossible to transfer far. Finally, the whole product must be carefully cooked in an oven, not just warmed over a fire. Bread, in short, is only possible in a settled culture that works at food preparation; it cannot be found on the ground or cooked over a campfire.

Consumed by the circle of the Ring, Frodo has begun to be shut up within himself and his own endless desires, and can no longer even remember the taste or desire for simple, civilized food. At the end, of course, Frodo will try to make the Ring his own, giving in to the lust for power, and will only be saved by a mysterious mercy and providential grace. Even so, just as with Adam and Eve, there is no simple road back after the fruit has been taken. For Frodo, nothing in Middle Earth can any longer give him rest, for he lives in a constant ache and itch for the lost Ring of power and in pain from the wounds that he has received. In Tolkien's Christian view, even the most wonderful stories, so far as they are limited to the unredeemed earth, must be ultimately filled with a sense of loss, and Frodo's is no different.

The Ring of Power is a symbol of the Forbidden Fruit, symbolically referencing the Fall of Humanity and so connecting this desire for corrupting power and control with the desire that all human beings feel. Through this connection it also, of course, is making various important moral points concerning both our own moral lives and the moral character of each person who interacts with this terrible temptation.

Lord of the Lembas: Another Symbol Considered

Bread is the food of the hearth and of community, a food that must be prepared, and in the Christian tradition, it is also the symbol of the Bread of Life: Jesus, broken on the cross (John 6:35). The most obvious symbol of the Eucharist in *LOTR*, however, is not plain bread, but the wondrous Elvish bread, Lembas.

Lembas, Tolkien tells us, is a light, airy bread made only by certain elves from a plant that they brought from the land where the Valar, the divine beings in charge of earth, dwell. While incredibly light, it gives great sustenance, and more, as its eaters rely on it alone (Wood 2003: 55). The connections to Catholic Eucharistic wafers are obvious: though light and airy, they give spiritual life and strength to the believer. The movie makes the connection even clearer by designing the lembas like a wafer that is split into four pie quarters (much as many Eucharistic wafers are made today in Catholic and Episcopal churches). As Sam breaks it and shares it with Frodo, we watch them eat a Communion-like meal together, symbolizing their close relationship. As Frodo begins to break down under the Ring, we watch his fellowship with Sam suffer, but Sam's own deep humility and trust in his master saves their relationship and ultimately saves their mission. Because Sam forgives all of Frodo's insults and continues to come back and support him and *speak* and *eat* with him, Frodo is never deprived of community the way that Gollum was and is. Though Gollum is now with Frodo and Sam all of the time, and even begins to trust Frodo a little, he is never able to enter their communion, and this is signified by his inability to partake of their food. Gollum refuses to eat a cooked and prepared rabbit, and when he tries to eat Sam's and Frodo's lembas, he chokes. What he eats, and what he cannot eat, both defines and demonstrates his evil, isolated, and warped character.

While the Eucharist is the clearest referent for lembas, other interesting and related possibilities are the manna God sends the Israelites in the wilderness (Exodus 16:31) and the "daily bread" Jesus instructs his disciples to pray for (Matthew 6:11). Food becomes a symbol of Sam's hope as he and Frodo finally approach Mordor, the land of evil, where they must destroy the Ring. In a touching scene, we find Sam counting all of the food they have left, and making sure that they have enough for the return trip as well. Never, until near the very end, does Sam give up hope that there will be a return journey. Just as there was always enough manna for each day in Israel's journey through the wilderness, but never enough to gather up and store for later (Deuteronomy 16: 14–32), so there always seems to be just enough lembas for what must be done. In the character of Sam, we watch as he must slowly give up his self-sufficiency and begin to trust that there will always be his daily bread. Here the multiple referents for the lembas deepen the symbol, emphasizing its communal aspects and its spiritual strength, but equally drawing upon its connection to faith in God's providential care.

You Are What, and How, You Eat: Food and Characterization

Tolkien and Jackson use eating to demonstrate the essential character of various people in *LOTR*. As we saw in the introduction, the hobbits love feasts and parties, generous and joyful affairs where food and drink flow freely. These simple creatures are characterized (literally) by their love for simple pleasures, whether a tavern song and dance or a pipe of tobacco. Rohan, an agrarian country that Gandalf, Aragorn and their companions help to save from Sauron, likewise delights in roaring feasts. After a solemn toast to fallen heroes, a feast commences, complete with drinking games and dancing on the tables!

In stark contrast, we have the culture of the orcs. Orcs are evil creatures, bred or created for the purposes of Sauron and other evil beings. A band of orcs captures Merry and Pippin, and through much of the second film, *The Two Towers*, carries or runs them through the territory of Rohan toward their master. The orcs feast, but this is no joyful celebration! Rather than lembas, they get energy from drinking a dark, blood-like substance similar to wine that the hobbits experience as horrible and yet effective, almost like a drug. In the movies, they also appear to be willing to eat both hobbits and other orcs. Several of the orcs demand to be allowed to eat their prisoners, and one tries to sneak up and kill them. The leader of the band chops off the offending orc's head, and as the head flies through the air, calls, "Looks like meat's back on the menu, boys!" followed by intestines being flung into the air. Rather than demonstrating community in their feasts, the banquets of the orcs are bloody, violent, and competitive affairs in which you'd better watch your back or you might become the next entrée. Notice that the feasting of evil characters such as Gollum or the orcs is a distortion of proper feasting. The liquor of the men, hobbits, and elves that gives refreshment, energy, and fun becomes a vile, bloody substance that burns and gives a manic, destructive force to the drinker, while the generous table of the hobbits becomes the scrounging gluttony of orcs feeding on each other.

The most powerful example of food being used to show a moral bent, however, comes from a character who was clearly good at one point, but has become warped by fear and pride: the Steward of Gondor, the father of Boromir. Gondor is the only remaining great kingdom of human beings, but its last king died centuries before and the city is now run by a line of stewards. While they originally ruled in the name of the absent king until a new one should appear, there is little doubt that the current steward has no intention of ever surrendering rule again. The main city of the realm, Minas Tirith, comes under attack as the third movie of the trilogy opens, and the Steward is both too proud in their lineage and strength and too afraid of Sauron's power, both overly confident in his own abilities, and overly fatalistic that the city will soon fall. In his fear, and having already lost his older son, Boromir, who dies at the end of the first film as Merry and Pippin are captured, we see the Steward send Faramir, his wiser and kinder younger son, on a suicide mission to reclaim a nearby city, apparently as an irrational punishment for surviving while the favored older son died.

Even as Faramir leaves the hall, the Steward sits down to a huge, sumptuous feast. The table overflows with a whole chicken, a plate of vegetables and of cheese, fried foods and sliced meats, and a large jug of wine. Though others, including Pippin, stand nearby, the Steward, the one who is to *serve* the king, sits down to this kingly meal alone, now served by others. Fastidiously pulling up his sleeves, the Steward begins to daintily pick with his fingers from the massive piles before him, piling his plate high with delicacies. As he eats, both hands are constantly full of food, ambidextrously filling his ravenous mouth even as he continues to talk. As Faramir and the soldiers of Gondor ride to their deaths on a suicide mission, we watch and hear the Steward crunch down on a tomato, the squirting juice reminiscent both of the blood of his men as they fall and of Gollum's earlier eating of the fish. Mercilessly, Jackson juxtaposes brutal scenes of war with the Steward's oddly fastidious and yet bestial eating, all the while showing us Pippin's disgusted reaction as he tries to sing for him of the fading of all good things. Clearly the Steward lives as he eats: gluttonously.

Just as he fastidiously chooses his food, so he snobbishly rejects one son in favor of the more warlike one, then ravenously chews up men's lives and spits them out in his thoughtless conduct of war. From the time that Faramir rides out, the Steward has a thin rivulet of red juice running down his chin, dripping from his mouth; the camera intimately studies his oddly choosy yet ravenous fingers and mouth as they dance among the sumptuous feast, tearing meat and dripping blood and juice, yet keeping his mouth permanently full, even overflowing. Dressed in his sumptuous finery, the Steward sits in a city that is under siege and starving, yet he feasts alone and bestially. In the same way, the Steward is clothed in all of his pride and selfishness, ignoring the good of his city and sending his ill-loved younger son to his death. The wastefulness of his eating symbolizes the wastefulness of his life, his lack of real love for both his sons, and even the death that he will soon suffer as he throws himself on a burning pyre to avoid having to struggle against the evil that is coming. A powerful and potentially very good man, the Steward has become twisted by his fear and pride till he is no longer truly a steward or a man. His eating demonstrates more powerfully than any description could that he has become an animal.

Conclusion

Often details regarding food and eating are included in movies, books, songs, and artwork, and in stories more generally, because of the symbolic and moral value of food metaphors: they quickly, insightfully, and powerfully refer to other instances of eating and food in other contexts (the symbolic meaning of the text) and so add depth of meaning and significance to a story. They also illustrate the character of the person(s) involved in an immediate and visceral way (the moral meaning of the text). Contemporary pop culture makes frequent use of such symbols, and informed viewers can understand all aspects of the artifact more fully if they are aware of these deeper levels of meaning. Of course, understanding and appreciating such symbols requires not only an awareness that such symbols can be used, but also a familiarity with the cultural heritage of Western society, including and especially the Bible that Western pop culture so often references. Such a familiarity cannot be achieved either quickly or easily, but its possession is well worthwhile and carries with it great rewards, both in ability to more fully appreciate pop culture today, and in the beauty and worth of the heritage itself.

Summary

- Scenes involving food and drink have a unique role to play in books and films because eating and drinking are so central to human life, and are part of both our nature and our culture.
- Food and drink often operate as symbols that refer to other occasions of eating and drinking, such as references to the fruit in the garden of Eden or to the Last Supper.
- By referencing these other stories, the artist can give his or her artwork more meaning and more nuance that the careful reader or viewer can interpret.
- One important way that eating and drinking can show us more meaning is by revealing to us the nature of various characters.
- Thus, we can judge if characters are good or bad by paying attention to the context and seeing what they eat, how they eat, whom they eat with, and when they eat.

Discussion Questions and Activities

- What other common elements appear in artwork that can be used as symbols and tools for characterization the way that food is used? Consider, for example, the way that people treat animals, or the clothing of the characters.
- Why do we so immediately understand that someone who eats alone and in a bestial manner is expressing an evil character? Is this just our own cultural bias, or is there some deep truth about human nature and food expressed here?
- Why are so many food references religious? Does this say something about food and human nature, or just about Western culture and Christianity?
- How should we understand the consumption of alcohol and especially wine in *LOTR* and other works of art? What might wine and similar drinks reference, what further nuance might they give a scene, and how does their consumption help to characterize the people in the film?
- An ancient practice in nearly every religious tradition to understand the power of food in your life (and to begin to gain control over that power) is fasting. Try fasting for 24 hours (make sure you drink water!), and

consider the effects of fasting. How much did you think about food? Did you feel like you could not continue without food? When was it hardest not to eat? Was it at meal times, or more just when you were bored?

Glossary

Filicide   Killing your own son.

Gluttony   A term for the vice of eating in a disordered manner, which may include eating fastidiously, ravenously, excessively, sumptuously, or too hastily (FRESH).

Literal meaning   The obvious sense of the text in its immediate context.

Moral   A broad term meaning roughly how good or bad someone or something is.

Reference   A symbol or artifact in a text that refers to something else.

Spiritual meaning   A medieval term for the various further symbolic meanings that a text has.

Symbol   As Augustine used the term (in Latin, *signum*, or sign), something—whether a word, a story, or a thing—that refers to or is a sign of something else.

Bibliography

Augustine (1960) *The Confessions of Saint Augustine*, ed. John K. Ryan, New York: Image Books.

Augustine (1984) *City of God*, tr. Hentry Bettenson, London: Penguin Books.

Beichner, Paul E. (1967) "The Allegorical Interpretation of Medieval Literature," *PMLA* 82:1 (March): 33–38.

Bower, Anne L. (2004) "Watching Food: The Production of Food, Film, and Values," in Anne L. Bower (ed.) *Reel Food* (pp. 1–14), New York: Routledge.

Ferry, Jane F. (2003) *Food in Film: A Culinary Performance of Communication*, New York: Routledge.

Isaacs, Neil D. and Zimbardo, Rose A. (eds.) (1968) *Tolkien and the Critics: Essays on J. R. R. Tolkien's The Lord of the Rings*, Notre Dame: University of Notre Dame Press.

Kass, Leon R. (1994) *The Hungry Soul: Eating and the Perfecting of Our Nature*, New York: The Free Press.

Konyndyk-DeYoung, Rebecca (2009) *Glittering Vices: A New Look at the Seven Deadly Sins and their Remedies*, Grand Rapids, MI: Brazos Press.

Fitzgeral, Allan D. (ed.) (1999) *Augustine through the Ages: An Encyclopedia*, Cambridge: Wm. B. Eerdmans.

Wood, Ralph (2003) *The Gospel According to Tolkien: Visions of the Kingdom in Middle-earth*, London: Westminster John Knox Press.

11 Television

The Big Bang Theory and Lived Religion

Dan W. Clanton, Jr.

Introduction

I first watched an episode of the CBS TV series *The Big Bang Theory* (2007–2019) in December of 2010. I'm a *huge* fan of comic books and assign several in my First-Year Seminar on "Heroes." That class was just ending when my Teaching Assistant Catie Niedermeyer emailed me to tell me I should watch the episode called "The Justice League Recombination." Therein, a group of three scientists and one engineer—all of whom could be classified as nerds—enter a Halloween costume contest dressed as the titular Justice League and win, thanks to their buxom and pretty neighbor Penny agreeing to be their Wonder Woman. It was funny and I enjoyed the peek into comic fan culture, so I started watching. I'd always been an avid TV watcher even since before VCRs (ask your parents) existed, so I love a good **sitcom**. This particular episode was smack in the middle of Season 4 of the series, so I started over with Season 1. What I soon realized is that *The Big Bang Theory* consistently includes religious references and jokes, mostly centered on Howard Wolowitz (the engineer, who's Jewish); Sheldon Cooper (one of the scientists, an atheist) and his overtly Christian mother Mary; and occasionally one of the two remaining scientists, Rajesh Koothrappali (who identifies as a Hindu). Maybe it's because I'm Jewish, or maybe it's because Christians on prime-time TV are more common than Jews, but I became interested in how Howard's Judaism was depicted, the choices made in what the writers showed us, and which aspects of Jewish life were highlighted. So, I watched every episode that had been released (and eventually the entire series) and meticulously took notes, looking for any mention of **religion**. Pretty soon, I felt I had enough material to try and put a paper together to share something about what I was thinking with other scholars.

That first time I tried to analyze the role that Judaism plays in Howard's life as it's presented to us in the series, I examined the treatment of what I considered to be Jewish issues and tropes.[1] That is, I paid attention to how the series depicts central components of Jewish identity by focusing on food; holidays, religious practices and observances; Howard's Jewish mother; and intermarriage. My thinking was, if I can isolate how the series treats these issues then, obviously, I'll be able to make some claims about

DOI: 10.4324/9781003079729-13

Howard's Jewish identity. After all, these are the basic things that Jews do and care about if they're good Jews, right? In just a minute, I'll give a sampling of this approach, then I'll talk about why this probably isn't the best way to approach the issue of **religious identity**. First, though, let's unpack that term and talk about what I think will be a better way for us to examine *The Big Bang Theory*.

Theory and Method

In my essay in the first edition of this book, I focused on the scholarly debate surrounding how to define religion and used the ABC TV series *NYPD Blue* (1993–2005) as a case study (see Clanton 2012). I noted that there are substantive and functional ways to define religion, the former seeking to identify some kind of underlying substance or core element that marks religion off as something distinct from other phenomena, while the latter focuses on not what religion is, but what it does. Again, my thinking was, if we're able to define religion in a nuanced way, then talking about religion in *NYPD Blue*—or any aesthetic product, for that matter—would be easier.

So, I produced a list of a few definitions of religion from reputable scholars and influential thinkers, then proceeded to discuss selected scenes from the TV series that depicted religious practices and/or religious language. Afterwards, I came to (what I thought) was a fascinating conclusion: the series demonstrated *both* kinds of definitions of religion. Looking back, though, I now see that this conclusion isn't so earth-shattering. For one thing, any time a series is on long enough to rack up 261 episodes, there's a good chance lots of subjects will be treated in nuanced, rounded ways. Second, I now see that the definitions of religion I used to frame my inquiry treat religion as an immaterial idea, a collocation of terms like "arbiter" and "system of symbols" and "cultural form" and "belief" and even "neurosis" (Clanton 2012: 90–91).[2] While these make fine definitions in the abstract, I now think they're not as helpful as analytical tools as they should be. Religion is a multi-valent, splendiferous thing that defies our nebulous attempts to pin it down. Whenever we think we have, religion finds a way to spill out the sides and overflow from whatever conceptual box we've placed it in. More than anything, though, religion is a *lived* phenomenon. Any attempt to capture the essence and/or function of religion that doesn't pay attention to how real, flesh-and-blood people live out/enact their beliefs misses a vital *performative* aspect to what it means to talk about religious identity (see Mikva 2018: esp. p. 132; and Bell 1998).

This is the argument that sociologist Meredith B. McGuire makes in her 2008 book, *Lived Religion: Faith and Practice in Everyday Life*. Right from the beginning, she claims that "standard notions of religion [like the ones I used] are wholly inadequate" (4, cf. 12). Then, she suggests that "we think of religion, at the individual level, as an ever-changing, multifaceted, often messy—even contradictory—amalgam of beliefs and practices that are not necessarily those religious institutions consider important" (4). That is, instead of focusing on how scholars or even religious institutions feel religious folk ought to behave, we should accept that people's views and practices and contexts and identities change. As such, "At the level of the individual, religion is not fixed, unitary, or even coherent. We should expect that all persons' religious practices and the stories with which they make sense of their lives are always changing, adapting, and growing" (12).

McGuire's focus on "individuals' religions, as lived in a particular time and cultural setting," helps her to understand **lived religion** as "the actual experience of religious persons," as opposed to "the prescribed religion of institutionally defined beliefs and practices" (12). However, McGuire warns us not to think of this "lived religion" as solely individual or subjective or nothing more than a "frame of mind." Instead, she reminds us that "people construct their religious worlds together, often sharing vivid experiences of that intersubjective reality," and that these worlds and experience need not be "logically coherent" as long as they're practically coherent for the individual (12 and 15). Put differently, McGuire argues that "individual religion is ... fundamentally social" as well as "embodied," meaning that the performance of one's religious identity finds expression in various social groupings and is made manifest via what one wears on, takes into, and generally does with one's body (13).

At this point, it's helpful for us to take a moment to revisit McGuire's claim that "all persons' religious practices ... are always changing, adapting, and growing." A few years after her book was released, the Pew Research Center published the results of its massive Religious Landscape Study, which, according to its website, "surveys more than 35,000 Americans from all 50 states about their religious affiliations, beliefs and practices, and social and political views."[3] Two of the most surprising and (for some) jarring findings in the Study were that the number of respondents who identify with traditional religions is declining, while respondents who identified with no religious tradition (aka the **"nones"**) rose dramatically between 2007 and 2014. These trends have continued, as can be seen in the results from a new Gallup poll released at the end of March 2021. That poll indicated "religious membership in the U.S. has fallen to just 47% among those surveyed—representing less than half of the adult population for the first time since Gallup began asking the question more than 80 years ago" (Neuman 2021).

There are a number of potential causes for these findings from Pew and Gallup. For example, in their work focusing on those who choose to be "nonreligious," Joel Thiessen and Sarah Wilkins-Laflamme write that,

> In the larger social context currently found in the United States, Canada, and Europe ... religion has lost much of its social authority and relevance, there is greater religious diversity than in the past, there is what is often seen as a competing scientific worldview, and individualism is rampant.
>
> (2020: 41)

Similarly, but more specifically focused on the U.S., Conrad Ostwalt argues,

> When religion loses its privileged position in society through disestablishment, as was the case in America, then religion is forced to compete not only against other religions but also against other cultural forms. So in American society, religion has found itself in the position of wooing its clients for allegiance, often against rival suitors as diverse as Friday night dates and Sunday afternoon football games.
>
> (2012: 42)

This competition is predicated on the idea that people can now make volitional choices regarding their religious identity, i.e., they no longer have to go along with whatever faith in which they were socialized or reared. Given these conditions, humans now have a plethora of choices before them as they try to decide on what McGuire called the "religious practices and the stories with which they make sense of their lives," even if those "religious practices" don't fall into commonly accepted religious traditions.

For Ostwalt, these practices and choices can include opting for cultural forms (such as sports or films or literature or social groupings like fandom) that *function* religiously for the person experiencing/embodying them. That is, "we can think about literature, film, music, art, and other cultural products, along with traditional religious structures and new religious groups, as vehicles that carry and transport our religious longings, rituals, and beliefs" (2012: 33). In sum, the rise of the "nones" coupled with the loss of adherents. Traditional religious groupings led to a reevaluation of religious identity in which it became clear that the search for meaning and relationships hadn't ceased; rather, it had found new outlets of expression, whether those were found in cultural/aesthetic products or alternative social groupings. In the wake of these seismic shifts in American religion it seems clear we need a different way to talk about religious identity.

One example of a new way to do this is found in Rachel B. Gross's 2021 book, *Beyond the Synagogue: Jewish Nostalgia as Religious Practice.* Her main argument—which echoes Ostwalt's—is that,

> American Jews participate in a broad array of ostensibly nonreligious activities—including visiting Jewish historic sites, conducting genealogical research, purchasing books and toys that teach Jewish nostalgia to children, and seeking out traditional Jewish foods—that are properly understood as religious.
>
> (4)[4]

Gross understands "religion" in a broad sense, writing that it is "best understood as meaningful relationships and the practices, narratives, and emotions that create and support these relationships" (6). Viewing religion in this relational way allows Gross to "see the significance of purportedly secular activities and organizations," that is, to "consider how individuals who do not regard themselves as 'religious' make meaning in their lives, as well as how those who do see themselves as religious find meaning outside of traditional practices" (6). This consideration is best done, Gross argues, through the "lived religion" approach I just mentioned, as it "focuses our attention on the ways in which people enact their religious identities on a daily basis, through ordinary activities such as eating, cooking, shopping, reading, or entertaining" (7). Focusing on these activities, Gross finds evidence that problematizes the Pew Study findings and belies the concerns among some Jewish scholars that Judaism in America is in crisis. According to her, both the Study and these Jewish scholars focus too narrowly on traditional and institutional models of Jewish religiosity, models that pay attention to markers of Jewish identity and practice like synagogue attendance, ritual observances, intermarriage, and public engagement with Jewish topics like the Holocaust and the state of Israel (Gross 8–12).[5] If some of these sound familiar, then you've been paying attention; I used a few of these same characteristics in my first attempt to gauge Howard's Jewish identity in *The Big Bang Theory* (See Clanton 2013). And Gross would critique my approach for being too narrow, for attending to institutional affiliation instead of material culture, for counting references to Jewish ritual practices instead of the number of briskets Howard's mother makes him, for imposing a concept of Jewish identity from the top down instead of listening to how Howard himself constructs a way of being Jewish that's meaningful for him.[6]

In order to demonstrate why I think the "lived religion" approach is more helpful in understanding Howard's Jewish identity, I'm going to give an example of my old approach, then an example of this new one. And because we can't discuss everything, we'll focus on one specific trope in the series: food.

Case Study

Examining food in *The Big Bang Theory* is a "gimme." That is, it seems as if a majority of scenes in the series take place during meals, whether in the apartment of the two main characters, Leonard and Sheldon; the cafeteria at the University where all the male characters work; or at The Cheesecake Factory, where the main female character, Penny, worked in the early seasons. In all of these locales, mention is made of Howard's culinary choices. This interest in the connection between Howard's religious identity as a Jew and his dietary decisions isn't limited to this specific television series. As Jonathan and Judith Pearl note, "The most prominently featured 'Jewish symbol' on television has been Jewish food," and *The Big Bang Theory* is no different (1999: 55). So, I thought, here's a great opportunity to gauge Howard's Jewish identity using a common trope surrounding Jews and television. Surely how the series talks about and shows Howard interacting with traditional Jewish customs regarding food will tell me a lot about his Jewish identity, right? What follows is how I saw it at first.

I noted that the series takes pains to establish Howard as a Jew but is equally insistent that his Judaism isn't defined by *kashrut*, which is the name used to refer to the complex of dietary laws and restrictions that are present in the Torah and that have been augmented by rabbis and leaders in the past, and today. Common restrictions for "eating kosher" or following these rules include not eating pork or shellfish, and not eating milk or milk-products (like cheese) and meat at the same meal. I focused on four specific examples—from a very large pool—to prove this claim: three superficial ones and one I felt was more revealing.

(1) In an episode titled "The Griffin Equivalency," everyone—as is common in the series—is eating Chinese food. Leonard asks, "Who was the shrimp with lobster sauce?" Howard responds, "That would be me. Come to papa, you un-kosher delight!"[7]

(2) In Season 3, Sheldon is stuck on a physics problem, so he decides to take a menial job that will allow his higher brain functions to work in the background. His choice: server at the Cheesecake Factory where Penny worked then. As he serves Howard his food, he notes, "Alright, one bacon cheeseburger, breaking two Jewish dietary restrictions simultaneously. Kudos." Howard then makes an appreciative gesture.[8]

(3) In a later episode, while eating Chinese food, the fourth main male character Raj—Howard's best friend and an astrophysicist from India—asks Howard, "Do you believe you're going to hell for eating sweet and sour pork?" Howard replies, "Jews don't have hell. We have acid reflux."[9]

These humorous, if superficial, exchanges aside, one of the scenes I thought was especially telling regarding food takes place between Howard and Raj. In an episode titled "The Financial Permeability," everyone is preparing to eat Chinese food (again) when Leonard tells Howard, "You owe me another two dollars. The price of moo shu pork went up." Howard sighs and replies, "It's getting tougher and tougher to be a bad Jew." Later, Howard complains that "This moo shu pork's burning a hole through my duodenum." Raj replies, "Tsk tsk tsk. Leviticus 11:3: 'Only that which parteth the hoof and cheweth the cud among the beasts shall ye eat'."[10] Looking grumpy and holding his stomach, Howard retorts, "Hey, do I mock you with the Bhagavad Gita every time you scarf down a Whopper?"[11] Not to over-explain the joke here, but Howard's naming a Hindu text and reminding Raj that traditional Hinduism would forbid him to eat beef.

In my research, I then argued that these four examples show us three things about Wolowitz and his Jewishness. First, it's obvious that dietary restrictions don't define Howard's Jewish identity in any kind of routine way, except perhaps in a negative fashion, i.e., the fact that he doesn't regularly adhere to *kashrut* is highlighted as a way of indicating that the series playfully casts him as a "bad Jew." Second, I claimed that the fact that Raj, a Hindu, is able to quote the Leviticus passage regarding food from memory, whereas Howard's response implies he's unaware of that specific text, portrays Raj as being more knowledgeable about Jewish texts and Law than Howard. Finally, I argued that even though these examples might lead one to conceive of Howard's Judaism as devoid of any gastronomical content, it seems that he's both proud of and informed about traditional Jewish dishes, such as *kreplachs*,[12] the mythical "tur-briska-fil,"[13]—a turkey stuffed with a brisket stuffed with gefilte fish—and his mother's famous brisket.[14] Additionally, I claimed, Howard does keep kosher during the High Holy Days, a fact that perhaps mitigates his self-description as a "bad Jew."[15] In conclusion, I posited, there's more evidence that Howard's Jewish background runs deeper than one might expect, but precious little data that implies that background is anything more than minimally determinative for his actions.

From the perspective of "lived religion," I now see I made several unhelpful assumptions. The most important of these is that I presumed there's a prescriptive reality that all Jews should attend to regarding food regulations—some sort of historically unconditioned notion of *kashrut*—when in reality Jews construct their identities in multiple ways surrounding food based on multiple contexts, identities, and affiliations (like culinary heritage or veganism or one's view on environmental sustainability). Scholars like Jenna Weissman Joselit have demonstrated how American Jews have creatively disentangled then re-entangled themselves with the ideas and practices behind *kashrut* based on factors like geography, economics, the "scientific" approach to food preparation, and the dividing line between private and public identities and practices (see especially Joselit 1994: 171–218). So, I shouldn't have been surprised that even though Howard dines out on bacon cheeseburgers, he also keeps kosher during the High Holy Days, as I mention above.[16] And I certainly shouldn't have used his food practices to make claims regarding his level of Jewishness.

Bringing us back to our new focus, Marie W. Dallam helpfully connects our emphasis on food with the "lived religion" approach I discussed earlier. She writes,

> In recent decades scholars have embraced the fact that a real understanding of American religious phenomena cannot focus only on doctrines, leaders, and institutions but must also include the vernacular beliefs and practices of members. In other words, the study of religion now includes studying *lived practices* in addition to the ideals put forth as official teachings and official behaviors. The study of religious foodways is a clear example of this new approach to comprehending history and culture.
>
> (2014: xix; my emphasis)

A focus on how Jewish foodways function to inform and define Howard's Jewishness, then, allows us to understand how his identity is constructed not from any external criteria (these would include Dallam's "doctrines, leaders, and institutions") but instead from his own location, contexts, and practices.

To demonstrate what a "lived religion" approach to Howard and food might look like, let's focus on an episode from Season 8 called "The Leftover Thermalization."[17] Three episodes earlier in this Season, Howard's mother unexpectedly dies on a trip to Florida, and evidently is cremated there, since two episodes earlier the airline loses her ashes,[18] prompting Howard to have a near-anxiety attack.[19] In our episode, the power goes out at Howard's Mom's house, and Howard is horrified that all the food in their freezer will be ruined, as it's "the last food my mother ever made."[20] So, he decides to invite everyone over for one last meal ("It'll be like Ma's feeding us one last time") that serves as a kind of makeshift, secularized, yet poignant *shivah*, a commemorative, collective exercise in mourning (see, e.g., Dosick 1995: 308–310).

The episode is both touching and funny, and most of the jokes revolve around the tropes I mention above, especially food as a marker of Jewish identity. For example, as he's cleaning out the freezer, he discovers that his Mom saved a piece of cake from his Bar-mitzvah. Howard's wife Bernadette asks if his mother ever threw anything away, and Howard remarks, "If I find my foreskin, I'm gonna kill myself." Again, Raj is listing all the food, including "three briskets, four meat loafs, one lasagna," but Howard corrects him, "No, that's noodle kugel." Raj responds, "Okay, Jewish lasagna," and continues, "Two pound cakes that are about eight pounds each, and one giant container of matzo ball soup." At the mention of the soup, Howard wistfully notes, "Ma always kept some on hand in case I got sick. She thought she could cure anything with her cooking." Howard has a very difficult time with all this, and at one point whimpers, "I'm never gonna talk to her again." Instead of focusing on his despair, though—this is, after all, a sit*com*—Howard reiterates his desire to host everyone, and the episode moves on to funnier material. For example, when Leonard and Penny arrive, Penny remarks how pretty the house looks when lit by candlelight. Stuart comments, "Yeah, turns out half a dozen menorahs really sets a mood." Again, once everyone arrives, Howard reminds everyone that "tonight's not a sad occasion." Bernadette adds, "We just want to have the kind of dinner that we've all had here so many times before," after which Howard quips, "Good food, good friends, and sometime around midnight heartburn that makes you pray for death." True to their word, the dinner is a happy time, at which talk turns to (you guessed it) comic books and popular culture. Even when a previous argument between Leonard and Sheldon breaks out again at the table, it's handled in a humorous way. Bernadette orders them into the living room and scolds them off-camera in a voice that obviously mimics Howard's late mother.[21] The episode even ends with a biblical pun: after dinner, everyone is resting in the living room, and Penny notes that she doesn't think she's ever eaten that much. Howard responds, "That's why my people wandered the desert for forty years: took that long to walk it off."

What does this episode tell us about Howard's Jewish identity from a "lived religion" perspective? First, it's obvious how deeply meaningful and intimate Howard's relationship with his mother was. Since Howard's father left them when Howard was only 11 and he was almost completely raised by her, this shouldn't be too surprising. This is something I noted in my previous research, and I also pointed out the long history of Jewish mothers in popular culture and how they've been stereotyped for comedic effect.[22] However, I also made reference to Howard's intense affection and appreciative devotion for his mother, and this leads us to our second point. Howard's emotional connection to his mother is bound up with their domestic religious practice.[23] True, Howard is a member of a synagogue, but not a regular attendee.[24] Instead, when the series shows us Howard's Judaism, it's mostly focused on the house he's shared with his mother. This all leads to the third and most important point of this episode: when Howard mourns his mother, he does so not in the context of a funeral or a formal *shiva*; he does so in her house through the consumption of clearly Jewish food she cooked which he shares with his social community of friends and family while he reminisces and recalls her lovingly. That is, Howard's deep appreciation and love for his mother is demonstrated through his engagement with the food she prepared and preserved for him in their home. As Gross explains,

> American Jewish foodways provide individuals with a sense of community and belonging across time and space. In keeping with broader understandings of religious practice as meaning-making activities, it becomes clear that American Jewish cuisine is an example of *lived religion*, activities that practitioners might not recognize as religious but that provide meaningful structures to their lives. Preparing and eating certain types of food places American Jews in a nostalgic network of sacred relationships with family members, friends, and coreligionists living and dead, historical and mythical.
>
> (2021: 158; my emphasis)

Gross's claim here resonates strongly with what we're shown in this episode. Howard's nostalgic commemoration of his mother in the company of family and friends functions religiously, as it serves to preserve those relationships Gross mentions through the medium of Jewish foodways. Put differently, instead of treating Howard's consumption of food from an "**etic**" or outsider vantage point of some supposed authority on how Jews *should* be eating in order to be *properly* religious in the abstract, it's more helpful for us to focus on how Howard (and his mother) constructs his own Jewish identity. And it's clear from this example that he places enormous value on and finds meaning in "the organic Jewish connection ... between food, family, domesticity, and identity," as he demonstrates what he treasures in *his* Jewish practice (Joselit 1994: 217).

Conclusion

In his critique of my first attempt to understand Howard's Jewish identity, Noah Berlatsky makes a point that helped me to recognize the shortcomings of my approach. He wrote, "There are lots of different ways to be Jewish" (2019). Berlatsky's point sounds simple, but it reminded me that a top-down approach to gauging religious identity is not especially helpful. That approach assumes that there's some sort of agreed-upon concrete standard or accepted list of practices/observances against which we can measure Howard's Judaism. And as we've seen, this isn't the case. It's much more helpful, then, to approach the issue of Howard's Judaism through the lens of "lived religion," as this takes seriously the ways in which individuals construct and conceptualize their own religious thought, beliefs, and practices—which may or may not include traditional religious observances, attendance, or ideologies. Doing so helps us understand not only Howard's religious identity as a 21st-century American Jew; it also helps us make sense of the enormous changes to both the concept of "religion" and to our world.

Summary

- In order for scholarship to advance, it's both okay and expected for scholars to change their minds about their work. If you discover a different or better approach to your data, then you can take a second or third look at it.
- Adherence to traditional religious identities is declining, and more people are self-identifying with "none of the above" in terms of religious identity.
- This decline and the rise of the "nones" is causing us to reevaluate how we understand and think about "religion."
- A "lived religion" approach is more useful in examining religious identity than an approach that assumes standards and ideals that don't actually exist.
- Applying a "lived religion" approach to *The Big Bang Theory* helps us understand Howard's Jewish identity as he constructs it, as opposed to how the more traditional, authoritarian, and restrictive approaches I mention above might prescribe it to be.

Discussion Questions/Activities

(1) What are some ways that you see "lived religion" in your own context (family, school, community, etc.)?
(2) Are there activities in which you engage that you'd consider "religious"? If so, why would you call them "religious"?
(3) Speaking of "religion," do you think it's possible for religion to be portrayed in depth in a television series? In the case of *Big Bang Theory*,

can a show constructed around the genre of a serialized, episodic television show beholden to advertising monies depict religion adequately? If so, what are some examples? If not, why not?

(4) Let's talk about stereotypes. In his critique of my work, Berlatsky also pointed out that "Howard is a Jewish stereotype [and] a bigoted trope" (2019). Jane Arnold claims that "stereotypes (like caricatures) are not necessarily inaccurate descriptions; they are simply unbalanced. Stereotypes might be described as the distilled essence of the public perception of particular groups of people" (1987: 275). Certainly the characterization of Howard includes persistent stereotypes about Jewish men, but the series includes an impressive 279 episodes. Surely over such a long period Howard has gained far more depth than simply a stereotypical Jewish man. Even so, Berlatsky's comment reminds us that we need to be aware of such stereotypes and the harm that a caricatured performance inflicts on popular understandings of Jews in television and film. So, have you seen stereotypical Jewish characters on television or in film? What made you think they were stereotypes? What other stereotypes can you think of in television and film? Is Arnold's description of "stereotypes" too mild? Why or why not?

(5) Here's an idea for your own research project. Using the "lived religion" approach I describe above, gather, synthesize, and hypothesize about data from *The Big Bang Theory* dealing with the Christian religious identity of Sheldon's mother Mary. You should pay special attention to her dialogue and actions in episodes like "The Maternal Combustion" (Season 8, Episode 182; originally aired 4-30-15); "The Convergence Convergence" (Season 9, Episode 207; originally aired 5-12-16); and "The Holiday Summation" (Season 10, Episode 219; originally aired 1-5-17).

Glossary

Etic A term used to indicate an analysis of a culture or phenomenon from an external point of view, i.e., an analysis performed by someone outside of a culture, who doesn't share in the practices or history or worldview(s) within that culture. Its opposite is "emic," which would designate an internal analysis. For example, if I wrote about football (American or otherwise) it would *definitely* be from an "etic" point of view, since I do not play.

Lived Religion as defined by Meredith McGuire, "the actual experience of religious persons." That is, the spectrum of beliefs and behaviors real people enact in order to demonstrate their religious identity, which may or may not include actions and ways of thinking prescribed by traditional religions.

Nones a term used to designate those who chose "none of the above" when asked to identify their religious affiliation on the Pew Religious

Landscape Study in 2014. The steep rise of the "Nones" is an indication of the changing face of "religion" in the U.S., and—along with the decline in mainline Christian denominations—means we need to rethink how we understand "religion."

Religion   A term of great elasticity, it is understood in the essay above as a spectrum of cultural forms, practices, and/or beliefs geared to the maintenance of a series of relationships along two axes, a vertical one (that cultivates ties with the sacred, the divine, gods or God) and a horizontal one (that tends to relationships with other humans, past, present, and future).

Religious Identity   A term used to describe the way(s) in which individuals self-identify with one or more of the cultural forms, practices, and/or beliefs that are understood as "religion" (see above). This identity is culturally and historically conditioned, and intersects with other attributes such as gender, sex, and racial identity (a collocation of features that are expressed in the term "intersectionality"; see *Keeping It 101: A Killjoy's Introduction to Religion* [2020]).

Sitcom   A genre of television, the "situation comedy" is one of the central forms of televisual expression. An episodic, most commonly serialized, exploration of a single or multiple contexts (or situations) from a comedic point of view (comedy here meaning both physical and cerebral humor) that can also explore more serious topics. Jane Feuer calls this "the most basic program format known to the medium" of television (1992: 109–110). Feuer goes on to list the sitcom's "salient features: the half-hour format, the basis in humor, the 'problem of the week' that causes the hilarious situation and that will be resolved so that a new episode may take its place the next week." John Hartley further dissects "sitcom" into "two main types [viz.] the drama of family comportment (often mixed with sibling rivalry) and the drama of sexual exploration. The former was routinely set in a home environment, the latter in the workplace" (2015: 96–98, 97). As this chapter explains, *The Big Bang Theory* hybridizes those settings, "joining family comportment (living together, couch-centric) and workplace (sexual exploration, flirt-centric) as other classic sitcoms such as *Friends* and *Seinfeld* did (Hartley 2015: 98).

Notes

1 I presented this research first at the Rocky Mountain/Great Plains Regional AAR/SBL Meeting in April 2013. I was then lucky enough to publish part of that paper under the title "The (Not-So) Jewish Tao of Howard Wolowitz" (Clanton 2013). More recently, I updated my research and presented it at the Annual Conference of the Popular Culture Association/American Culture Association in April 2017.

2 These terms come from the definitions of Rita M. Gross, Clifford Geertz, Conrad Ostwalt, E.B. Tylor, and Sigmund Freud, respectively.

3 The results of this Study can be found online at https://www.pewforum.org/religious-landscape-study/

4 Surprisingly, Gross doesn't use or mention Ostwalt's work in her book, even though the similarities are obvious.

5 Gross doesn't directly address the Pew Study, but her comments on other researchers are nonetheless applicable.

6 More immediately, my claims were (rightly and helpfully) critiqued by Berlatsky (2019). Berlatsky's comments prompted much reflection on my part and ultimately led me to the reevaluation in this chapter.

7 "The Griffin Equivalency," (Season 2, Episode 21; originally aired 10-13-08). Following this, Howard, as he is wont to do early in the series, tries to flirt with Penny, saying, "I'm not necessarily talking to the food." In Season 8, we also learn that Mrs. Wolowitz has a fondness for shellfish, as Howard mentions that she loves to eat shrimp at Benihana. See "The Prom Equivalency" (Season 8, Episode 167; originally aired 11-6-14).

8 "The Einstein Approximation," (Season 3, Episode 54; originally aired 2-1-10).

9 "The Spaghetti Catalyst," (Season 3, Episode 60; originally aired 5-3-10). Obviously, there's much more to be said regarding the Jewish practice of eating Chinese food. The early history of this connection is explored in Joselit, 1994: 214–215.

10 An abridgement and misquotation of the King James Version translation of the Bible. The full text reads, "Whatsoever parteth the hoof, and is clovenfooted, and cheweth the cud, among the beasts, that shall ye eat."

11 "The Financial Permeability," (Season 2; Episode 31; originally aired 2-2-09).

12 In "The Panty Piñata Polarization," (Season 2; Episode 24; originally aired 11-10-08), the guys are playing Klingon Boggle, and Howard calls out the word "kreplach." Raj objects, noting, "That isn't Klingon. It's Yiddish for 'meat-filled dumpling." Weakly, Howard responds, "Well, as it turns out, it's also a Klingon word [meaning] a hearty Klingon dumpling."

13 From "The Pirate Solution," (Season 3, Episode 44; originally aired 10-12-09).

14 References to Mrs. Wolowitz's brisket are too numerous to recount. One of the most amusing appearances of Mrs. Wolowitz's most famous dish is in "The Adhesive Duck Deficiency," (Season 3, Episode 48; originally aired 11-16-09). Howard, Leonard and Raj go out to the desert to watch a meteor shower, but wind up eating pot-laced brownies they're given by some fellow campers. At one point, their hunger almost overwhelms them, but Howard discovers his mother has wisely packed an extra brisket.

15 Also in "The Panty Piñata Polarization," Penny recounts Howard's order at The Cheesecake Factory: "Shrimp Caesar salad with no almonds for the highly allergic, kosher-only-on-the-High-Holidays Howard."

16 In "The Panty Piñata Polarization," Penny recounts Howard's order at The Cheesecake Factory: "Shrimp Caesar salad with no almonds for the highly allergic, kosher-only-on-the-High-Holidays Howard."

17 Season 8, Episode 177; originally aired 3-12-15.

18 Her ashes are lost in "The Intimacy Acceleration" (Season 8, Episode 175; originally aired 2-26-15). This in and of itself is of interest to us, as it shows Howard's mother is cremated, not given what we think of as a "traditional" Jewish burial. There is also a continuity error here, as in "The Vacation Solution" (Season 5, Episode 103; originally aired 2-9-12), Howard mentions that, "Ma and I have a primo double cemetery plot at Mount Sinai [presumably a Jewish cemetery] right near the guy who played Mr. Roper on *Three's Company*."

19 Mrs. Wolowitz dies in "The Comic Book Store Regeneration" (Season 8, Episode 174; originally aired 2-19-15). The character of Mrs. Wolowitz was written out of the show after the death of Carol Ann Susi in November 2014. Susi provided Mrs. Wolowitz's inimitable voice, as she virtually never appeared on-screen and was instead simply heard. In "The Comic Book Store Regeneration," as Howard and Bernadette leave for Florida, the rest of the cast share memories of

Mrs. Wolowitz then have a collective farewell and toast to her memory. And it is hard to avoid the impression that the actors themselves aren't thinking of Susi in this moment.

20 This is obviously before Howard and his wife Bernadette move into his dead mother's house, which happens in the subsequent episode in Season 8, "The Skywalker Incursion" (Season 8, Episode 178; originally aired 4-2-15).

21 Howard even asks his remaining dinner guests if they've ever noticed that Bernadette sounds like his mother, to which they all reply in the negative, feeling very uncomfortable. This isn't the first time the series has made this humorous, if somewhat Oedipal connection. See also "The Habitation Configuration," (Season 6; Episode 118; originally aired 11-8-12).

22 As is well known, literature, television, and film have long portrayed Jewish mothers as affectionately overbearing, lovingly controlling, and compassionately critical towards their sons especially. One of the best cinematic examples of this trend is found in Woody Allen's short film "Oedipus Wrecks," contained in *New York Stories* (1989), along with short films by Martin Scorsese and Francis Ford Coppola. Since its debut in 2013, the ABC series *The Goldbergs* has provided viewers with a textbook Jewish "smother" in the character of Beverly Goldberg. In his work, Zurawik describes these portrayals as "the castrating Jewish mother," (2003: 84) while Antler bemoans the "tired stereotypes of possessive, manipulating Jewish mothers" (2000: 53).

23 In "The Zarnecki Incursion" (Season 4, Episode 82; originally aired 3-31-11), Sheldon wants Howard and Raj to go somewhere with him right away, but Howard says he can't go, since "Tonight's the Sabbath and my mother and I have a tradition of lighting the candles and watching *Wheel of Fortune*." More generally, the set of Mrs. Wolowitz's (and later Howard and Bernadette's) house is filled with Jewish objects and *tchotchkes*.

24 In "The Friendship Contraction," (Season 5, Episode 102; originally aired 2-2-12), Howard proudly shows Leonard and Raj a press release from NASA announcing his upcoming trip to the ISS, and notes, "This is going right into my synagogue's newsletter."

Further Reading

Clanton, Jr., Dan W. (2013). "The (Not-So) Jewish Tao of Howard Wolowitz." *Moment Magazine*. Posted on 1 May 2013. Online at http://www.momentmag. com/the-not-so-jewish-tao-of-howard-wolowitz/
This is an abridged version of my first attempt to synthesize my conclusions about Howard's Jewish identity. The above essay refers to this attempt and explains why I now feel it's not the most helpful way to approach the data from the series.

Gross, Rachel B. (2021). *Beyond the Synagogue: Jewish Nostalgia as Religious Practice*. New York: New York University Press.
Gross's book explores the idea that activities most people would consider non-religious actually function religiously for American Jews. In separate chapters, she examines topics like genealogical research, heritage tourism, the transformation in Jewish delis, and purchasing products for children. All of these, she claims, are evidence of a nostalgia for an Eastern European Jewish past and should be seen as examples of lived religious practices.

McGuire, Meredith B. (2008). *Lived Religion: Faith and Practice in Everyday Life*. New York & Oxford: Oxford University Press.
McGuire's book is a key resource for those interested in the approach I advocate in the above essay. Her work is sociological in its foundation, and she examines

groups (Latinos, Latinas, and southern white Evangelical Christians in the U.S.); bodily religious practices; and the impact of gender as examples of how individuals collect and synthesize their own forms of "invisible religion."

Ostwalt, Conrad (2012). *Secular Steeples: Popular Culture and the Religious Imagination*. 2nd Edition. London & New York: Bloomsbury.

This work has been central in my own understanding of the reciprocal relationship between religion and (popular) culture. Ostwalt argues for two trends in contemporary society: one in which traditional religious institutions adopt/implement secular forms and practices ("secularization of the sacred"), and another in which secular cultural forms take on the function historically located within religious traditions ("sacralization of the secular"). Implicit in these trends are a number of assumptions and claims about the pervasiveness of our human search for meaning despite the fact that traditional religions seem to be in decline.

Bibliography

Antler, Joyce (2000). "Not 'Too Jewish' for Prime Time." Pages 23–88 in Neal Gabler, Frank Rich, and Joyce Antler, *Television's Changing Image of American Jews*. New York: The American Jewish Committee and The Normal Lear Center.

Arnold, Jane (1987). "Detecting Social History: Jews in the Works of Agatha Christie." *Jewish Social Studies* 49, 3/4:275–282.

Bell, Catherine (1998). "Performance." Pages 205–224 in *Critical Terms for Religious Studies*. Edited by Mark C. Taylor. Chicago & London: Chicago University Press.

Berlatsky, Noah (2019). "The Loosey-Goosey Judaism of Howard Wolowitz." *Splice Today*. Posted 21 May 2019. Online at https://www.splicetoday.com/moving-pictures/the-loosey-goosey-judaism-of-howard-wolowitz

Clanton, Jr., Dan W. (2012). "On the Job and among the Elect: Religion and the Salvation of Sipowicz in *NYPD Blue*." Pages 89–103 in *Understanding Religion and Popular Culture*. Edited by Terry Ray Clark and Dan W. Clanton, Jr. London & New York: Routledge.

——— (2013). "The (Not-So) Jewish Tao of Howard Wolowitz." *Moment Magazine*. Posted on 1 May 2013. Online at http://www.momentmag.com/the-not-so-jewish-tao-of-howard-wolowitz/

Dallam, Marie W. (2014). "Introduction: Religion, Food, and Eating." Pages xvii–xxxii in *Religion, Food, and Eating in North America*. Edited by Benjamin E. Zeller, Marie W. Dallam, Reid L. Neilson, and Nora L. Rubel. Arts and Traditions of the Table: Perspectives on Culinary History. New York: Columbia University Press.

Dosick, Wayne (1995). *Living Judaism: The Complete Guide to Jewish Belief, Tradition, and Practice*. New York: HarperCollins.

Feuer, Jane (1992). "Genre Study and Television." Pages 104–120 in *Channels of Discourse, Reassembled: Television and Contemporary Criticism*. 2nd Edition. Edited by Robert C. Allen. New York & London: Routledge.

Gross, Rachel B. (2021). *Beyond the Synagogue: Jewish Nostalgia as Religious Practice*. New York: New York University Press.

Hartley, John (2015). "Situation Comedy, Part 1." Pages 96–98 in *The Television Genre Book*. 3rd Edition. Edited by Glen Creeber. New York & London: Palgrave Macmillan & British Film Institute.

Joselit, Jenna Weissman (1994). *The Wonders of America: Reinventing Jewish Culture, 1880–1950*. New York: Henry Holt and Company.

Keeping It 101: A Killjoy's Introduction to Religion (2020). "Intersectionality" (Episode 202). Posted 16 September 2020). Online at https://keepingit101.com/e202

McGuire, Meredith B. (2008). *Lived Religion: Faith and Practice in Everyday Life.* New York & Oxford: Oxford University Press.

Mikva, Rachel S. (2018). "Six Issues that Complicate Interreligious Studies and Engagement." Pages 124–136 in *Interreligious/Interfaith Studies: Defining a New Field.* Edited by Eboo Patel, Jennifer Howe Peace, and Noah J. Silverman. Boston: Beacon Press.

Neuman, Scott (2021). "Fewer Than Half of U.S. Adults Belong to a Religious Congregation, New Poll Shows." *NPR.* Posted 30 March 2021. Online: https://www.npr.org/2021/03/30/982671783/fewer-than-half-of-u-s-adults-belong-to-a-religious-congregation-new-poll-shows

Ostwalt, Conrad (2012). *Secular Steeples: Popular Culture and the Religious Imagination.* 2nd Edition. London & New York: Bloomsbury.

Pearl, Jonathan and Judith (1999). *The Chosen Image: Television's Portrayal of Jewish Themes and Characters.* Jefferson, NC & London: McFarland & Company.

Thiessen, Joel and Sarah Wilkins-Laflamme (2020). *None of the Above: Nonreligious Identity in the US and Canada.* Secular Studies. New York: New York University Press.

Zurawik, David (2003). *The Jews of Prime Time.* Brandeis Series in American Jewish History, Culture, and Life. Lebanon, NH/Hanover & London: Brandeis University Press/University Press of New England.

12 Popular Music with Biblical Themes

FKA twigs' *MAGDALENE* and the Liberating Power of Myth

Siobhán Jolley

Introduction

As a music fan and biblical scholar, there is little that I find more exciting than listening to new tracks and recognizing names, images and stories that have companions in the Bible. Fortunately for me, Gilmour (2017: 76) is only slightly hyperbolic in his assertion that "the sounds of the Bible are all over popular music and its influence on that art form is inestimable." Despite this, popular music receives far less systematic scholarly attention in the field of biblical reception studies than visual arts, film and literature. I, too, am guilty of this faux pas—most of my work and training is in visual reception. However, as someone who enjoys playing a range of musical instruments and who listens to music for several hours of most days, it was probably inevitable that I would eventually write this chapter. I have a particular love for the art of the long play album (which streaming services and shuffled playlists threaten to overshadow). Even though this digital revolution means I am more selective about when I purchase a physical copy of a record or CD, I still enjoy setting aside time to listen to a full album straight through for the first time. My primary research focus, alongside reception, is Mary Magdalene, and so when my eclectic musical tastes led me to FKA twigs' 2019 album *MAGDALENE*, my attention was unavoidably piqued. I hope, however, that this is more than pure self-indulgence![1] Musicologists—including Gilmour (2005)—have demonstrated variously that religion is key to the analysis of the way in which popular music interacts with culture more broadly. With this significant connection in mind, this chapter will consider how analysis of the reception of the Bible in popular music can be generative for the study of the afterlives of biblical texts in our wider cultural sphere.

As Forbes (2017)—amongst others—has observed, defining what actually constitutes "popular" music is a task which demands increasing nuance. The demise of general "Top 40" charts into genre-specific measures, and the wide array of music made more accessible by the rise of streaming models, means that "pop" as a genre is no longer easily defined, nor necessarily the most popular! The formula offered by Nachbar and Lause (1992: 5), namely that "the popularity of a given cultural element [...] is directly proportional

DOI: 10.4324/9781003079729-14

to the degree to which that element is reflective of audience beliefs and values," is potentially instructive here. By this measure, popular music is any music that has mass appeal because of its coalescence with the beliefs, values, and norms of the audience. This chapter accordingly treats popular music as a category (in contrast with, for example, worship music) rather than a genre, though a case could well be made for genre specific study too.

The cultural reception of the Bible is communicated across a range of popular media in several modes, and the use of the Bible can be overt or latent. Overt examples demonstrate direct interface with biblical material that is intentional and are constructed with the connection in mind, as in Coolio's use of Psalm 23 in "Gangsta's Paradise"(1995).[2] Latent examples, by contrast, arise more from the enduring influence of Christianity on Western Culture in a broader sense, as appears to be the case in the eclectic blend of biblical images in Coldplay's "Viva La Vida" (2008).[3] Across both categories, the engagement can be indirect, encountering the text via its mythologized cultural expression rather than close reading of the text itself. Such indirect engagement is not necessarily latent, as demonstrated by Lady Gaga's "Judas" (2011). Whilst there is nothing latent about the way she evokes the biblical figure, it is also clear that this is not a direct **exegesis** of text, either.[4]

Mythologization, per Roland Barthes (1957), is useful as an interpretive key for conceptualizing how ideas, events and persons from the biblical texts are transmuted as they are culturally mediated in popular music. This chapter looks at one such example as a case study, the presence of the mythologized Mary Magdalene in FKA twigs' 2019 album, *MAGDALENE*. By exploring the interplay between biblical text, its reception, and the processes of mythologization, it will make the case that such music opens up new interpretive potential for encountering Christian texts, and that indirect and secular engagement with the Bible is nonetheless theologically generative.

Theory and Method

Religion is "much more than what happens during services or prayer times" (Clark 2006: 475). More, as Rycenga (2003: 338) has pointed out, the shared components of "performance and ritual" in the expression of popular music and religion means they are fruitful conversational partners. This chapter is concerned particularly with how the relationship between religion and popular culture is expressed using the Bible in "secular" music. It therefore takes a reception critical methodological approach. **Reception criticism**, as summarized by Morse (2014: 253), "describes a critical and creative practice that is concerned with the interpretation and influences of the Bible in the past as well as in the future." It is an umbrella term for the methodological approaches that seek to incorporate the hermeneutical process that is traditionally referred to as **"reception history"** alongside other non-historiographical methods which utilize reception.[5]

The fourfold typology of the interaction between religion and popular culture offered by Forbes (2017: 11–21) sets the parameters for any discussion of this nature with four categories:

(1) *Religion in popular culture*
(2) *Popular culture in religion*
(3) *Popular culture as religion*
(4) *Religion and popular culture in dialogue*

Substituting the word "religion" with "scripture" in this framework allows us to recognize how interaction between the Bible and popular culture might be modeled similarly. Any study of the Bible in popular music might fall into his first category; however, the reception critical method utilized here is equally characterized by dialogue between culture and scripture. It is important to note that any such approach is inherently situated but not inherently **ethnographic**. In his prelude to *Musicking*, Small (1998: 13) articulates the complex ways that music can be understood to be a dynamic confluence of several relationships, "between person and person, between individual and society, between humanity and the natural world and even perhaps the supernatural world." Accordingly, biblical reception expressed in popular music is highly subjective, and as dependent on the audience as it is on the composer and performer to make meaning.

Any form of reception typically entails the exegesis or adaptation of written material, the drawing together of cultural memory and traditions and the experience and insights of the creator. Traditions of interpretation and adaptation in reception of biblical texts frequently attach themselves to the text through mythologization. Mythologization, after Barthes (1957), is the process by which an object (including persons such as the Magdalene) is imbued with a cultural significance beyond its contextual meaning. The history of how the object came to represent this new idea is not immediately apparent, and so there is a risk that the new meaning is understood as objective truth (see Barthes, 1957: 113–117). In the case of Mary Magdalene, mythologization under patriarchy has developed the sparse accounts of her life in the canonical Gospels into a rich narrative of sexual sin and repentance, expressed in reception.

Edwards (2005: ix) has characterized popular culture as "in a constant state of retelling, reinterpreting and re-appropriating biblical stories, characters and figures," and understanding the relationship between myth and text is key to making sense of this mode of biblical literacy. One of the ways in which myth gains traction is through its cultural codification, including in works of biblical reception. As such, reception criticism necessarily critiques and analyses myth, which is received alongside the biblical source material. As Wyman Jr. (2020: 72) notes when appraising the role of the Bible in American culture, "The Bible that is floating around in popular culture often is not the Bible as text, word for word, steeped in history, at all." Works of reception are both influenced by and contribute to the process of mythologization and, as in the examples earlier, are frequently neither a straightforward reworking of a biblical narrative, nor a simple retelling of the stories of biblical figures.

Hutcheon (2006: xvi) describes such adaptation as "repetition without replication" and its analysis invites new insights into the biblical text it receives as well as the popular culture which frames the reception. As demonstrated by FKA twigs, the encounter with mythologized biblical texts can nonetheless be generative of new and resistant readings of texts made familiar through their popular afterlives. *MAGDALENE* offers an adaptation via awareness through culture, subverting tropes about gender and social expectation and repurposing Biblical ideas that are contingent in our Western cultural inheritance as tools for thinking with rather than given narratives.

FKA twigs' *MAGDALENE* and the Liberating Power of Myth

FKA twigs' critically acclaimed second album, *MAGDALENE*, is named for and inspired by the biblical figure of the same name and addresses broader ideas about gender and sexuality. However, analysis of the lyrics and twigs' commentary reveals a Mary Magdalene that is only loosely aligned with the woman described in the Gospels. This chapter uses *MAGDALENE* as a lens through which to explore the complicated relationship between scripture and myth borne out in reception. It will argue that, despite various attempts to the contrary, mythologization is inherently part of the feminist conceptualization of the Magdalene, and cements her enduring interest and relevance in popular culture.

Tahlia Barnett, releasing music under the name FKA twigs since 2012, is a musical polyglot; her contemporary electronic pop veers effortlessly from opera to jazz via hip-hop without second thought. She is a singer, songwriter, actor, dancer, and producer, and much more in between! Her work is at once deadly serious, profoundly personal and, often, incredibly funny.

MAGDALENE is twigs' second full-length studio album, released via Young. Its nine tracks run for 39 minutes, with twigs writing, performing, and producing almost all of the content. Despite what Apple Music has described as "futurist textures and careful obfuscations," the album offers a raw feminist exploration of what it means to be a woman in relation to self, spirituality, and society. The introduction of the Magdalene as the prism through which these themes are addressed adds an additional dynamic: the question of myth.

The Mythologization of Mary Magdalene

The strand of myth which presents the Magdalene as hyper-sexualized, a sexual sinner or sex worker, arguably reaches its full expression in the Italian Counter Reformation (c. 1545–1648) and has remained dominant ever since in the West. Canonical biblical source material regarding the

Magdalene is surprisingly scant. The only extended narrative is in John 20:1–18, which describes her witness to the resurrection, and she is more typically presented in passing as part of a group of women who travel with Jesus. With the notable exception of Luke 8:2, all specific references are in the context of the passion and resurrection narratives.[6] Notably, none of this material mentions sin—sexual or otherwise.

The only qualifying information in these accounts is the reference to the Magdalene having had "seven demons," cast out (Luke 8:2; Mark 16.9). There has been a tendency to read this as referring to a serious sin in line with the view proffered by Gregory the Great (1990: 269) in his 591 homily XXXIII, wherein he also conflates the Magdalene with the sinful anointing woman (in Luke 7:36–50) and Mary of Bethany (from John 11 and 12). It is not implausible by any means to connote sexuality in the descriptions of the anointing woman's loose hair and physical contact, both of which cross social boundaries of expectation with a male stranger. However, the term used to describe the woman as a sinner, *hamartōlos*, is not in itself sexual and that she is known in the city still demands an interpretive leap to arrive at the common conclusion that she was a sex worker. Nevertheless, Gregory's papal exposition set an authoritative precedent for this interpretation and the Magdalene's link to sexual sin became, tenuously, anchored in scripture.[7]

The wide circulation of *The Golden Legend* (de Voragine 1275) further contributed to the consolidation of Magdalene myth. Drawing upon a range of earlier accounts, this text describes the later life of the Magdalene, living an ascetic life in the wilderness, eventually clothed only by her hair, and having daily ecstatic experiences. This combination in visual art only furthered the sexualization apparent. The Magdalene is often noted as being exceptional in the Catholic artistic canon for being painted from non-biblical narratives despite the new priorities for art set out at the Council of Trent (1545–1563). However, it is equally clear that mythologization had already taken so significant a hold, that her characterization as a penitential sexual sinner was already conceptually attached to the biblical text.

The mythologized Magdalene is thus commonly considered a hyper-sexualized outlier in Christian tradition despite being a saint. This idea is evidenced unexpectedly across popular culture which often includes the idea as an unexplored given. Culbertson (2010) has explored at length the stranglehold which this idea appears to have on the popular understanding of the character of the Magdalene in music. He notes examples from the 1980s (Culbertson 2010: 68), such as references to the Magdalene as a sex worker in the Rainmakers' "The Wages of Sin" and Redgum's "Working Girls" but this is an ongoing phenomenon. Bob Dylan's 2012 "Scarlet Town" refers to the Magdalene as "mistress Mary" with "legs that can drive men mad." On stage, in *Jesus Christ Superstar*, the character of Mary Magdalene has been singing "I've had so many men before" regularly for over 50 years in "I Don't Know How to Love Him" (Rice and Lloyd-Webber 1970). These examples, from many, are united by the fact that the idea of the Magdalene as a sexual sinner is presented as normative and unexamined.

twigs' Remythologized Magdalene

As a consequence of these problematic norms, Magdalene scholars such as Haskins (2005) have long since called for her demythologization. However, in twigs' work, we see a different expression of myth that may not be so easily rejected.

In her commentary on Artemisia Gentileschi's *Mary Magdalene in Ecstasy* for Google's *Artzoom* project (Google Arts & Culture 2020), twigs cites the influence of typical portrayals of the penitent Magdalene on her own shifting attitude to the character:

> When I was researching about Mary Magdalene and I was looking at a lot of paintings of her, she seemed so poised and so together. But the irony is in finishing my music, I found a deep wildness, a looseness, an acceptance, a release.

For the album cover art and related imagery, Matthew Stone combined photography with 3D digital mapping to create a three-dimensional rendering with the stucco and visible brushstrokes of the Magdalene artworks that twigs admired and rejected in research (Stone and Josephs 2019). Yet, despite the clear influence of this early visual reception, in twigs' various descriptions of the Magdalene as "herbalist," "healer" and "Jesus' closest confidante" (Spanos 2019; Dunn 2019), we are presented with an alternate mythologization that reimagines her as a liberating, rather than limiting archetype. Mythologization never takes place in isolation, and so is tangibly linked to the dominant epistemologies and systems of power. Despite this, mythologization is not intrinsically problematic, especially in the context of women's histories where source material, as with the Magdalene, is frequently limited. The goal of feminist re-mythologization as we see in this album is not historical reconstruction of a "true" or "lost" Magdalene, but to reconsider how her mythologization is shaped by patriarchal norms and knowledge construction.

By her own account, twigs does not consider the Magdalene as an individual woman or biblical figure, but rather as an emblematic archetype. In an interview with Zane Lowe on Apple's *Beats 1* (2019) shortly after release, she summarized:

> I didn't look at her as a character, a person in the Bible. It was more looking at her as a woman and what she represented, what her archetype was, what was her true story, how was it manipulated, how does that relate to the matriarchy in general, and how that story is manipulated.

In engaging with this complex interplay between received mythology and archetypal potential in the album, twigs contributes to her own myth making—bypassing the quest for an objective historical figure, in favor of re-mythologization in the tradition of feminist objectivity, which aims to avoid centering patriarchal perspectives as universal. Advocated by scholars such as Haraway (1988) and Harding (1992), feminist objectivity recognizes what MacKinnon (2013: 1026) has called "the simple falsity of the standard post-Enlightenment opposition between particularity and universality." This is problematic not only because it frequently limits and harms those whose experiences are not centered as universalizable, but also because it is, as Stefaniw (2020: 264) argues, "counterfactual" by the experiences it excludes. As Berdini (1997) has observed of visual artworks, reception offers a specific codification of an artist's reading of a text, not the text in abstract objectivity. Thus, when twigs offers us a mythologized Magdalene that contradicts the dominant myth of the sexual sinner, she does not do so by attempting to reconstruct an objective historical reality, but rather deploys feminist objectivity to provide a resistant counter-narrative.

MAGDALENE

MAGDALENE begins with the clashing echoes and electronic distortion of the opening "thousand eyes", where the production almost overwhelms the vocal line. twigs cites the influence of Gregorian chant and medieval chord structures, which adds a traditional Christian framing to a very modern composition (Apple Music). This effective evocation of the loss of the Magdalene's voice under the gaze and commentary of others sets the tone for the re-mythologization that is about to occur; twigs is concerned with re-vocalization and restoring agency, and those central themes pervade the remaining eight tracks.

The themes of being pulled in multiple directions, the object of expectation and the desire to escape received patterns are picked up in "home with you" and "sad day," before "holy terrain" (featuring the rap artist Future) begins to offer the alternative. Future is an "interesting" choice of collaborator, given his own creative output—one review called him "one of rap's most successful misogynists" (Cummings-Grady 2019). Yet, for twigs, it was what she calls his "patriarchal energy" (Apple Music) that allowed him to communicate the core message of this track: equality that elevates women without somehow demoting men. This is essential for her conceptualization of the connection between Jesus and the Magdalene, which is the focus of the literal centerpiece, "mary magdalene."

In discussing the track on Apple Music, twigs explains:

> Let's just imagine for one second: Say Jesus and Mary Magdalene are really close, they're together all the time. She's his right-hand woman, she's his confidante, she's healing people with him and a mystic in her own right [...] the idea of people thinking that might happen is potentially really dangerous. It's easier to call her a whore, because as soon as you call a woman a whore, it devalues her. I see her as Jesus Christ's equal.

This is a powerful statement, if apparently social rather than Christological, but it sums up the purpose of her reimaging in a nutshell: patriarchal myth has devalued the Magdalene by reducing her to a lustful caricature.

In the bemoaning of unrequited feelings in "cellophane," something of the ardent romanticism of the mythologized Mary Magdalene who falls for the oblivious or desexualized Christ is apparent. "Didn't I do it for you/ Why don't I do it for you/Why won't you do it for me/When all I do is for you." Yet, a more complex tapestry is woven, with notes of the *John* 20 Magdalene distraught at the tomb: "When you're gone I have no one to tell/ And I, just want to feel you're there/And I don't want to have to share our love /I try but I get overwhelmed." This is more than the superficial lust and unrequited crush that is so often attributed to the Magdalene under patriarchy. Rather, this is the complex love that transcends the romantic that allows twigs to imagine the depths of the connection between Jesus and the Magdalene. It restores gravitas and esteem lost under patriarchal myth, without denying the nuances of her experience as a woman.

"cellophane" is the final track of the album, the culmination of a second act which navigates this careful balance between holding the Magdalene in high regard and not allowing her to become decontextualized. twigs told Pitchfork magazine that there is an oppression to enforced empowerment:

> As a woman of color, this idea that I need to be a Nubian queen all the time is very stressful. I do find it problematic to always feel like your icons are always strong and always OK. If that is somebody's idea of slaying in this time, it's wildly off the mark.
>
> (Myers 2019)

There is a raw vulnerability across this final quartet—"fallen angel," "mirrored heart," "daybed," and "cellophane"—that deals with pain, illness, depression, and vulnerability as much as it addresses empowerment, restored agency and intimacy.

That this is an artist playing with an archetype not simply embodying a character is made plainest in "home with you," where a reflective narrator remarks that "Mary Magdalene would never let her loved ones down." At other times, the boundary is more blurred, and the song could quite easily be from the biblical Magdalene's perspective rather than the personal account of twigs as a Magdalenesque woman. It is both twigs' Magdalene, and the self she is casting in her image, that is "powerful and independent," "vulnerable and sensitive" (Myers 2019).

The Liberating Power of Myth

In addressing the issue of sexual objectification in Magdalene myth, feminist responses have been dominated by two opposing approaches. The real merit of twig's account is the third way that it navigates, avoiding potential pitfalls of both.

One approach sets out in defense of Mary Magdalene's purity through refutation of the so-called "myth of prostitution." There are clear merits to this position in relation to the lack of convincing evidence that Mary Magdalene engaged in sex work. We know that the conflation with the woman in Luke 7 is a harmonization conjecture and even if we accept it, that she is a sex worker or sexual sinner is little more than hearsay.

However, it is important to note that appeals to historical objectivity are problematic—and one reason why reception criticism that takes a liberative focus is necessary. Firstly, the Gospel texts themselves are a form of reception with a degree of removal from any historical reality. As such, it serves us to be cautious of making absolute and objective claims based on these accounts, however authoritative we consider them to be! Secondly, the pervasiveness of this strand of imagery illustrates aptly how difficult it is to deconstruct mythologization. Mythologized knowledge is not typically rooted in empirical evidence and therefore cannot be easily refuted by the absence of it, no matter how harmful or oppressive the resultant reading can be. This is key to the third, and perhaps most pressing, case against the defending honor mode of response—as shown by Ipsen (2014), this approach is harmful for those who relate to the Magdalene's sexuality and especially her identification as a sex worker. When taken to its fullest conclusion, this approach is ultimately based in a notion that it is problematic for the Magdalene to be inaccurately regarded on equal terms with sex workers, which reflects a potentially unchecked bias against them.

In contrast with this approach is the idea that sexuality is heralded as the Magdalene's sole contribution to empowerment. In many regards this is offered as the more enlightened position, where sex workers and advocates for female sexual liberation use the Magdalene's social and theological capital to advocate for those marginalized by centrist and conservative attitudes to female sexuality and sex work.

However, this approach still participates in a binary model of female sexuality, and its troubling perpetuation of whore-virgin archetypes. This is particularly acute in relation to the Magdalene, since in Christian imagery she embodies the so-called "whore" when held in condemnatory opposition to Mary the Mother. Mary is the archetype par excellence of unattainable perfection, while the Magdalene is the archetype of avoidance. Whilst there is of course value to elevating the voices subjugated by this binary, as a means of historical redress, this approach still accepts the terms defined under patriarchy, whereby women's sexual identity remains a site of scrutiny and conflict. Further, as bell hooks (1984:149) accurately notes, resonant with twigs' concerns about enforced empowerment, "the assumption that one 'should' be engaged in sexual activity [...] is one expression of sexual coercion." Associating rampant sexuality with masculinity and sexual availability with femininity is a variant expression of sexual objectification.

Synthesizing the merits of these two positions, twigs offers a subversion rather than inversion of the systems of power and oppression. In the title track, "mary magdalene," twigs explores the dichotomy of the whore/virgin binary, countering the reductive instrumentalization of both women. The space her re-mythologized Magdalene occupies is made plainest with the double entendre "I do it like Mary Magdalene." In the Pitchfork interview (Myers 2019), twigs summarized her characterization thus: "She represents both things. And in both is when [women] are the most powerful." The sexuality of the Magdalene (and other women) is one aspect of her being, and thus ultimately incidental to her ontological worth. She is a complex, multidimensional character (just as other women are multidimensional) and her sexuality is one component of the re-mythologized archetype.

The Merits of Magdalene Myth?

The manner in which biblical themes and characters are embedded in western culture more broadly affords popular media a particular utility as a lens for assessing complex imagery, including the way ideals about gender and femininity are communicated. In *MAGDALENE*, the complex presentation both draws upon and subverts the way in which Mary Magdalene is conventionally characterized, and thus offers a challenge to the subsequent types in which other women are cast. twigs' reclaiming of archetypal narratives that perpetuate patriarchal ideas about Mary Magdalene is a germane example of a liberative reading that focuses on texts as used and received rather than appealing to historical objectivity.

Considering the scarcity of biblical source material, mythologization is an inevitable consequence of attempts to construct knowledge around the figure of Mary Magdalene. Though this mythologization is typically understood in terms of a patriarchally shaped narrative of sexual sin, marginalization and conflation with other women, twigs' press descriptions of Mary Magdalene as a "herbalist," "healer," and "Jesus' closest confidante" are equally rooted in myth. Yet *MAGDALENE* demonstrates how reclaiming mythic narratives can function as an effective feminist exegetical tool for re-platforming female agency and exploring what is left unsaid in the biblical texts. Any attempt to demythologize the Magdalene will ultimately be limited by the insufficiency of these accounts; attempts to remythologize, on the other hand, are a generative reflection of the importance of story in feminist meaning-making *and* popular culture.

The story of the mythologized Magdalene continues to outrun the comparatively mundane biblical alternative. Rather than attempting to circumvent this fact, using reception as a means for engaging other forms of text embraces the fact that the Magdalene's significance can be rooted in a current context rather than a past context. twigs has described the Magdalene as "a male projection and [...] the beginning of the patriarchy taking control of the narrative of women." (Apple Music). Her re-mythologized *MAGDALENE* is equally all-encompassing as a means of reclaiming that control.

Shortly before the album dropped, twigs posted some of the cover art on her Instagram page with a caption that explained the profound personal impact of her engagement with myth. She concluded, "i stopped judging myself and at that moment found hope in 'MAGDALENE'. to her i am forever grateful" (FKA twigs 2019). Far from the removal from reality that Barthes imagined when he theorized mythologization, feminist myth making offers what FKA twigs has described as "grounding" and a "duality," recognizing the tension between myth as received and myth as created (Myers 2019). It is through this that even a highly mythologized *MAGDALENE* can set those cast in her image free.

Conclusion

The consequences of reading such interplay between the biblical text and its adaptation in popular media are varied. As well as enriching our understanding of work such as *MAGDALENE*, greater insight into the core text is afforded when undertaking this type of reception criticism. As noted by Exum (2019) in her model of visual criticism, reception and the text become mutually engaged. For some, this might be the flashpoint of the perceived decline in biblical literacy—where engagement with popular reception supersedes engagement with the text itself. However, when a text becomes so ubiquitous and its content so familiar in the cultural sphere, there are many benefits to approaching the biblical material with a new lens. Collins 2005: 90 has pointed out that biblical literacy may well function differently in "our postmodern digital age" and that we can "recognize a plurality of 'ways of knowing' about the Bible." Against Gilmour (2017: 67) who recognizes "a decline in biblical literacy evident in recent generations," it seems fairer to consider that popular biblical literacy is changed rather than lost.

Music, like other art forms, has both shared and distinctive capacities to communicate biblical myth. That popular culture, and popular music in particular, is rarely considered high culture ought not diminish its significance as biblical reception. As observed by Copier, Kooijman, and Vander Stichele (2010: 191), "[e]ven though these appropriations are often intended as 'fun', they remain quite powerful in their triviality." Indeed, as illustrated by the example of *MAGDALENE*, "serious" themes including feminism, grief and loss are frequently explored through this medium. Key to the definition of popular music offered in this chapter is the notion of shared experience and communality, so it should come as little surprise that such works can engage social, cultural, and religious themes too.

Summary

- Popular music in the West is replete with religious themes and the use of biblical imagery, both directly and indirectly, in ways that are latent and overt.

- Mythologization means that ideas related to the biblical text become attached to, and result in, wider reception of those texts.
- FKA twigs' *MAGDALENE* is an example of the way in which biblical ideas about the Magdalene can be developed, de- and re-mythologized, to have an enduring cultural significance.
- *MAGDALENE* illustrates that popular music has the same capacity to contribute to reception studies as artworks associated with so-called "high culture" and is generative for the study of biblical texts.

Discussion Question and Activities

- Select a piece of popular music with biblical themes and analyze how it engages with the text. Is the connection overt or latent? Is it direct or indirect? Is it replication or adaptation?
- How do musical retellings of Biblical stories help hearers to understand biblical texts differently? Think about how we encounter music and why music is such an important part of people's lives.
- Does music have a unique capacity for biblical reception? Why?
- What makes a piece of popular music 'secular' or 'sacred'?

Glossary

Adaptation   As theorized by Linda Hutcheon, it is the continuous creative practice that is central to the story-telling imagination. Adaptation is, "derivation that is not derivative" (Hutcheon 2006:9), and is the process by which reception can deviate from the biblical text without diminishing its influence.

Ethnography   The descriptive study of a particular group or culture, which demands immersion in the culture or community that is the object of study.

Exegesis   The critical interpretation and explanation of scripture.

Latent Biblical Imagery   Imagery that is present within works of reception as a consequence of the pervading presence of such imagery in culture more broadly.

Overt Biblical Imagery   Imagery that is developed by use of explicit biblical themes and motifs, which may take the form of direct quotation or the inclusion of recognizable characters or events.

Mythologization   As theorized by Roland Barthes, is the process by which an object can be transformed independently from its context to be endowed with ideological symbolism through a social construction of its meaning.

Reception   A term used to describe both works that are produced as a form of adaptation or expression of biblical texts and the process by which they are created.

Reception Criticism   An umbrella term for the methodological approaches that seek to incorporate the hermeneutical process that is traditionally referred to as 'reception history' alongside other reception-oriented theories in such a way that it can be utilized as a theological method rather than a theological record.

Reception History   A term that best describes an approach that seeks to identify and catalogue the trajectories and tropes found within the history of a text's received interpretation.

Notes

1 Self-indulgence for me would look more like an appraisal of biblical themes across the Beatles' back catalogue or biblical women as characters in contemporary folk music. I make no promises that I can resist this forever, though!

2 Coolio quotes Psalm 23:4: "As I walk through the valley of the shadow of death," but then diverges with "I take a look at my life and realize there's nothin' left."

3 The lyrics explore falls from grace, kingship, war and make regular mention of Jerusalem and characters such as St. Peter. The instrumentation for the track includes church bells.

4 The song is sung from the perspective of a character who references the behavior of women towards Jesus in the Gospels as their own but focuses on this narrator's love for Judas.

5 **Reception history** forms a part of reception criticism that is descriptive rather than applicational. Conversely, reception criticism is concerned with analyzing both the process (i.e., the act of receiving the text) and the cultural objects produced consequently (i.e., reception—in this case, a song or performance).

6 Matthew 27:56, 61; 28:1; Mark 15:40, 47; 16:1, 9; Luke 24:10; John 19:25; 20:1–18.

7 The Catholic Church only changed the readings for the feast of Mary Magdalene from Luke 7 to John 20 as part of the liturgical reforms of the Second Vatican Council and did so without comment (Moore 2015:44–45). However, Gregory articulated but did not innovate this merging of characters.

Further Reading

Barthes, Roland (1957) *Mythologies* (The Noonday Press: New York).
This is a series of essays which explores his notion of mythologization in a range of popular culture from advertising to wrestling.

Culbertson, Philip (2010) "'Tis a Pity She's (Still) a Whore: Popular Music's Ambivalent Resistance to the Reclamation of Mary Magdalene," in Elaine M. Wainwright and Philip Culbertson (eds.), *The Bible in/and Popular Culture: A Creative Encounter* (Society of Biblical Literature: Atlanta, pp. 61–80).
This chapter gives an overview of the reception of Mary Magdalene in popular music, with reflections on teaching this topic.

Gilmour, Michael J. ed. (2005) *Call Me The Seeker: Listening to Religion in Popular Music* (Continuum: New York).
This edited volume introduces the broader study of religion and popular music.

Haskins, Susan (2005) *Mary Magdalen: Myth and Metaphor* (Pimlico).
This is a highly readable but comprehensive overview of Magdalene myth as it has developed in western culture.

Morse, Holly (2014) "What's in a Name? Analyzing the Appellation 'Reception History' in Biblical Studies," *Biblical Reception*, 3: 243–264.
This work outlines various methodological approaches in reception studies, including the definition of reception criticism.

Bibliography

Althusser, Louis (2008) *On Ideology*. Verso: London.

Apple Music. "MAGDALENE by FKA Twigs on Apple Music." Accessed February 25th, 2022. https://music.apple.com/ch/album/magdalene/1477652618?l=en

Barthes, Roland (1957) *Mythologies*. The Noonday Press: New York.

Beats 1 (2019) "FKA Twigs and Zane Lowe 'MAGDALENE' Interview." On *New Music Daily*. Apple Music. Accessed February 25th, 2022. https://www.youtube.com/watch?v=FU88-ILTX5A

Berdini, Paolo (1997) *The Religious Art of Jacopo Bassano: Painting as Visual Exegesis*. Cambridge University Press: Cambridge.

Clark, Lynn Schofield (2006) "Introduction to a Forum on Religion, Popular Music, and Globalization." *Journal for the Scientific Study of Religion*, 45: 475–479.

Coldplay (2008) *Viva la Vida*. Parlophone: Capitol.

Collins, Matthew A. (2005) "Loss of the Bible and the Bible in Lost: Biblical Literacy and Mainstream Television," in Katie B. Edwards (ed.), *Rethinking Biblical Literacy*. T&T Clark: London.

Coolio (1995) "Gangsta's Paradise." Tommy Boy, Warner Bros, MCA.

Copier, Laura, Jaap Kooijman, and Caroline Vander Stichele (2010) "Close Encounters: The Bible as Pre-Text in Popular Culture," in Elaine M. Wainwright and Philip Culbertson (eds.), *The Bible in/and Popular Culture: A Creative Encounter* (pp. 61–80). Society of Biblical Literature: Atlanta.

Culbertson, Philip (2010) "'Tis a Pity She's (Still) a Whore: Popular Music's Ambivalent Resistance to the Reclamation of Mary Magdalene," in Elaine M. Wainwright and Philip Culbertson (eds.), *The Bible in/and Popular Culture: A Creative Encounter*. Society of Biblical Literature: Atlanta.

Cummings-Grady, Mackenzie (2019) "Is Future Problematic? A Look at One of Rap's Most Successful Misogynists." Popdust, August 27th. https://www.popdust.com/is-future-problematic-2640047407.html

de Voragine, Jacobus (1275) "The Golden Legend (Aurea Legenda)."

Dunn, Frankie (2019) "FKA Twigs Reveals the Meaning Behind Every Track on 'Magdalene'." *Vice* [Print and Online], November 8th. https://i-d.vice.com/en_uk/article/evj9jn/fka-twigs-magdalene-meaning-track-breakdown-lyrics

Dylan, Bob (2012) "Scarlet Town." Columbia Records.

Edwards, Katie B. (ed.) (2005) *Rethinking Biblical Literacy*. T&T Clark: London.

Exum, J. Cheryl (2019) *Art As Biblical Commentary*. T&T Clark: London.

FKA Twigs (2019) *MAGDALENE*. Young Turks.

Forbes, Bruce David (2017) "Finding Religion in Unexpected Places," in Bruce David Forbes and Jeffrey H. Mahan (eds.), *Religion and Popular Culture in America*. University of California Press: Oakland, CA.

Gilmour, Michael J. (2005) "Radios in Religious Studies Departments: Preliminary Reflections on the Study of Religion in Popular Music," in Michael J. Gilmour (ed.), *Call Me The Seeker: Listening to Religion in Popular Music*. Continuum: New York.

Gilmour, Michael J. (2017) "The Bible and Popular Music," in Christopher Partridge and Marcus Moburg (eds.), *The Bloomsbury Handbook of Religion and Popular Music*. Bloomsbury: London & New York.

Google Arts & Culture (2020) "FKA Twigs Reflects on a 17th Century Feminine Tribute to an Iconic Woman." *Artzoom*. Accessed 25th February 2022. https://artsandculture.google.com/asset/fka-twigs-reflects-on-a-17th-century-feminine-tribute-to-an-iconic-woman/SQGV3yl3-zzuhQ?hl=en

Gregory the Great, Pope (1990) *Forty Gospel Homilies*. Cistercian Publications: Kalamazoo, MI.

Haraway, Donna (1988) "Situated Knowledges: The Science Question in Feminism and the Privilege of Partial Perspective." *Feminist Studies*, 14: 575–599.

Harding, Sandra (1992) "Rethinking Standpoint Epistemology: What Is 'strong objectivity'?" *The Centennial Review*, 36: 437–470.

Haskins, Susan (2005) *Mary Magdalen: Myth and Metaphor*. Pimlico: London.

hooks, bell (1984) *Feminist Theory from Margin to Centre*. South End Press: Boston.

Hutcheon, Linda (2006) *A Theory of Adaptation*. Routledge: New York.

Ipsen, Avaren (2014) *Sex Working and the Bible*. Routledge: London and New York.

Lady Gaga (2011) *Judas*. Streamline, Kon Live Interscope.

MacKinnon, Catharine A. (2013) "Intersectionality as Method: A Note". *Signs: Journal of Women in Culture and Society*, 38: 1019–1030.

Moore, Rebecca (2015) *Women in Christian Traditions*. NYU Press: New York.

Morse, Holly (2014) "What's in a Name? Analyzing the Appellation 'Reception History' in Biblical Studies." *Biblical Reception*, 3: 243–264.

Myers, Owen (2019) "The Sacred and Profane Genius of FKA Twigs." *Pitchfork*, October 22. https://pitchfork.com/features/cover-story/fka-twigs-interview/

Nachbar, Jack, and Kevin Lause (1992) "In Introduction to the Study of Popular Culture: What Is This Stuff that Dreams Are Made Of?," in Jack Nachbar and Kevin Lause (eds.), *Popular Culture: An Introductory Text*. Bowling Green University Press: Bowling Green, OH.

Rainmakers (1986) "The Wages of Sin". Mercury Records.

Redgum (1984) "Working Girls". Epic Records.

Rice, Tim, and Andrew Lloyd-Webber (1970) "I Don't Know How To Love Him". Decca, MCA.

Rycenga, Jennifer (2003) "Religion and Spirituality," in *Bloomsbury Encyclopedia of Popular Music of the World, Volume I: Media, Industry and Society*, 335–345.

Small, Christopher G. (1998) *Musicking*. Wesleyan University Press: Middletown, CT.

Spanos, Brittany (2019) "FKA Twigs Strips Off Expectations on Her New Album 'Magdalene'." *Rolling Stone*, November 11. https://www.rollingstone.com/music/music-features/fka-twigs-magdalene-interview-new-album-909005/

Stefaniw, Blossom (2020) "Feminist Historiography and Uses of the Past." *Studies in Late Antiquity*, 4: 260–283.

Stone, Matthew, and Mathew Josephs (2019) "FKA Twigs – MAGDALENE Artwork". Accessed February 25th, 2022. https://www.matthewjosephs.com/fka-twigs-magdalene-artwork

Wyman Jr., Jason A. (2020) "The Bible and Popular Culture," in Claudia Setzer and David A. Shefferman (eds.), *The Bible in the American Experience*. SBL Press: Atlanta.

13 The Tarot as Material Religion

Cynthia A. Hogan

Introduction

One crisp October evening when I was in my late teens, I managed to get myself out of both homework and chores to take my father's El Camino down to the local shopping mall. Shivering as I parked the car, I breezed through the Café Square entranceway by the movie theaters. I escape past the din of the video arcade but can't avoid the booming 80s music or the rumble of roller skates echoing from the above roller rink to weave my way through the crowds of Friday night shoppers who are between me and my favorite store. Waldenbooks is the only source in my very small city of the latest in popular culture offerings. Breathing in the dueling aromas of movie theater popcorn and pizzeria pizza that permeate the whole mall, I glance through the latest mystery novels before the label "Metaphysical" captures my attention. The Metaphysical section consisted of a tall, narrow white bookshelf that contained a sadly limited selection of books on UFOs, ghost stories, angels, channeling, magic, witchcraft, and something called "**Tarot**," of which I had only two choices. The first was *The Mythic Tarot: A New Approach to the Tarot Cards*, which listed authors Juliet Sharman-Burke and Liz Green along with illustrator Tricia Newell on the front of a black cellophane-wrapped box with a picture of a crowned woman in a flowing dress and with equally flowing hair standing in a wheat field. The second was *The Rider-Waite Tarot Deck* with its cover illustration of an intimidating man garbed in a red and white robe holding a strange implement up behind an altar. Since mythology had always enchanted me, I opted for the black box and the mysteries it promised to reveal. Without a second thought, I shelled out my hard-earned allowance and bought *The Mythic Tarot* and eagerly drove back home with my new treasure. *The Mythic Tarot* had a set of lavishly illustrated cards, a guidebook to explain what the cards meant and how to use them, and a black polyester cloth stamped with outlines for the cards to be laid in a specific manner. This was my first Tarot deck. As I write these words from my desk, I can peek over to a basket filled with an assortment of different Tarot and **oracle decks** that I've since collected. The basket is lined with the same black cloth from *The Mythic*

DOI: 10.4324/9781003079729-15

Tarot, a physical connection to an odyssey begun many years before that led to a life-long study of religion, **material religion**, and popular culture.

What Is the Tarot?

At its simplest, the Tarot is a deck of cards. Standard tarot decks tend to be based on the seventeenth–eighteenth century *Tarot de Marseille*, which provided Arthur Edward Waite (discussed in greater detail below) a model for his *Rider-Waite Tarot Deck* (also known as *The Rider Tarot Deck* or *The Smith-Waite Deck*). We do have Tarot cards from as early as the fifteenth century but not a complete deck (Dummett 1980). The Tarot is much more than a regular deck of playing cards since its imagery combines symbol and **allegory**, expressing in different ways the spiritual quest from ignorance to enlightenment, the mystical journey of the soul through stages of development, or the exile from and return to the divine (Place 2005). Tarot decks have a unique structure, and standardized decks based on the *Marseilles Tarot* or the *Smith-Waite Tarot* have 78 cards that are divided into the **Major Arcana** and **Minor Arcana** (*arcanum*; plural of *arcana*, comes from the Latin for "hidden" or "secret").

The Major Arcana consists of 21 numbered cards and the unnumbered "Fool" card. The Fool has a multitude of meanings but generally represents the individual in their spiritual journey. The final card of the Major Arcana is "The World" card that possesses numerous meanings such as the ultimate destination, completion, mastery, or one's return to the source all of things. The Minor Arcana consists of 56 cards that are divided into the four suits of Wands, Cups, Swords, and Coins, with each suit containing 14 cards. The four suits reflect the four classical elements of matter, which are fire (Wands), water (Cups), air (Swords), and earth (Coins), known from ancient Greek philosophy and used in contemporary Pagan traditions. Suit cards are numbered from the ace to ten with an addition of four court cards: Page (alternatively a prince or princess), Knight, Queen, and King. Some imagery from the Tarot deck may have had precedents in the Islamic world, particularly the Marseilles Tarot's use of curved swords, but its historical origins have been traced to fifteenth-century Italy, possibly in Milan, Bologna, or Ferrara (Dummett 1980).

The Tarot was originally a card game not much different from other playing card games with rules, players, winners, and losers. Given that the Tarot possessed more detailed imagery and its historical context was the Christian social world of Renaissance Italy, the picture cards suggested additional allegorical meanings that became infused with the game of Tarot (Place 2005). As this game diffused across Europe, it came to the attention of eighteenth-century **occultists** such as Antoine Court de Gébelin, Jean-Baptist Alliette (Etteilla), and Èliphas Lèvi, each of whom saw a different purpose for the cards. These occultists invented an esoteric heritage for the origins of the Tarot decks with associations to alchemy, astronomy, ceremonial magic, numerology, and **divination**. It was Court de Gébelin who inaccurately devised an ancient Egyptian provenance for the Tarot. Through the network of European occultists, the constructed history of the Tarot and its esoteric meanings came to the attention of Arthur Edward Waite (1857–1942) in the early twentieth century.

Waite commissioned artist Pamela Coleman Smith to craft the images for his deck, infusing the deck with esoteric and **occult** symbolism drawn from a variety of European traditions and currents such as astrology, numerology alchemy, and ceremonial magic, but also including recognizable Christian imagery. Waite corrected de Gébelin's fictitious history of the cards, placing them in the European context, but enhancing their esoteric associations. One of Waite's *Golden Dawn Society* contemporaries, the notorious Aleister Crowley (1845–1947), created his own deck, co-producing *The Crowley-Thoth Tarot* with Egyptologist and artist Frieda Harris (1877–1962), which was published posthumously in 1977. Both Tarot decks interweave deeply complex systems of symbolic language invoking mystical themes such as the soul's spiritual quest and offering inexhaustible interpretations. With the Tarot now in the hands of ceremonial magicians and occultists, new allegorical meanings and symbolic images took shape.

In the early twentieth century the Tarot was known in artistic circles through T.S. Eliot's poem *The Waste Land* (1922), recalling the clairvoyant Madame Sosostris and her "wicked pack of cards" (ll. 43–56). Eventually, the Tarot was popularized in "New Age" cultural currents and the explosion of interest in alternate spiritual paths from the 1960s forward. The Tarot has proliferated in the late twentieth century and continues to morph into new digital platforms. Each year dozens of new Tarot decks are designed and books on the Tarot are published. Conferences are built around Tarot culture, and countless websites devoted to the Tarot are widely popular today. What accounts for this continued interest in all things Tarot? Perhaps one of the reasons is that Tarot can be simultaneously spiritual, religious, and material.

Theory and Method

In and of itself, the Tarot might not constitute what scholars would traditionally consider a "religion." Given the variety of competing theoretical approaches for defining religion, one helpful model proposed by Ninian Smart (1927–2001) may help us situate the Tarot into a larger religious framework. Smart suggests that there are seven dimensions to religion: (1) narrative/mythological, (2) philosophical/doctrinal, (3) ethical/legal, (4) social/institutional, (5) emotional/experiential, (6) **ritual**, and (7) material (Smart 1999). Smart's model is not the only way to understand the religious elements of the Tarot. It could be read through other theoretical approaches, but let's take a look at how the Tarot intersects with Smart's dimensions since we will explore the Tarot as **material religion** as well as a form of religious popular culture.

The Major Arcana of most Tarot decks tend to be based on the Smith-Waite system and follow the journey of the unnumbered Fool card through various stages of development. The movement across the 21 numbered Major Arcana cards allegorically reflects the development of the soul (represented by the Fool) on its journey from ignorance (or alternatively, physical embodiment) across the major stages and challenges represented by each of the 21 cards. The final card of the Major Arcana, the World card, can represent the soul's transcendence, enlightenment, or return to the divine source of all things.

Each Tarot deck incorporates symbols into the Major Arcana cards, which can take on different meanings for different people in the same way that paintings of biblical stories may be interpreted differently by different viewers depending on their understanding of the Bible. For some, the story of Adam and Eve in Genesis 1–3 may be understood as the sacred story of human origins, or it may be read as an allegory for the exile from and return to God. Most Tarot decks are grounded in a cultural or religious tradition, work of literature, or popular culture that reflect larger spiritual themes that visually unfold across the five suits of the deck. Each new year brings many new Tarot decks with different narratives, mythologies, and themes, but even the 2021 *Disney Villains Tarot* (Insight Editions, November 2021) by Minerva Siegel and Ellie Goldwine includes a Death card featuring Hades from Disney's 1997 film *Hercules*, reflecting the soul's path through the land of the dead and its re-emergence or resurrection into the land of the living. Robert M. Place's *The Vampire Tarot* (based on Bram Stoker's 1897 novel *Dracula*) considers life, death, and immortality, while *The Labyrinth Tarot Deck* by Minerva Siegal (based on Jim Henson's 1986 film *Labyrinth*), allegorizes the soul's descent into the unknown, the battles and challenges it must face, and its triumphant emergence into the light.

We might also consider the Tarot within Smart's philosophical/doctrinal and ethical/legal dimensions since each Tarot deck promotes an internally consistent moral or religious framework that draws on traditional values for the greater good. Further, Tarot decks tend to be internally coherent within their own visual narrative structures. Though there are multiple types of Tarot decks available, each Tarot conforms to its own consistent narrative frame. For example, *The Mythic Tarot* (which we'll explore below in more detail), is based on Greek and Roman mythology as a whole, but each of its five suits demonstrates traditional moral or religious themes such as exile and return, disobedience and redemption, sacrifice and loss, pride and humility.

Applying Smart's social/institutional and experiential/emotional dimensions, we can see how communities are formed and the bonds which connect Tarot users to each other as well as to Tarot as a spiritual practice. There are now regularly scheduled Tarot conferences, workshops, and trainings. New courses are being offered on Tarot both in person and online through Tarot Readers Academy, the Seatle Tarot School, or the Soul Tarot School, and others. Though Tarot practitioners can work alone, they can also find social and supportive communities both in person and virtually. There is little doubt that Tarot is experiential. Practitioners engage with the cards on different levels—symbolically, psychologically, and spiritually depending on their facility with the cards. Most Tarot practitioners would agree that using the Tarot is an intuitive process, the goal of which is to reveal knowledge that is not yet fully conscious. Tarot works to uncover hidden emotions and feelings, often in surprising ways. As a contemplative or meditative tool, Tarot offers its practitioners ways to reflect on guilt and forgiveness, devotion and peace, mystery and awe, or ignorance and truth through interactions with the images, the physical manipulation of the cards, the narrative frame provided by the guidebook, and their own intuitive readings of the cards. In the next section, we will consider how the Tarot cards align with Smart's ritual and material dimensions since Tarot is performed through certain prescribed or conventional practices that engage the senses while the cards themselves convey spiritual and religious meaning.

What Is Material Religion?

The term "religion" is a modern category, shaped by nineteenth-century European Christian scholars grappling with how to appropriately categorize, theorize, and systematize the worlds' various belief systems. The giants in the early fields of anthropology and psychology each had their own definition of religion (Pals 2014). Contemporary theorists informed by critical social and cultural theories have extended definitions of religion into new realms of inquiry and opened up new lenses of inquiry. Scholars such as Sally M. Promey, David Morgan, and S. Brent Plate consider the material, embodied, and performative dimensions of religion by pushing back against traditional text-based approaches which have long dominated the field of religious studies (Morgan 2021). With this shift occurring in the past 20-years or so, critical attention to the material dimensions of religion has produced serious and compelling scholarship, which moves us beyond traditional monotheistic foci on text and beliefs into exciting new arenas of study, such as the body's role in religious expression and performance, the function of the senses in religious worship, and other material aspects of religious practice, such as space, place, and objects, and of course, popular culture.

The study of religion took a material turn with the work of David Morgan and S. Brent Plate, who launched *Material Religion: The Journal of Objects, Art, and Belief* in 2005. And this theoretical attention on the material can help us understand Tarot practice in a more nuanced way. Previously, the academic approaches to the Tarot tended to view it as superstition and divination, which was the purview of either anthropology or psychology, while the study of its iconography was considered the domain of art history. Now, though, religion scholars can benefit from these new approaches to the materiality of religion. The Tarot as **material religion** can be explored in several ways, three of which include the following interconnected nodes: (1) embodiment through the senses of visuality and tactility, (2) performance of ritual, and (3) community interaction. Each one of these nodes, however, intersects across various networks including popular culture, commodity, media, constructs of sacred time and place, etc. Because the Tarot is first and foremost a deck of cards, one must experience it through the senses of touch and sight, whether this is through the actual physical manipulation of the cards by the practitioners' hands, or the use of hands to access digital versions online though computer interfacing hardware.

Further, the Tarot is an embodied **ritual** practice. Using Tarot cards requires the use of the physical body, specifically the eyes, arms, and hands in a prescribed manner. Often, Tarot practitioners will take a moment to meditate on a question or key issue that they would like the cards to illuminate for them, either when holding the whole card deck in their hands or while actively shuffling it. Tarot practitioners may say a prayer to a deity for assistance and burn incense while working with the Tarot deck to enhance the connection to larger spiritual or divine forces. As **haptics** are involved in the handling, shuffling, grasping, and manipulation of the cards, Tarot practitioners believe that there is a connection between their hands and the cards. That physical connection enhances the spiritual connection, which is revealed when the cards are read and seem to respond to the particular question. Other practitioners maintain that a relationship builds up over time between the Tarot deck and its owner. Sometimes the use of a quick "knock" on the cards clears the deck of residual energies from a previous reading or when someone other than the owner of the cards has touched them. Another way to cleanse the cards is to pass them through burning smoke from incense, recalling the traditional use of incense in religious rituals from around the world, and creating a sense of the sacred surrounding the use of the cards (Sharman-Burke and Greene 2018).

The sense of touch is involved in a deeply integrated way with the sense of sight through engagement with Tarot imagery and symbolism. Though readers will differ in the particular layouts they prefer to use, all readers must in some way interact with the cards, or by extension interact physically with a computer if using online Tarot tools. The body performs Tarot as a ritual, shaping the experience and being shaped by it. Rituals must be performed correctly in order to produce the desired result. Tarot readers are free to follow traditional Tarot ritual preparations and layouts or not; however, Tarot procedures generally follow a particular order. The **querent** formulates a question or sets an intention. The deck is then shuffled, sometimes in a particular manner and for a determined length of time. Cards must be chosen somehow, either dealt or drawn out by the querent. The cards are then placed in a prescribed format or layout that the Tarot reader has chosen to best address the question or aim. Sometimes this may take the form of a three-card spread representing Past/Present/Future or Obstacle/Action to Take/Outcome, or any number of larger spreads such as the Celtic Cross ten-card layout depending on the preference or knowledge being sought.

One then reads or interprets the cards in order, in relation to each of the other cards, and each card's position in the layout. Meanings of the cards may not necessarily be fixed, but they are bounded. In some ways, each card is limited by a set of prescribed meanings. In this way, there are unlimited possibilities of readings in the same way that many verses in religious texts do not have fixed meanings and are interpreted. In Tarot, the overall message or meaning is produced through the interpreter's intuition alongside or above the meanings provided by the authors/designers of the deck in a guidebook. Sometimes Tarot practitioners ignore the guidebook completely and rely on their own interpretations of the cards. Tarot practice is a performance of religious ritual that engages the body, connecting the material of the Tarot cards to the non-material aspects of the spiritual knowledge and insights sought.

As a form of material religion, Tarot operates within communities, whether they are real, physical locations or virtual spaces. **Tarot culture** has a large community with networks and connections across continents and cyberspace. The Internet connects Tarot communities in new ways; entire virtual Tarot communities exist in the non-physical world. Deep connections are often built between professional Tarot readers and with **querents**, either in person or online. Tarot practitioners connect regularly through podcasts, vlogs, blogs, workshops, conferences, and in schools or workplaces. Those connections are built in virtual spaces, in bookstores, at metaphysical shops, or psychic fairs, reinforcing Tarot practice not only in its ritual and material dimensions but also as popular culture.

Case Studies

The Smith-Waite Tarot Deck

The Rider-Waite Deck or *The Smith-Waite Deck* is one of the most easily recognizable Tarot decks available and many Tarot beginners cut their proverbial teeth on this deck. Its symbolic system is entrenched in Tarot culture so much so that other Tarot decks either tend to follow it or reject it, either way engaging with it on some level. As such, *The Smith-Waite Deck* tends to serve as a standard in Tarot culture. The narrative arc in *The Smith-Waite* deck captures the universal journey of the human spirit from birth to death broadly understood allegorically, symbolically, and metaphorically. The mystical journey of the soul through life, death, and rebirth is expressed across an expansive range of images evocative of medieval Christian European culture. Specific cards of the Tarot reflect back to readers the many possibilities open to them. The cards may also reveal obstacles or a startling depth of self-knowledge might unfold across the Tarot layout. Hence the Tarot as a system of symbols may be read at different levels. Waite himself famously wrote, "The true Tarot is symbols; it speaks no other language and offers no other signs" (1922: 4). In other words, the Tarot is an inexhaustible interpretive source from which readers construct their own stories and meanings. To see how this works, let us proceed with a reading from *The Smith-Waite* deck. As the reader, you might think of a question. In the spirit of Tarot, the deck is shuffled, and a random card is drawn from the deck. The card drawn is The Fool.

As noted above, the Fool card is placed either at the beginning of the **Major Arcana**, or at the end since it is the only card of the **Major Arcana** that was originally not numbered. In *The Smith-Waite* deck, however, there is a clear number "0" at the top. The Fool card features a youth dressed in colorful medieval garb. In one hand, the youth holds a staff that lays gently across one shoulder and has a fabric bag tied to the end. The figure faces away from a bright yellow sun shining behind him in the top upper right, which is the source of light and forms the yellow background of the top two-thirds of the card. In the youth's other hand is a tiny white rose. In the background behind the figure lies a jagged range of white-topped mountains that cuts across the card, dividing it diagonally. In the foreground, we see the youth standing on what appears to be a ledge. The figure seems to be in motion and at the figure's feet is a small white dog leaping up on its hind legs. The gaze of the youth is upward. Is the figure about to step off the ledge into a terrifying abyss as the dog rises up to warn him? Or is the ledge not a ledge but merely a step and the dog is simply playing? Traditionally, the Fool has been understood as the soul or spirit about to embark on a journey. In *The Mythic Tarot* deck, which we will consider below, the artists have depicted the young god Dionysius as the Fool emerging from a cave—recalling birth and rebirth since Dionysius as the son of Zeus was born twice (Sharman-Burke and Greene 2018).

One can read the Fool of the Tarot as a naive, innocent, and trusting youth who is blindly oblivious to what's ahead. Waite describes the fool as "the spirit in search of experience" (1922: 155). Tarot scholar Rachel Pollack suggests that the Fool "belongs anywhere in the deck in combination with and between any of the other cards" and that the Fool acts as "the animating force giving life to the static images" of the Tarot cards (Pollack 2007). Indeed, the Fool often represents the life spirit or soul in each of us as we seek experience and journey through the difficult stages of life revealed across the other cards of the Major Arcana. Tarot practitioners know that each card of the Major Arcana is a stage of learning for the Fool, and the Fool must pass through each stage by confronting each figure or mastering each experience in order to achieve wholeness, which is represented in the last card, "The World." Most Tarot decks either imitate or slightly vary the *Smith-Waite* ordering of the other 21 cards of Major Arcana which are: I. The Magician, II. The High Priestess, III. The Empress, IV. The Emperor, V. The Hierophant, VI. The Lovers, VII. The Chariot, VIII. Strength, IX. The Hermit, X. The Wheel of Fortune, XI. Justice, XII. The Hanged Man, XIII. Death, XIV. Temperance, XV. The Devil, XVI. The Tower, XVII The Star, XVIII. The Moon, XIX. The Sun, XX. Judgement, XXI. The World.

It is interesting to note that in the Smith-Waite deck, the Death Card is not the final card. In fact, it is in the middle of the Fool's journey and as such, the Death Card does not represent physical or mortal death. Each card of the Major Arcana as well as the Minor Arcana can have positive or negative associations. When interpreting the cards, then, Tarot practitioners will note the positions of each card to other cards for clues to the overall message within the **spread**. Each card has multiple possible meanings and links to numerological, astrological, and the elemental associations that must be considered. When working with a whole 78-card Tarot deck, cards from the Major Arcana that appear in a spread indicate that significant forces are at work. The meanings of the Tarot cards continually evolve within the spiritual practice of its users, often reflecting greater self-knowledge and deeper religious significance the longer one works with them.

The Mythic Tarot

The creators of *The Mythic Tarot*—authors Juliet Sharman-Burke and Liz Greene, and illustrator Giovanni Caselli—craft their Tarot on the myths and stories of ancient Greece and Rome, and explicitly base their approach on Swiss psychoanalyst Carl Jung's (1875–1961) theory of the collective unconscious. Jung believed that beneath a person's individual unconscious lies the collective unconscious, which contains shared **archetypal** human experiences (such as birth, death, rebirth, motherhood, fatherhood, child-hood, shadow, exile, etc.) that can impact one's individual psyche when a psychological wound or trauma is activated (Jung 1991). As Tarot devotees know, the list of archetypes and **archetypal** experience is not confined to these few examples.

Our investigation of *The Mythic Tarot* will take us more deeply into the allegory of the exile and return of the soul. In our first case study of the *Smith-Waite* deck, we considered the Fool as the initiator of the soul's journey through the Major Arcana. In *The Mythic Tarot*, we will use one of the suits of the Minor Arcana to demonstrate this same theme. A shuffle of *The Mythic Tarot* and we draw three cards, the Ace of Cups, the Six of Cups, and the Nine of Cups. The Suit of Cups in *The Mythic Tarot* visually narrates the myth of Psyche (Soul) and Eros (Love), which have been popularly retold by recent authors such as M. Charlotte Craft and Kinuko Y. Craft in their 1996 illustrated novel *Cupid and Psyche* (HarperCollins) and Wendy Higgins's 2019 *Soul in Darkness* (Barnes and Noble). Perhaps one of the most popular retellings of the Greek myth comes from Rick Riordan's Percy Jackson series, particularly *Percy Jackson's Greek Heroes* (Disney-Hyperion 2017). The myth of Eros and Psyche is an archetypal tale of how passion fuels the soul to its greatest height, though the ascension is fraught with trials that must be overcome.

Each of the numbered cards in *The Mythic Tarot's* Suit of Cups visually depicts a stage in the development of the Soul's evolution from ignorance to enlightenment, told through the actions of a mortal princess named Psyche who had inadvertently insulted the goddess Aphrodite and is condemned to death. Aphrodite's son Eros is sent to execute Psyche, but instead falls in love with her. The two are married, though Psyche is not to look on the face of her husband, who visits her only under the cover of darkness. Psyche is oblivious to her immortal husband's divine identity. Psyche, living in a perpetual childlike state, is content in this ignorance until her sisters visit her and suggest that she has married a monster. Psyche betrays her promise and learns that she has indeed married the god Eros. Eros, enraged at her betrayal, leaves their palace and Psyche is confronted with her loss. Seeking redemption, she seeks out Aphrodite to learn what she must do to prove herself worthy and win Eros back. Aphrodite sends her through numerous trials including a journey to the realm of Hades, the land of the dead. Psyche overcomes each trial and is reunited with Eros, eventually ascending with Aphrodite and Eros to the immortal realm of the gods on Mt. Olympus.

The illustration for the Ace of Cups is based on the ancient Greek poet Hesiod's *Theogony* (ll.188–195), where he describes the birth of Aphrodite as she rises whole from the sea. The image on the Ace of Cups differs from Hesiod's tale with the addition of her holding an enormous golden chalice in one hand, reflecting the theme of the Suit of Cups. Like the Major Arcana, each numbered card of the Minor Arcana has a particular association. Aces generally mean something new or raw is manifesting but not yet formed. One meaning offered by the Ace of Cups is that of the raw power of undifferentiated love and force of nature, and the card suggests powerful forces are at work.

On the Six of Cups, Psyche sits alone on a rockface at the edge of the sea. Five cups are upright just below her on the rock and she stares contemplatively into the sixth. Psyche is neither despondent nor sorrowful. Instead, she appears pensive and accepting, ready to face what must come next. The Six of Cups suggests the maturity that comes with one's acknowledgment of past mistakes, a necessary step toward spiritual growth. Our last card is the Nine of Cups, which represents what Tarot practitioners refer to as the "Wish Card." It is the card of completion, joy, celebration, and victory. Psyche has emerged from her trials victorious and is reunited with Eros. Aphrodite approves the union since Psyche is now worthy of her son. On a coastal shore, six golden chalices form a pyramid. Psyche and Cupid gaze at one another, each holding a cup, while Aphrodite uses her cup to bless their union. Psyche (Soul) and Eros (Passionate love) stand face to face acknowledging and accepting each other as equals joined by Aphrodite (Divine love).

In Tarot, the Suit of Cups is associated with water, which is considered the symbol of spiritual life. In the *Smith-Waite* Tarot, the Suit of Cups incorporates specific Christian references, and its Ace of Cups includes the dove symbol of the Holy Spirit, the Eucharistic Host, and Chalice (Waite 1922). Like the *Smith-Waite* deck, *The Mythic Tarot's* Suit of Cups expresses the soul's transition from mortal to immortal, the soul's mystical union with the divine, and one of the enduring religious themes of the Tarot overall.

Tarot decks are material objects that are used in service of spiritual or self-knowledge. Tarot decks can incorporate imagery from popular culture, myth, literature, art, and religion but each deck encodes its cards with spiritual, religious, and psychological significance. Tarot practice is a ritual performed for self-knowledge, spiritual enlightenment, contemplation, and meditation, often carrying religious value in the same ways as other recognizable religious objects such as prayer beads, icons, or ceremonial objects used in services. Tarot cards connect the practitioner with something greater than themselves. Once fully embedded in the Christian culture of Europe, as Tarot becomes more and more popular, it becomes more and more diverse.

The Tarot can be read, but it is not a book, and it offers no simple or easy answers. This may be why it is such a compelling expression of material religion.

Conclusion

The Tarot is becoming more and more common in popular culture. No longer the purview of the few, the Tarot is finding its way into new films, such as Aaliyah-Janay Williams's 2021 short film *Tale of Tarot*, and inspiring countless YouTube videos. Each year new decks are designed by individual artists on their own or mass produced by corporations like the *Lo Scarabeo* brand, which introduces new Tarot editions of high quality. *The New York Times* has been covering Tarot for the past several years, with a recent article from April 1, 2021: "How to Get Started with Tarot" by Gabrielle Drolet. Tarot has historically appeared in film, literature, and mystery novels, and is now found on T-shirts, drinkware, and graphic art—one only needs to begin paying attention to see how abundant Tarot culture is. Tarot cards today draw deeply from the world's great religious and cultural traditions to express symbolism and divinity in significant new ways that represent the human spectrum of identities and spiritual paths. Tarot decks are as varied and inclusive as the communities who create them, share them, and build their identities around them. More and more people are turning to Tarot cards for self-knowledge, self-expression, and artistic expression as well as for comfort, kinship, and healing, or to connect with something greater than themselves.

Summary

- The Tarot deck originally arose in fifteenth-century Europe as a card game and many Tarot decks retain the Christian imagery and allegorical meanings of its medieval heritage.
- Tarot decks are informed by the great religious and cultural traditions and express symbolism and divinity in ways that represent the human spectrum of identities and spiritual paths.
- The Tarot is a form of material religion since decks encode psychological, spiritual, and religious values into material objects, which are accessed through the performance of ritually laying out the cards to be read and interpreted.

- From novelty decks based on television series, cinematic franchises, and popular literature, to new expressions of the world's spiritual teachings, Tarot decks and communities continue to proliferate across global popular culture.

Discussion Questions and Activities

- Search for different Tarot decks. If you compare them, in what ways are they similar or different? Do you see connections across decks? In what ways?
- Do Tarot's images, narrative frameworks, and ritual use reflect other aspects of religion that you are familiar with?
- How would you describe the ways that Tarot practice builds community and connects people worldwide?
- If religion can be studied materially, what other forms of popular culture might be understood as "material religion"?
- With numerous Tarot decks created and published each year, do the meanings of Tarot cards offer an inexhaustible source of interpretation?

Glossary

Allegory   narratives, imagery, or poetry that use symbols to reveal hidden meanings of a moral, religious, or political nature. The Tarot can be seen as an allegory of the spiritual or mystical quest from ignorance to enlightenment.

Archetype (adjective, archetypal)   An often universally shared recurrent image, symbol, or motif that appears across human cultures and is reflected in art, literature, poetry, or mythology, such as the Queen archetype or the Hero archetype. Swiss psychoanalyst Carl Jung popularized the analysis of archetypes through his writings on the collective unconscious, which he believed was the source of archetypes as psychological actors in an individual's unconscious.

Cartomancy   The use of playing or picture cards for fortune-telling or divination.

Coleman-Smith, Pamela (1878–1951)   The illustrator hired by Arthur Edward Waite, who created the images for *The Rider Waite Tarot*, originally published in 1909.

Divination   Often known as "fortune-telling" or a practice of using objects to determine the will of supernatural beings, to gain knowledge through supernatural techniques, or to uncover otherwise hidden knowledge of self or others.

Haptics   Refers to the sense of touch, the study of nonverbal communication through touch, and interactions between the human sense of touch and technology.

Major Arcana   Twenty-one cards that make up the "fifth suit" of most Tarot decks. The Major Arcana also usually includes one unnumbered card, the Fool.

Marseilles Tarot   The deck sold today under the title "Marseilles" is a repro-
duction of a seventeenth–eighteenth-century French deck that is based
on an earlier deck produced in fifteenth-century Italy. The Marseilles
Deck contains 78 cards, 22 in the Major Arcana, and four suits (wands,
cups, swords, and coins) of 14 cards, each numbered from ace to ten,
with four court cards: page, knight, queen, and king. The Marseilles
Deck provides the standard model for today's Tarot decks, which either
uphold the 78-card structure or adapt this model in innovative ways.

Material Religion   An interdisciplinary approach to studying religion that
considers the material and embodied dimensions of religion and that
employs a variety of theories and methods to study the ways meaning
is negotiated in the interactions between people and things, which tends
to be social and practice-oriented rather than object-oriented.

Minor Arcana   The four suits of most standard Tarot decks include Coins
or Pentacles, Swords, Wands or Batons, and Cups that are numbered
from one or ace through ten, with court cards representing a page,
knight, queen, and king. Tarot deck authors may substitute princess or
prince for either the page or the knight.

Occult   The term derives from the Latin *occultus* for something that is
secret or hidden. In contemporary parlance, occult often refers to supernatural, mysterious, mystical, or esoteric experiences or phenomena.

Oracle Cards   A deck or set of cards that does not follow the traditional
suit structure of Tarot decks and is used either in lieu of Tarot decks or
alongside Tarot decks for the purposes of self-reflection, self-development, or divination.

Querent   The person seeking knowledge from the Tarot deck.

Rider-Waite Tarot Deck   The Tarot deck commissioned by Arther Edward
Waite and illustrated by Pamela Coleman Smith in 1909 that has
become recognized as a universally used or standard Tarot deck.

Ritual   A prescribed set of actions or performances that reflect meaning for
particular individuals and communities.

Smith-Waite Tarot Deck Another name for *The Rider Waite Tarot* deck
which gives credit to the artist Pamela Coleman Smith for her Tarot
illustrations.

Spread   A variety of recommended layouts for reading Tarot cards after
the querant has drawn them. Commonly used spreads include the Celtic
Cross ten-card spread, the three-card spread, and the five-card spread.
Tarot readers can even draw a single card of the day, the week, or the
month. Though the Tarot reflects prescribed rituals, there is no obligation to use any particular spread, allowing readers and querants to
adopt the spread that works best for their purposes.

Tarot   A deck of 78 cards that generally has two parts, the Major Arcana
consisting of 22 cards and a Minor Arcana consisting of four suits of
numbered and court cards. Tarot decks are often used for divination
purposes, but more often today are used for self-knowledge in
self-development.

Tarot Culture   The culture that revolves around the use of Tarot in communities and among practitioners past and present, Tarot history, Tarot art, Tarot usage, Tarot debates, Tarot authors, Tarot books and decks, and more that combine into an ever-growing component of popular culture.

Trumps (*Trionfi*)   The "fifth suit" that was added to the standard four suit playing card deck in fifteenth-century Italy and an alternate name for the Major Arcana.

Waite, Arthur Edward (1857–1942)   British author and occultist responsible for popularizing occult and mystical meanings of Tarot cards while simultaneously correcting inaccurate claims about the ancient Egyptian origin of the Tarot.

Further Reading

Auger, Emily E. (2016) *Cartomancy and Tarot in Film: 1940–2010*. Chicago: The University of Chicago Press.

———— (2014) *Tarot in Culture Volume Two*. Ontario: Valleyhome Books.

———— (2014) *Tarot in Culture Volume One*. Ontario: Valleyhome Books.

Auger is one of the pioneers for the academic study of Tarot. Auger's anthologies and collections are an excellent starting place for assessing the role of Tarot in popular culture.

Aveni, Anthony (2003) *Behind the Crystal Ball: Magic, Science, and the Occult From Antiquity through the New Age*, rev. ed. Boulder, CO: University Press of Colorado.

Aveni offers a readable history of the use of divination tools from antiquity forward.

Decker, Ronald, Thierry Depaulis, and Michael Dummet (2002) *A Wicked Pack of Cards: The Origins of the Occult Tarot*. London: Gerald Duckworth & Co., Inc.

This volume takes up where Dummett's volume (see below) leaves off and explores the origins of the occult use and significance of Tarot in Western esoteric traditions from the eighteenth century up to the end of the nineteenth century.

Decker, Ronald and Michael Dummett (2002) *A History of the Occult Tarot*. London: Duckworth Overlook.

This accompanying edition to *A Wicked Pack of Cards* (above) traces the evolution of the use of Tarot in Western esoterica traditions starting in the late nineteenth century through the late twentieth-century.

Dummett, Michael (1980) *The Game of Tarot from Ferrara to Salt Lake City*. London: Gerald Duckworth & Co., Ltd.

Dummett's extensively researched monograph is the first evidence-based treatment of the history of the Tarot as a card game, though he does include one brief chapter on the use of Tarot in esoteric or occult circles beginning in the late eighteenth century.

Gray, Eden (1972) *A Complete Guide to the Tarot*. A Bantum Book. New York: Crown Publishers.

Gray's short book is a classic introduction to the Tarot cards and their uses.

Greer, Mary K. (2002) *Tarot for Yourself*. 2nd Edition. New Jersey: The Career Press, Inc.

Greer is a Tarot expert who has written several books on Tarot including the one listed here. Her website, marygreer.com, is also an excellent resource for the study of Tarot.

Kaplan, Stuart R. (2001) *The Encyclopedia of Tarot*, Volume I. Eighth Printing. Stamford, CT: U.S. Games Systems, Inc.
Kaplan's encyclopedic history of the Tarot may contain some inaccuracies according to Tarot scholars, but his multi-volume set is well worth reviewing when beginning the study of Tarot, including its history and the innumerable Tarot decks available today.

Morgan, David (2021) *The Thing About Religion: An Introduction to the Material Study of Religions*. North Carolina: University of North Carolina Press.
Morgan's textbook provides both scholars and students a superb introduction to the study of religion from the perspective that religious meaning is produced through the intersection of social realities, embodied practices, and materiality.

Place, Robert (2005) *The Tarot: History, Symbolism, and Divination*. New York: Penguin Group.
Place has written three other books on the Tarot and created four Tarot decks. This book delves deeply into history of the esoteric philosophy invoked by Tarot symbolism.

Pollack, Rachel (2007) *Seventy-eight Degrees of Wisdom: A Book of Tarot*. San Francisco, CA: Red Wheel/Weiser, LLC.
——— (2018) *Tarot Wisdom: Spiritual Teachings and Deeper Meanings*. Woodbury, MN: Llewelyn Publications.
Pollack is an expert in Tarot who has authored several books on Tarot as well as fiction, and created two Tarot decks of her own, *The Shining Tribe Tarot* (revised deck, 2001) and *The Raziel Tarot* (2019).

Waite, Arthur Edward (1922) *The Pictorial Key to the Tarot*. London: Wm. Rider & Son, Ltd.
Waite's monograph offers a detailed explanation for the *Rider-Waite Deck* that has become the most universally known Tarot deck.

Walker, Barbara (1984) *The Secrets of the Tarot: Origins, History, and Symbolism*. San Francisco: Harper & Row Publishers.
Walker's introduction is one of the standards of Tarot study.

Bibliography

Auger, Emily (2004) *Tarot and Other Meditation Decks: History, Theory, Aesthetics, Typology*. Jefferson, NC, and London: McFarland & Company, Inc., Publishers.

Curry, Patrick and Angela Voss (2007) *Seeing with Different Eyes: Essays in Astrology and Divination*. New Castle, UK: Cambridge Scholars Publishing.

Decker, Ronald, Thierry Depaulis, and Michael Dummet (2002) *A Wicked Pack of Cards: The Origins of the Occult Tarot*. London: Gerald Duckworth & Co., Inc.

Drolet, Gabrielle (2021) "How to Get Started with Tarot" *The New York Times*. https://www.nytimes.com/2021/04/01/style/self-care/tarot-guide-for-beginners.html

Dummett, Michael (1980) *The Game of Tarot from Ferrara to Salt Lake City*. London: Gerald Duckworth & Co., Ltd.

Giles, Cynthia (1992) *The Tarot: History, Mystery, Lore*. New York: Simon and Shuster.

Hanegraaff, Wouter J. (2012) *Esotericism and the Academy: Rejected Knowledge in Western Culture*. Cambridge: Cambridge University Press.

Jung, C.G. (1991) *The Archetypes and the Collective Unconscious*. New York: Routledge.

Kripal, Jeffrey J. (2017) *Secret Body: Erotic and Esoterica Currents in the History of Religion*. Chicago: University of Chicago.

Morgan, David (2021) *The Thing About Religion: An Introduction to the Material Study of Religions*. North Carolina: University of North Carolina Press.

—— (2018) *Images at Work: The Material Culture of Enchantment*. New York: Oxford University Press.

—— (2016a) "Divination, Material Culture and Chance." Pages 502–504 in *Material Religion*, 12: 4.

—— (2016b) "Materializing the Study of Religion." Pages 640–643 in *Religion* 46: 4.

—— (March (2012) "Things." in *The Embodied Eye: Religious Visual Culture and the Social Life of Feeling*. Berkeley: University of California Press.

—— (March 2011) "Things." Pages 140–147 in *Material Religion* 7:1.

Morgan, David (ed.) (2010) *Religion and Material Culture: The Matter of Belief*. London: Routledge, 2010.

Pals, Daniel (2014) *Nine Theories of Religion*. New York and Oxford: Oxford University Press.

Place, Robert (2005) *The Tarot: History, Symbolism, and Divination*. New York: Penguin Group.

Sharman-Burke, Juliet and Liz Greene (2018) *The New Mythic Tarot*. New York: St. Martin's Press.

—— (1986) *The Mythic Tarot*. New York: Simon & Schuster.

Smart, Ninian (1999) *Dimensions of the Sacred: An Anatomy of the World's Beliefs*. Berkeley: University of California Press.

Turner, Victor (2017) *The Ritual Process: Structure and Anti-Structure*. London and New York: Routledge.

Waite, Arthur Edward (1922) *The Pictorial Key to the Tarot*. London: Wm. Rider & Son, Ltd.

Walker, Barbara (1984) *The Secrets of the Tarot: Origins, History, and Symbolism*. San Francisco: Harper & Row Publishers.

Zeigler, Gerd B. (2017) *Tarot: Mirror of the Soul: Handbook for the Aleister Crowley Tarot*. 3rd Edition. Newhausen, Switzerland: AGM Urania.

14 Fandom as Religion
Cosplay, Community, and Identity

America Wolff

Introduction

The first time I considered studying **fandom** as religion was when I attended San Diego Comic-Con during the summer of my junior year in college. With only a general idea of what this **nerd**-Mecca might have in store for us, a group of friends and coworkers and I set to work sitting in lottery-based waiting rooms to get the coveted tickets, scouring the internet for the cheapest place to stay, and pooling together for a rental car to get us and all of our costumes from the middle of Missouri to sunny San Diego. As a young student of Religious Studies, it wasn't long before I began to take notice of how important these rituals were to the journey we were taking. With each step that we took toward the goal of Comic-Con, we were undergoing a fan transformation. We weren't just fans anymore; we were becoming Comic-Con fans. Once I stepped onto the streets of Downtown San Diego it became clear that there was something special not just about this place, but about the community that had sprouted up around it. Local businesses decked out their windows with Marvel characters and buildings were adorned with advertisements for the latest nerdy television shows and films. Everywhere you turned there were old friends reuniting after a year apart and brilliantly costumed attendees posing for pictures. Stepping into the exhibit hall we were met with a smorgasbord of fan merch and art from every conceivable nerdy subculture. It was in this situation that I experienced what religious studies theorist Émile Durkheim would call **collective effervescence** and that I started to recognize fandom as a uniquely powerful force in the lives of the people around me—not to mention my own! Participant observation has been a central point of my work on religion and fandom ever since fandom first caught my interest as a site of academic study and analysis. Being a member of fan communities offers me a unique insight into the power that these communities hold and offered me entry into fan spaces that have guided my work on religion and popular culture.

The term "**cosplay**" comes from a combination of the terms "costume" and "play," and is usually used in reference to individuals who recreate characters from popular media using costumes and makeup. In 2019 I had the opportunity to present work at a national conference relating to cosplay

DOI: 10.4324/9781003079729-16

and San Diego Comic Con. Though a strictly professional environment, I took the opportunity to play with the boundaries between fandom and academia by fashioning a cosplay comprised of my best conference blazer and the Captain Hammer costume I had worn to San Diego Comic Con the previous summer to present my paper. There may have only been a handful of folks in the room who recognized the iconic yellow circle with a hammer worn by Nathan Fillion in the popular web-series "Dr Horrible's Sing-Along Blog," but that wasn't the point. That "Professor Hammer" costume offered me a place to think and speak within both my identity as a Comic-Con attending fan as well as a scholar with a vested interest in the study of fandom.

Theory and Method

When we think about fandom our minds often wander to fans sleeping outside a convention center to see a popular panel or groups of cosplayers reenacting a *Lord of the Rings*-style battle. It may not be our first thought as we scroll through social media platforms like Tumblr that we are bearing witness to the practice of religious communities. I suggest that we should consider exactly that. Functional theorists of religion argue that religion can be understood not by looking at *what* people believe, but by looking at *how* they believe it. For example, Durkheim explains religion as an essentially social phenomenon founded in the nature of things. The world is split between the empirical or physical world (the **profane**) and the collective social (the **sacred**); as such, religion is understood as the purest essence of society (Durkheim 1965). To participate in a society, to interact and take part in the creation and maintenance of a structured, ritualized way of living, is to share in religious practice. Robert Bellah makes the claim that in the United States, Americans participate in a form of civil religion, or a unifying system of beliefs and sacred rituals and symbols that evoke a kind of loyalty to the nation state and collective identity through participation (Bellah 1967). This civil religion provides a meaningful order to the lives of individuals as they participate in American society. These theorists, among others, attempt to look at religion in terms of the system that it provides, how individuals navigate that system, and what roles it plays in their lives. Religion itself should be categorized not simply by its association with a particular deity or sacred text, but by its ability to orient us within our world. Religion is at its core the identity-building practices that position us within our contexts and allow us to produce meanings as individuals and as communities. It is where our beliefs and ideas about the world and what ought to be meet our choices and practices both for ourselves and for our communities. I argue that understanding participation in fandom as religious practice allows us to take seriously the identity building found within these communities and provides a more nuanced understanding of the meanings produced within them. What if consumers of popular culture, namely communities of fans dedicated to a particular piece of popular culture, are in fact practicing a kind of religion? Religion by this definition encompasses the processes by which individuals orient themselves in the world and produce meaning that is employed in the navigation of social systems. By focusing specifically on fandom as a religious practice we recognize the function of fandom and fan communities as they orient individuals in the world, and extend the categorical privilege enjoyed by the label of "religion." That is to say, we acknowledge the real-world impact of fandom on the lives and choices of fans as being rooted in a sacred set of norms and standards. In applying religion as an analytical frame, we can assert that fandom orients and produces meaning for its practitioners in such a way that these practices become set apart. In simple terms, to think about fandom and fan communities as religious communities is to take seriously the way that fandom shapes its adherents as human beings and in turn, how it is shaped by them.

But first, let me back up and consider how we get to this expanded definition of religion. In her book, *America: Religions and Religion*, Catherine Albanese recognizes religion as "a system of symbols (creed, code, cultus) by means of which people (a community) orient themselves in the world with reference to both ordinary and extraordinary meanings and values." Essentially, a religious system is one that embodies these four "Cs" and uses them to express and perform communal values and negotiate power through their exercise (Albanese 1981: 197). Both virtual and physical fan communities or "fandoms" are groups of fans with shared attachment to a particular genre, author, television series, film, book, etc., who participate in various physical locations alongside the internet in conversation and artistic/literary exchanges and can be recognized as adherents to this very sort of system. Beyond simply sharing a mutual interest in a certain video game or book series, these online communities in particular encourage members to participate in the maintenance and development of collective systems of belief (creed) through the acceptance of and upkeep of a standard canon. Simultaneously, these communities develop and preserve rules dictating the behavior of members (code) both toward one another and in the kind of content that will be accepted by the community and allowed to exist in shared spaces. Guided by an acceptance of this framework, individuals within the community participate in negotiations of those acceptable limits in order to perform values such as political ideology and ethics through rituals (cultuses). Rituals or cultuses are, according to Albanese, intended to "act out the understandings expressed in creeds and codes" (10). Rituals act as performances intended to marry the beliefs and ideals of a community, its creeds, with approved action, its code, in a way that evokes community values and unity.

The field of religion and popular culture has benefitted from a huge array of scholarship demonstrating the ways that popular culture is used as a vehicle for religious ideas and symbols. Michael Jindra's 1994 article in the journal *Sociology and Religion* discusses *Star Trek* fandom as being a new age religious movement, arguing that "the modernism that is exemplified by Star Trek is, in the final analysis, a faith itself that is practiced in the various types of communities that make up Star Trek fandom" (Jindra 1994). His argument is that the values of Star Trek fandom—in this case, that their belief in being optimistic about the future and the advancement of humans and their place in the universe—is equally as religious a worldview as a Christian who puts their belief in the second coming of Jesus and the final days. In this way, fandom is quite literally the religion of modernity, providing a base for the exploration of humanity in a worldly society. This optimism acts as the creed of the Star Trek community; the participation in online discussion and fan organizations dedicated to the expansion of the community are representative of the community's expected systems of behavior—their code. As for cultus, Jindra references conventions as ritualistic events. "Conventions are an opportunity to immerse oneself further in the [Star Trek] 'experience,' much as one immerses oneself in ritual" (Jindra 1994).

Markus Davidsen's "Culture and Religion: Fiction-based religion: conceptualizing a new category against history-based religion and fandom" makes the argument that fandom constitutes a "form of play" rather than a genuine form of religion (Davidsen 2013: 378). Taking his work on the validity of fiction-based religion into account, I make the argument that while fandom does certainly embody a kind of "play," we should analyze the function of fandom as religious practice without abiding by his caveat of "supernatural" belief and adherence. The "play" to which he refers takes on a much different meaning. The fictional play world he describes is in reality what I argue constitutes a ritualized space used to explore and understand the problems of the outside world away from the rigid organization it imposes. In fact, understanding religion itself as a form of play in which people construct and deconstruct identities in relationship with communities and ideas that are sacred to them can help us to think about religion not just as something that we have, but as something that we do. While neither Jindra nor Davidsen shares my theoretical framework in their own analysis of fandom and fiction-based religion, their work speaks to a scholarly line of inquiry that maintains there is something religious about the way that fan communities interact and perform in their space.

Catherine Bell, in her book *Ritual Theory, Ritual Practice*, understands ritual as a cultural performance of ethos and values through the exercise of power and dominance to discover meaning outside of structured space and time (1992). According to Bell,

> Ritualization does not embrace the lived tensions and values of social life as just one set of terms among others in its taxonomic elaborations... People do not take a social problem to ritual for a solution. People generate a ritualized environment that acts to shift the very status and nature of the problem into terms that are endlessly retranslated in strings of deferred schemes.

(106)

In the creation of **fan-fiction**, for example, the author manufactures an environment free of the ingrained structure of reality or canon—an alternate universe whose very status and nature are shifted so as to be conducive to the exploration of moral and ethical problems in a way that is not necessarily possible otherwise. Bell's understanding of ritual is particularly useful for the understanding of these fan practices because it does not rely heavily on personal belief as an integral part of the performance of ritual. Rather, active participation begets the essence of ritual, allowing for a diverse range of individuals to participate in the ritual as equally valid and functional actors negotiating in a shared space. Bell's understanding of ritualization is useful also in analyzing the ways in which cosplayers negotiate the boundaries between fantasy and reality with their embodiments of particular characters. The accuracy of the presentation holds minimal weight as cosplayers transition their character from the pages of the comic book to the convention floor; the process by which that character is constructed, embodied, and reproduced begets meaning. The following case study will show how I apply this expanded theory of religion as orienting practice in a study of cosplay and embodiment at San Diego Comic-Con.

Case Study

For a recent project, I had the opportunity to interview one of the people with whom I attended Comic-Con on my first trip. Now an avid cosplayer themself, my friend Taylor offered some insights on how they came to don one of their favorite and most popular cosplay characters—the Wicked Lady from the anime *Sailor Moon*. The Wicked Lady was a character that had spoken to Taylor since they were young. A child with magical abilities but whose voice goes unheard and unrecognized secretly transformed into a sensual and confident villain whose power threatens those who neglected her. The Wicked Lady's story held up a mirror to the struggles that Taylor experienced in their own life. When I asked them what drew them to the character they said:

> Maybe not having a voice, feeling like you have to force your voice, especially whenever I was younger, seeing a character like that pushing and making her own way and like sometimes if you aren't feeling heard and you feel like you have to make yourself be heard, it can make you feel like a bad guy. But she wasn't a bad guy, she was just a child who wanted to be listened to.

For Taylor, the Wicked Lady spoke to the young Black girl living in a predominantly white area of southern Missouri whose voice was not only ignored but villainized for reasons outside their control. She spoke to the adolescent who was learning who they were, discovering fashion and identity while still struggling to be seen and heard. She gave confidence to the young non-binary adult whose world was changing along with them as they explored their gender and sexuality. When the time came to make the yearly pilgrimage to San Diego Comic-Con, becoming the Wicked Lady meant finding space for all of the versions of Taylor that saw themselves in the beautiful and confident villain whose greatest crime was a desire to be seen. This deeply personal cosplay required more than just putting on a costume. This kind of work asked not only that Taylor know themself in the "real", but that they could imagine who they might be in a world otherwise. As an observer, it was magical to see Taylor in their Wicked Lady costume. The confidence that they exuded as we stepped into the convention area was apparent and contagious. It's no surprise that while they wandered the exhibit hall, they were asked to take photos with other Black *Sailor Moon* cosplayers who recognized the character and found a kinship with them. Taylor found a way to embody a character from their fandom of a fictional world at the convention that spoke powerfully, but cosplay is not limited to fiction. As we move through the following examples of cosplay and identity building, consider the ways that this religious embodiment and transformation are woven into the fabric of fandom.

Cosplay and Embodiment

Stepping into the halls of the San Diego Convention Center wearing the raincoat and backpack he wore to the 1965 "Bloody Sunday" march from Selma to Montgomery, Congressman John Lewis cosplayed as himself at the 2015 Comic-Con. In addition to public service and activist work, Lewis was the cowriter of the Eisner Award-winning graphic novel *March* based upon his own experiences during the Civil Rights Movement. Upon leaving his panel, Lewis (wearing the same clothing iconized by the graphic novel) led a group of enthralled fans and San Diego school children through the halls of the Convention Center and to the overflowing exhibition floor where they commanded the attention of vendors, media, and convention attendees alike (McDonald). Lewis's performance embraced cosplay by embodying the emotions of his character, invoking the Civil Rights movement, and bringing forth the opportunity for solidarity and awareness, as well as to call attention to the biographical novels. In donning his iconic costume, Lewis called forth the past and situated the struggle for equality and the pain of that struggle right in the heart of San Diego. While every performance by cosplayers does not have its root in reality-based experience, these performances nonetheless serve to connect members of the same communities through the medium of costume. In taking on the appearance of a recognizable character, the participant is taking part in a ritual that unites other members of their community through recognition and speaks to the values they hold. Lewis was attempting to ritually embody the values of racial equality and civil disobedience—values to which people identifying with the *March* demonstrate their connection and commitment through their consumption of the graphic novels.

It's essential that we frame cosplay as an exercise in community interaction and identity building. Even as costumes are created and donned by individual members, the interaction between cosplayer and fandom begets the production of meaning. For cosplayers, particularly those attending conventions and competitions, the donning of a costume is not akin to a child dressing up as a ghost for Halloween and going trick or treating door to door. The choice of what character/characters to embody is distinctly personal, requiring a level of emotional investment on the part of the cosplayer, as well as necessitating the formation of a relationship with the relevant fandom. It's worth noting that this relationship might be positive, with the cosplayer taking on the identity of a fan like Taylor with *Sailor Moon*, and their performance a communication of community values. Cosplay could also serve as critique, with cosplayers purposely mocking or demeaning a particular character or fandom. Further still, cosplay may be used for the purpose of bringing distinct fandoms together through the merging of characters. Like I was able to communicate with and embody two distinct identities in my "Professor Hammer" cosplay (the scholar and the fan), cosplay has the ability to make meaning for the individual by drawing from otherwise unrelated sources.

The physical articulation of both individual and community identity expressed in cosplay is essential to understanding fandom as religious practice. The bodily relationship to the character or characters being embodied by the cosplayer is, as Nicolle Lamerichs argues, "an affective process," bridging a gap between the fictional world and the reality of the practitioner. (Lamerichs 2018: 199) Cosplay functions not just as signifier to members of an in-group that the person self-identifies with a particular fandom, but rather it demonstrates an immersive practice in ritual experience. The expression of particular characters—real or fictional—serves as an act of ritual embodiment, recalling and asserting a particular universe or identity within a dedicated space. Beyond simply negotiating a relationship with other fans, cosplay functions as an affective experience for the cosplayers themselves. Rather than replacing themselves entirely with the character in question, cosplay demands a sort of merging of identities—this ritualized act produces a version of a particular character that is part fictional and belonging to the community, and part individual and tied intimately to the reality and bodily experience of the cosplayer. This transformation sets the individual apart from the rest of the convention goers not only as a member of a privileged group of embodied character-individuals, but by producing experiential meaning.

In her book *Productive Fandom: Intermediality and Affective Reception in Fan Cultures*, Lamerichs explains affect as "a fundamental condition that allows us to make sense of aspects of our life and valorize them," and more importantly as "an intensity that allows the subject to produce meanings" (2018: 205)." Expanding on Matt Hills' now-standard work *Fan Cultures*, Lamerichs argues that the emotional impact of cosplay on both the player and the communities they belong to goes beyond understandings of affect as "an overwhelming, ontological power" (2018: 206). Further, she prob-lematizes the oversimplification of fan identity as attachment primarily to text rather than to a community. Instead, Lamerichs outlines what she calls an affective process, focusing on the importance of affect as a developing state with multiple points of entry and objects of devotion. This deviates from scholarship which focuses on affect as the result of cosplay in its pro-duction of meaning within the context of bodily action (Lamerichs 2018: 208). More simply put, the affective process represents the emotional and embodied practice of cosplayers as an ongoing and transitional experience which allows for the articulation of meaning for both cosplayer and com-munity. This affective process described by Lamerichs is itself a process of ritualization, a shifting of the very nature of player identity for the produc-tion of meaning through embodied performance. What's being experienced by the cosplayer as well as the fandom communities connected to them is not that an individual is becoming or being replaced by a fictional being, but a transformation from fan to rearticulated character for the duration of the performance. This emphasis on the process, on the transformation itself, is essential to understanding how cosplay lends itself to building identity.

In his essay "Identity and Play at Comic-Con," Kane Anderson explains the relationship between fantasy and reality for spectators on the conven-tion floor by describing the relationship between cosplayers dressing as Wonder Woman and the importance of them to onlookers. He argues,

> I do not mean that all spectators view the presence of a real-life inter-pretation of Wonder Woman as proof that Olympian gods exist or that golden lassos can command others; instead, the reformation of percep-tion relies on a spectator simultaneously appreciating the actualized character while maintaining an understanding that this performer is not *the* Wonder Woman.
>
> (Anderson 2014: 305)

It's important to understand that the process of cosplay is not about embod-ying perfectly a fictional character to the point of bringing that character to life as they are written in canon. Rather, for both the cosplayer and the spectator, the product created at the intersection of the cosplayer's real-life identity and the embodiment of the fictional character belongs fully to nei-ther realm. Anderson goes on to explain that the intentionality of cosplay-ers is not to truly bring a character like Wonder Woman out of the pages of a DC comic book and into the real world, but that cosplayers "ultimately fashion their new bodies from the intersections of their materialism and their celebration of bodies that cannot, perhaps should not, exist in our phenomenological plane" (2014: 417). These forms of ritual embodiment are reflective of the orienting project of fandom as religion. The course of dressing up, forming a persona, and presenting it to a particular audience is the site of identity construction for the whole community as they partake in the consumption of cosplay.

Jennifer E. Porter analyzes the practice of creating "personas" or alternate personalities used by attendees, which allow them to reconstruct their identities in the context of the convention in her essay "To Boldly Go: Star Trek Convention Attendance as Pilgrimage." This allows them to frame interaction with other fans as they see fit. Though this practice does not necessitate the use of costuming, many attendees did participate in costuming, donning physical markers of their transformation. Gender, she argues, rests at the forefront of these identity articulations in the case of some Klingon (an alien race within the Star Trek universe) cosplayers attending the convention. She explains:

> It is this challenge to gender roles, and to the limited or constrained social roles that their everyday personas force them to adopt, which underlies their choice of Klingon costuming. Playing a Klingon in the convention context allows them to express, for example, a sexual side of themselves that their work personas require them to repress.
>
> (Porter 1999: 251)

This act of critical posture on the part of these cosplayers is not simply interested in venerating Star Trek, nor in promoting the exhibition of female sexuality for the pleasure of the male spectator. For the women in Porter's study, the purposeful performance of female sexuality articulates a real-world deficit in the production of identity outside of fandom. Neither fully human nor fully Klingon, these cosplayers are renegotiating the boundaries of their own individual identities as they construct a self that bears the markers of a sexually expressive woman foreign to the world outside of the convention. The real-world self-awareness makes her identity pointedly distinct from the Klingons of the Star Trek universe. This third category, the location of the newly constructed identity, is demonstrative of the meaning embedded in cosplay practice. It is religious insofar as it orients these women in the real world; it is fandom insofar as those orientations are rooted in the collective knowledge and love of the Star Trek community. The process of forming and performing the persona allows these women to play out parts of their real-world identities that they only feel comfortable exhibiting within fan spaces.

Another example of this critical expression of gender is found in Catherin Thomas's ethnographic essay, in which she describes an encounter with a cosplayer dressed in the iconic golden Princess Leia bikini—a particularly revealing garment often considered emblematic of the overt sexualization of female bodies in sci-fi/fantasy worlds. The golden bikini itself, seen in the 1983 *Star Wars* film *Return of the Jedi*, is worn by the character as a marker of her state of enslavement and deliberate sexualization by her captor. Popular culture media, including television shows such as *Friends*, have long pointed to this particular piece of clothing as an item of adolescent male masturbatory fantasy, with plotlines centered upon male characters requesting their female partners to wear the costume as a form of sexual foreplay (*Friends*: "The One With the Princess Leia Fantasy."[1] Thomas explains:

He was completely unshaven and he did not wear a wig to cover up his short, spiky hair. The bikini costume was too tight for his heavy-built body and so he was bulging at the seams. His costume managed to undercut the "sexiness" of the costume and his remarks (at times disturbingly sexist) seemed to suggest that the costume cannot obliterate who he essentially is—a man.

(2014: 608)

For this cosplayer, the use of the Princess Leia costume is doing several things at once. First, it speaks to the importance of the bikini as iconic of *Star Wars* fandom, and speaks to his situation within it. Second, it communicates to members of the fandom who are familiar with the character and costume through the intangible sexism of the canonical event (Leia being taken prisoner and forced to wear the bikini in the first place) and places it within the physical realm. This purposefully jarring display of sexualized and female-gendered clothing on a male-presenting body signals also to those spectators who do not know that this costume holds a relevance to the community to which it belongs. Third, the intentional communication of masculinity on the part of the cosplayer allows him to reconcile his own identity within the fandom with his identity outside of the cosplay space.

Not surprisingly, this particular form of gender subversion has become commonplace within fan spaces. In a 2016 interview with NPR, actress Carrie Fisher—original wearer of the gold bikini in *Return of the Jedi*—claimed that her favorite Princess Leia cosplayers were in fact men, particularly overweight men wearing the garment. Once again, the impact of this particular form of cosplay comes not just from the individual gain, but from reaction of the community to the negotiation of gendered sexualization within the *Star Wars* fandom. The abundance of cosplayers undergoing this affective process speaks to a negotiation within the fandom surrounding the need to problematize the oversexualization of female characters, while simultaneously reinforcing the bonds of community. The costume is not just caricatured as a problematic piece of a beloved canon, it is deconstructed and reproduced through a ritualized process, allowing the cosplayer to comment on and communicate with the fandom in order to produce new meaning. This is a commentary not just on where the gold bikini is situated within *Star Wars* fandom, but how fandom identity reflects the values or identities of the fans themselves. It is this work of critique and recreation that imbues fandom with its religious character.

Conclusion

For cosplayers, the performance of character is an affective process, demanding the concession of a real-world identity for the purpose of communication with a collective. Though carried out primarily by individuals, the practice itself speaks to the need of fan communities to negotiate the boundaries of fantasy and reality and situate fan identity as a piece of a larger identity tapestry. The process of constructing this marginal identity— one that situates itself on the boundaries of the real-life person and the embodied character—is orienting practice. Beyond simply critiquing or celebrating the canonical material of the particular fandom, cosplay articulates the ways in which that canon reflects the shortcomings of realty and the needs of the fans for whom that content is embraced. Where a heavy-set man cosplaying as Slave Leia may offer a critique of both the *Star Wars* universe and the oversexualization of women by members of the fan community, a female cosplayer may employ that same costume for the purpose of asserting their own identity within the fandom by embodying the pleasures conferred in that sexualization for her own purposes. Like the Klingon cosplayers at the *Star Trek* convention, the ability to personify that sexualization allows the individual to negotiate their identity and its fluidity as they transition from the workplace to fan-friendly spaces like conventions or social media platforms. In this way cosplay is in a constant state of negotiation between the cosplayers themselves, the larger fandoms from which they draw, and the spectators who consume their final product. Though without a doubt an enjoyable activity, the meaning endowed by this affective process sets it apart from the mundane. That is to say that insofar as religion is understood as practices which orient us within our world, the ever-changing and adapting rituals of cosplay communities become more than simply every-day practice. They are our religion.

Summary

- Functional definitions of religion offer us the flexibility to analyze non-traditional practices and communities through the lens of religion.
- Cosplay offers opportunities for practitioners to articulate their positionalities through an affective process.
- Though usually created by the individual, cosplay is a practice deeply influenced by community and interacting with others within and outside of the given fandom.
- Cosplay is best understood as a ritual process, by which an individual communicates and identifies with a particular fandom or character through embodied practice.

Discussion Questions and Activities

- What fandoms are you a part of? In what ways do your fandoms orient you in life?
- What is the benefit of talking about things like fandom as religious practice? How does it help us to better understand these important communities that we are a part of?
- Think of a fandom that you're a part of. For example, is there a sports team that you're an especially big fan of? Use Albanese's 4 Cs (creed,

code, cultus, community) to describe why that fandom does (or does not) meet these criteria to be a religion.

- Interview someone you know about fandoms they are a part of. Do you understand what these fandoms mean to them? How might other ideas about religion and popular culture from this book relate to that fandom and the way it may or may not function in their lives?

Glossary

Collective Effervescence A term coined by sociologist Émile Durkheim that refers to a particular feeling of connectedness and excitement brought about by the ritual actions of a community, and which reinforces the bonds of that community.

Cosplay A combination of the terms "costume" and "play," cosplay refers to the practice of costuming for the purpose of taking on an alternate persona.

Fandom A community made up of individuals with a shared interest or love for a particular person or piece of art.

Fan-fiction Creative literature written by fans of a particular piece of media that utilizes the characters and/or settings of the canonical works to tell non-canonical stories.

Nerd A sometimes-pejorative but often reclaimed term for someone with an unusually strong engagement with and interest in a particular fandom.

Participant Observation A method of studying a particular subject by observing and participating in the activities as they are conducted normally.

Note

1 *Friends*: "The One with the princess Leia Fantasy" (S3E1; originally aired 9/19/1996).

Further Reading

Hills, Matt. *Fan Cultures* (2002). London: Routledge, Taylor & Francis Group.
This volume offers a robust introduction to the study of fan communities and the history of fandom as the subject of academic study. Focusing on the theoretical implications of studying fandom, this volume offers a variety of theoretical pathways for thinking about fandom, collective identity, and how we as scholars can think productively about fan cultures. Further, Hills' use of "fan-cult" in thinking through the differences between someone with an interest in a fandom versus a pro-active and embodied member of the fandom will be of interest to students of new religious movements.

Lamerichs, Nicolle. *Productive Fandom: Intermediality and Affective Reception in Fan Cultures* (2018). Amsterdam: Amsterdam University Press.
In *Productive Fandom*, Nicolle Lamerichs takes a deep dive into the theoretical questions posed by Matt Hills in his crucial introduction to the study of fan

cultures. With a decade's worth of new fan communities emerging in both online and physical spaces, Lamerich's book offers a thoughtful new perspective on the ways that fandoms (both global/digital and local) act as a stage for mediating values through an exploration of play and affect.

Bolling, Ben, and Matthew J. Smith (2014). *It Happens at Comic-Con: Ethnographic Essays on a Pop Culture Phenomenon.* Jefferson, NC: McFarland & Company, Publishers.

Bolling and Smith's collection of ethnographic essays offers a unique view into the experiences of a group of young scholars exploring Comic-Con for the first time. Though it does not explore specifically the religious nature of fandom, it offers strong sociological perspectives on the goings-on of conventions, and the ways in which fans use cosplay as a form of communication both within the fandom and to the world. For students interested in ethnographic research, the volume demonstrates the rich materials that can be produced by these scholarly methods.

Bibliography

About Comic-Con International. (2015). Retrieved November 25, 2016, from http://www.comic-con.org/about

Albanese, Catherine. (1981). *America, Religions and Religion.* Belmont, CA: Wadsworth Publishing Company.

Anderson, Kane. (2014). "Identity and Play at Comic-Con." In *It Happens at Comic-Con: Ethnographic Essays on a Pop Culture Phenomenon*, edited by Ben Bolling and Matthew J. Smith. Jefferson, NC: McFarland & Company Publishers, 16–28.

Bell, Catherine. (1992). *Ritual Theory, Ritual Practice.* New York: Oxford University Press.

Bellah, Robert. (1967). "Civil Religion in America." *Daedalus* 96, no. 1: 40–55.

Bolling, Ben, and Matthew J. Smith. (2014). *It Happens at Comic-Con: Ethnographic Essays on a Pop Culture Phenomenon.* Jefferson, NC: McFarland & Company Publishers.

"Carrie Fisher Opens Up About 'Star Wars,' the Gold Bikini and Her On-Set Affair." *NPR* (28 Nov. 2016): www.npr.org/2016/11/28/503580112/carrie-fisher-opens-up-about-star-wars-the-gold-bikini-and-her-on-set-affair

Davidsen, Markus Altena. (2013). "Fiction-based Religion: Conceptualizing a New Category Against History-Based Religion and Fandom." *Culture and Religion* 14, no. 4, 378–395.

Durkheim, Émile. (1965). *The Elementary Forms of the Religious Life.* Translated by Joseph Ward Swain. New York: Free Press.

Hills, Matt. (2002). *Fan Cultures.* London: Routledge, Taylor & Francis Group.

Jindra, Michael. (1994). "Star Trek Fandom as a Religious Phenomenon." *Sociology of Religion* 55, no. 1: 27–51.

Lamerichs, Nicolle. (2018). *Productive Fandom: Intermediality and Affective Reception in Fan Cultures.* Amsterdam: Amsterdam University Press.

Macdonald, H. (2016). "San Diego Comic-Con Evolves." *Publishers Weekly* 263, no. 26), 36–40.

McGrath, J. F. (2015). "Explicit and Implicit Religion in Doctor Who and Star Trek." *Implicit Religion* 18, no. 4: 471–484.

Porter, Jennifer E., and Darcee L. McLaren. (1999). *Star Trek and Sacred Ground: Explorations of Star Trek, Religion, and American Culture.* Albany, NY: State University of New York Press.

Index